SARAJEVO

SARA

THE STORY OF
A POLITICAL MURDER

JEVO

JOACHIM REMAK

CRITERION BOOKS, INC.
NEW YORK

Designed by Sidney Feinberg

Sources for Illustrations

The Bettmann Archive: 2 and 20; Bildarchiv der Österreichischen Nationalbibliothek: 1, 3, 4, 8, 16, 18 and 21; Miloš Bogićević, *Le Procès de Salonique*, Andre Delpeuch, Paris: 7; Professor Vojislav Bogićević, Sarajevo: 9, 10, 11, 12, 13, 14, 15, 19 and 25; Heeresgeschichtliches Museum, Vienna: 5, 6, 17 and 22; The Hoover Institution on War, Revolution, and Peace: 23 and 24; Rudolf Lechner & Sohn, Vienna: 26.

To Roberta

Preface

Nearly five decades after Sarajevo, some of the details surrounding the crime that set off the First World War are still obscure, and are likely to remain so. For motives that should become apparent in the course of this book, some of the participants have been prevented from talking, while others have voluntarily kept silent; some have deliberately lied about the roles they played, while others have attested to facts of which in reality they had little or no knowledge. Yet a time has now arrived when enough evidence is available to separate truth from falsehood with some degree of accuracy, and to reconstruct a story of the plot that should be substantially correct. That is what this book has tried to do.

In writing it, I have profited very greatly from the aid and advice that were given by a number of people, and I should like to express some measure of my gratitude to them here. Especially I am indebted to Professor Frederick A. Breier, to Professor Bernadotte E. Schmitt, to Professor Wayne Vucinich, to Professor Thomas A. Bailey, to Dr. Miloš Martič, to Professor Charles Burdick, to Mr. Ray Morrison, to Dr. D. F. O'Brien, to Dr. Paul Sweet, and to Mrs. Mark Christine for their criticisms and suggestions concerning the manuscript. On the illustrations, gracious and generous aid was extended by Professor Vojislav Bogićević, by Duke Max of Hohenberg, by the Austrian Army Museum, and by the Austrian National Library. Permission to quote certain crucial material was very kindly granted by Éditions Payot, Paris, for Albert Mousset, *Un Drame Historique, L'Attentat de Sarajevo;* by Oxford University Press, for Luigi Albertini, *The Origins of the War of 1914;* and by Rudolf Lechner & Sohn, for the manuscript page from *Gavrilo Princips Bekenntnisse* shown in the illustrations.

A particular note of appreciation is owed to the Hoover Institution on War, Revolution, and Peace, at Stanford University, without whose unique resources in twentieth century European history this book could not have been written. So many members of the Hoover Institution's staff offered so much help and patience that I hope they will not misunderstand if I say that the assistance given by Mrs. Arline B. Paul and by Mrs. Agnes F. Peterson does call for a separate expression of gratitude.

A long-range debt, which has to do with my whole training as a historian, is owed above all to two men: to Professor Raymond J. Sontag, and to Professor Ernst H. Kantorowicz. This is not the sort of debt which can be adequately summed up, but I would at least like to indicate its existence.

As for the acknowledgments of individual sources, no footnotes are given in the text, in order not to interrupt the narrative. Instead, a bibliographical essay, listing and discussing all the sources used, will be found at the end of the book.

JOACHIM REMAK

Lake Grove, Oregon
March 21, 1959

Contents

List of Illustrations

xi

CAST OF PRINCIPAL CHARACTERS

NOTE: Serbo-Croat names have not been transliterated. The approximate English pronounciation of the letter č is tsh, of ć—tch, of j—y, of š—sh, of ž—j. Nedjelko Čabrinović thus is pronounced Nedyelko Tshabrinovitch, Grabež—Grabej, and Pašić—Pashitch.

MUHAMED MEHMEDBAŠIĆ
NEDJELKO ČABRINOVIĆ
VASO ČUBRILOVIĆ
CVIJETKO POPOVIĆ   Assassins
GAVRILO PRINCIP
TRIFKO GRABEŽ
DANILO IIĆ

ARCHDUKE FRANZ FERDINAND   Heir to the Throne
    OF AUSTRIA-ESTE   of Austria

SOPHIE COUNTESS CHOTEK,
    DUCHESS OF HOHENBERG   His Wife

GENERAL OSKAR POTIOREK   Governor of Bosnia
                              and Herzegovina

FRANZ JOSEPH I   Emperor of Austria and
                              Apostolic King of
                              Hungary

NIKOLA PAŠIĆ	Prime Minister of Serbia
BOGDAN ŽERAJIĆ	An Unsuccessful Murderer
VLADIMIR GAĆINOVIĆ	A Revolutionary
DR. LEON VON BILINSKI	Minister of Finance of Austria-Hungary
MILAN CIGANOVIĆ	Bosnian Exile in Belgrade
COLONEL DRAGUTIN DIMITRIJEVIĆ, CALLED APIS	Chief of Intelligence, Serbian General Staff
MAJOR VOJA TANKOSIĆ	Dimitrijević's Aide
VELJKO ČUBRILOVIĆ	Teacher in Priboj and Agent on the Underground Route
MITAR KEROVIĆ	Farmer; father of Jovo, Blagoje, and Nedjo Kerović
MIŠKO JOVANOVIĆ	Cinema Manager in Tuzla and Agent on the Underground Route
DR. GERDE	Commissioner of Police in Sarajevo
PRINCE ALFRED MONTENUOVO	Imperial Lord Chamberlain
ALOIS VON CURINALDI	President of the Sarajevo Court
FRANJO SVARA	Public Prosecutor

Max Feldbauer
Konstantin Premužić
Felix Perišić   Defense Counsel
Franz Strupl
Rudolf Zistler
Wenzl Malek

Nikola Forkapić
Branko Zagorac
Cvijan Stjepanović
Marko Perina   Friends of the Assassins
Ivo Kranjćević
Lazar Djukić
Dragan Kalember

SARAJEVO

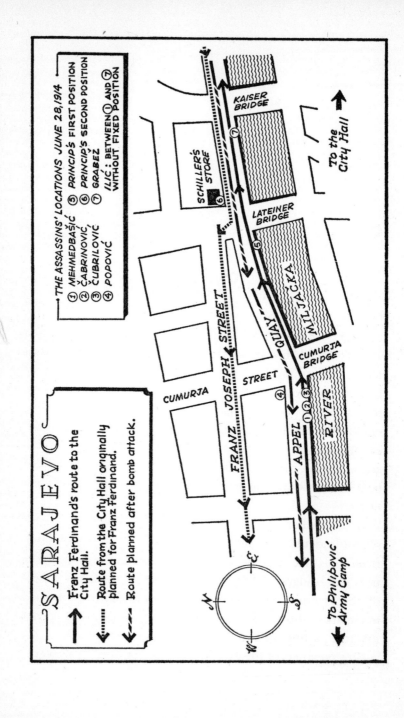

SARAJEVO

→ Franz Ferdinand's route to the City Hall.

⋯⋯ Route from the City Hall originally planned for Franz Ferdinand.

- - - Route planned after bomb attack.

THE ASSASSINS' LOCATIONS JUNE 28, 1914

① MEHMEDBAŠIĆ
② ČABRINOVIĆ
③ ČUBRILOVIĆ
④ POPOVIĆ
⑤ PRINCIP'S FIRST POSITION
⑥ PRINCIP'S SECOND POSITION
⑦ GRABEŽ
ILIĆ : BETWEEN ① AND ⑦ WITHOUT FIXED POSITION

KAISER BRIDGE

SCHILLER'S STORE

LATEINER BRIDGE

To the City Hall

MILJAČKA

QUAY

CUMURJA BRIDGE

CUMURJA STREET

FRANZ JOSEPH STREET

APPEL

RIVER

To Philipović Army Camp

N E S W

Sarajevo, June 28, 1914

ON THE MORNING of June 28, 1914, seven young men took up the positions they had previously agreed on along an avenue called the Appel Quay in Sarajevo, capital of the then Austrian province of Bosnia. The first post, near the building of the Austro-Hungarian Bank, was that of a Moslem carpenter. A few yards away from him, near the teachers' training college, stood a typesetter, who had spent the earlier part of the day having his picture taken, with an anti-Austrian paper in one hand, and a bomb in his inside coat pocket so that, as he said later, "a memory would remain."

A bit further up, by a bridge, stood two Sarajevo high-school students. Two more students who had recently come from Belgrade together had placed themselves near the next two bridges leading across the river. The last member of the group, a twenty-four year old schoolteacher and newspaper editor, had no fixed spot of his own but spent his time passing up and down between the others.

Five members of the group were not yet twenty; all were

3

natives of Bosnia or of its sister province, Herzegovina. All, except for the Moslem, were Serb-Orthodox Catholics. All were armed with Belgian army revolvers and small bombs of Serbian manufacture, and carried vials of cyanide to poison themselves with later in the day.

At about a quarter past ten, several cars approached. In the first sat the Mayor and the Police Chief of Sarajevo; in the second, the Heir to the Austrian Throne, Archduke Franz Ferdinand, his wife Sophie, and the Governor of Bosnia, General Oskar Potiorek. Three more cars bearing various members of Franz Ferdinand's and Potiorek's suites followed behind them.

As, cheered by the crowd, the procession passed his post, the carpenter thought that just then a policeman had stepped directly behind him. Torn between indecision and fear, he did nothing. The typesetter, who was next, had stronger nerves. When he saw the Archduke's car, he took his bomb from his pocket, knocked its cap off against a lamp post, stepped forward, and hurled it at Franz Ferdinand.

The bomb fell on the folded hood of the car's open roof and bounced off into the street. There it exploded with a loud detonation and badly wounded several spectators as well as an aide of General Potiorek's who had been riding in the next car. The Archduke himself appeared unhurt. Having made sure that the wounded were receiving medical attention, he turned to his suite saying: "Come on, the fellow is insane," and the procession continued on its way to the City Hall. As it did so, none of the remaining five conspirators took any action, some because they thought that the attempt had succeeded, others because their courage failed them.

CHAPTER I

Franz Ferdinand

A Royal Education

Of fairly heavy build and medium height, with slightly
protruding, steel blue eyes and an upturned, thick black
moustache, Franz Ferdinand in 1914 had the physical appearance of the not uncommon type of Austrian army officer whose world was limited by his military duties, and
whose interests outside his career were circumscribed by
good food and good company. Actually, Franz Ferdinand
was an extraordinarily complex and difficult person, whose
reported plans for Austria-Hungary's future served to make
him one of the most puzzling—and occasionally one of the
most feared—of men to his contemporaries.

Franz Ferdinand was born in Graz, capital of the Austrian province of Styria, on December 18, 1863, the eldest
son of Archduke Carl Ludwig and his wife Maria Annunciata. His father was the second youngest brother of the
Emperor of Austria, Franz Joseph I. His mother was the
daughter of the late Bourbon King of the Two Sicilies, Fer-

dinand II. Maria Annunciata was a beautiful, frail woman, who despite the warnings of her doctors bore her husband three more children—Otto, Ferdinand Carl, and Margaretha Sophie—until she died of tuberculosis in 1871 at the age of twenty-eight.

Archduke Carl Ludwig, left a widower for the second time (his first wife, a Saxon princess, had died within two years of their marriage) remarried in the summer of 1873. His new wife was the eighteen year old Maria Theresia, daughter of Dom Miguel, the Infanta of Portugal. She treated Carl Ludwig's children with great love and devotion. There were to be few people with whom Franz Ferdinand was as close and trusting as with his Portuguese stepmother.

His youth, in general, was spent in the manner customary for a Habsburg prince not destined for the succession: in his father's picturesque castles and hunting lodges on the Danube and in the Tyrolean mountains, or in the family's town house in Vienna. His education was private and of the sort that goes far toward explaining why there are so few ruling monarchs left in the world. Some of his tutors were excellent men, such as the liberal and intelligent Prior Godfried Marschall, his tutor in religion, who went on to become Bishop of Vienna. More typical, however, were men like Dr. Onno Klopp, his instructor in history. Klopp, a man of violently clericalist and monarchist bent, felt that not one among the existing historical textbooks was fit reading for a descendant of Charles V and Maria Theresia since none did enough justice to the House of Habsburg. He therefore taught history to Franz Ferdinand on the basis not of texts but of lectures he himself prepared, dwelling in particular detail on those Habsburg emperors who had distinguished themselves as leaders in the Counter-Reformation. Franz Ferdinand, bright and quick-witted, stood all this perhaps better than most, but still the haphazard tutorial system left some very serious gaps in his education, above all in his working knowledge of languages.

At twenty, an examination presided over by his father ended his formal schooling. His next step—again an obvious one—was to take up his military career in earnest. Joining a regiment of dragoons in Upper Austria as a first lieutenant, he saw service with an infantry regiment in Prague, with the hussars in Hungary, and again with the infantry in Bohemia. His promotions, as was to be expected in the case of a Habsburg prince came fast: captain in 1885 at the age of twenty-one, major in 1888, colonel in 1890, general in 1896, and Inspector General of the entire armed forces of Austria-Hungary in 1913.

His relations with his fellow officers lacked warmth, for Franz Ferdinand had a strong tendency to hold himself aloof, but this did not mean that the young Archduke spurned the usual diversions of the Austrian officer and gentleman. He would often leave his dull garrison town in Upper Austria for his apartments in the family palace in Vienna. He was even then a passionate hunter; he was also not averse—as his tactful biographer, Rudolf Kiszling, puts it—to "other pleasure trips, about which many interesting details were then told in society." He was abetted in these escapades by his gay and charming younger brother Otto, who had a disarming knack for letting Franz Ferdinand pick up the bill for both of them.

Mayerling and the Succession

Thus far, Franz Ferdinand's life had run along a smooth and entirely predictable course. Then, within the space of a few years, three events occurred which gave it a wholly new direction: his becoming the Emperor's heir apparent, his illness, and his morganatic marriage.

On January 30, 1889, the Emperor's son, Crown Prince Rudolf, for reasons and under circumstances that are still not entirely clear, shot himself at his hunting lodge at Mayerling. Under Habsburg house law, the succession now passed to Franz Ferdinand's father, Archduke Carl Ludwig. (First in line to succeed the Emperor, had the Mexicans not shot him, would have been Carl Ludwig's older brother Maximilian.)

Greatly devoted to his family, Carl Ludwig was a very kind and a very sociable man, who had neither the inclination nor the ability to hold high office. It was generally assumed after Mayerling, therefore, that Franz Ferdinand was the new heir to the throne. Seven years later, he became the Heir Apparent in law as well as in fact, after his father had died of too much piety. On a pilgrimage of the Holy Places, in 1896, Carl Ludwig would not be dissuaded from stooping down by the river Jordan in Palestine and drinking from its waters. He caught dysentery and died that same spring.

An Un-Austrian Austrian

At that particular moment, Franz Ferdinand himself was so ill that there was considerable speculation over the succession's passing to his brother. Franz Ferdinand's health had never been robust. He was much affected by throat trouble, and in 1885 he had to travel to Greece and Palestine to regain his strength. Whatever relief the Mediterranean climate brought him was short-lived. Between 1892 and 1893 he went on a trip around the world, in the course of which he visited the United States. His American itinerary included Yellowstone Park, the Grand Canyon, Salt Lake City, Chicago, and Niagara Falls, and ended in New York, where he had the all but obligatory dinner at Delmonico's. "There is no doubt," he later wrote about his impressions of New York's high life,

> that it [Delmonico's] is a restaurant of the first rank and of great fame. We were offered not just roast beef and lamb chops, but select products of French cooking. A distinguished public filled the elegant rooms.
>
> We ended the evening at Koster and Bial's Music Hall, which is connected with a restaurant. We attended a performance of the kind offered by Ronacher's in Vienna, and were more than a little pleased when three girls, apparently Austrian, sang the "Blue Danube." We were less stimulated by a ballet performance at the end of the show based on a fête at the Court of King Louis XVI; décor and dancing left as much to be desired as the dancers, most of whom were far removed from the days of their youth.

About a year after his return, in 1895, Franz Ferdinand fell extremely ill again. The blunt diagnosis of his personal physician was that he was suffering from tuberculosis. An extensive stay in the milder and dryer climates first of the Tyrol, then of Egypt, and finally of Switzerland brought about a major improvement of his condition, and in 1898 he was considered to be entirely well again.

His illness, however, left two deep scars. One was that for the remainder of his life, he had to take pains not to catch as much as the mildest of colds. He was forbidden to ride or walk too hard, or to remain in city air for too long. To exercise so much physical restraint meant torture to a man of Franz Ferdinand's active and passionate nature. "I will never forget," wrote one of his aides, "his terribly sincere and plaintive words when one hot summer day the two of us climbed a rather steep hill: 'Oh, it's easy for you; you don't even get warm.' "

An even more crucial result of this period was an all too understandable feeling of bitterness. During the worst part of his illness, most people at Court had been convinced that there was little hope for him, and had turned their attention to his popular and handsome brother Otto. Otto was given the military advancement reserved for a crown prince, and the Foreign Minister prevailed upon the Emperor to grant Otto the personal retinue of an Heir Apparent, since Franz Ferdinand was "lost anyway." An article in a Hungarian paper which came to Franz Ferdinand's attention even expressed some ill-concealed glee over his illness and the expectation of his impending death.

Had the Archduke been more of a Stoic, he might have looked back on these incidents with gratitude, for their effect was to give him an angry determination to get well. He had been anything but an easy patient; the Hungarian editorial made him observe his doctor's orders punctiliously. As it was, the period only pointed up his less attractive character traits.

Potential savior of the Austrian monarchy, and passionately dedicated to the cause of Austria, Franz Ferdinand essentially was the most un-Austrian of Austrians. The mood of *fin de siècle* Austria, and particularly of Vienna, was one of tolerance and mellow irony. "The situation," reads the famous if mythical Austrian war communiqué, "is desperate but not serious." The mood of Franz Ferdinand was one of distrust and autocratic aloofness. "You think that every man is an angel at the outset, and have unfortunate experiences afterwards," he told one of his close associates. "I regard everyone whom I meet for the first time as a scoundrel, and wait until he does something to justify a better opinion in my eyes."

A man of gigantic pride, he was at the same time dangerously thin-skinned. It was not just that he was unable to stand direct criticism; he also had a constant dread of not being taken seriously enough or of being underrated. If an associate should imply that he considered himself to be Franz Ferdinand's intellectual superior, a verbal explosion would inevitably follow. No really outstanding person would remain in his entourage for long; broken friendships and associations dissolved in anger were the marks of his career.

He was, as even an admiring biographer, Theodor von Sosnosky, is forced to concede, "the natural autocrat; had he lived in more ancient times, he would probably have become a despot."

This dark side of his character—to which must be added the further un-Austrian traits of misanthropy, religious bigotry, and miserliness—made him one of the least loved of figures in Austrian life. He did not seem to care. Partly it was his pride, nourished by his decided convictions about the divine origins of royal power, and partly his choleric temperament which made him show the same unconcern for public opinion that had ultimately cost his ancestress Marie Antoinette her head a century or so earlier.

His failings might have mattered less had they not been accompanied by lack of moderation and balance. It seemed that he could only love or hate, not like or dislike. Many of the things he touched had a tendency to lose their normal proportions, to become much larger than life. This even applied to his favorite pastimes of hunting and antique collecting.

Franz Ferdinand was a dedicated hunter and a fabulous

shot. During his trip around the world an Indian maharajah he was visiting produced a professional marksman who entertained his audience by tossing coins high up into the air and riddling them with bullets. Franz Ferdinand watched, then tried the same trick and beat the startled professional. When he was recuperating from tuberculosis in the Tyrol two years later, he once amused himself by shooting, from the deck chair in which he was sitting, small twigs from a larch tree about thirty feet distant with such uncanny accuracy that it finally looked as though the tree had been clipped with a gardener's shears.

But in Franz Ferdinand's hands, hunting changed from an aristocratic sport into mass butchery. During his world tour, he sometimes shot game from the windows of his moving train. In 1897, at the age of thirty-three, he killed his thousandth stag; in 1910 his five thousandth. Single hunts in which he killed up to 2,000 pheasants were not rare.

No one discouraged him from going on these rampages. As one of the monthly reports from the Archducal forest administration had it: "His Royal and Imperial Highness' most devoted of servants very humbly begs to report that in the Kozli district 380 hares have been counted, all of whom are already looking forward with unbounded joy to being shot by His Highness."

When collecting antiques, he was similarly voracious. Unappreciative of music or literature ("Goethe and Schiller," he said indignantly during the unveiling of a Goethe monument in Vienna, "get their statues, while many Austrian generals who have done more for our country are neglected!"), he started an art collection whose chief claim to distinction lay in its quantity. His special fondness was for *objets d'art* showing representations of Saint George and the Dragon. Over the years, often after some shrewd bargaining on his part, he collected some 3,750 pieces bearing a likeness of the knight and the beast: paintings, coats of mail, pieces of furniture, inn signs, letter weights, clocks, coins, carpets, cups, bookbindings, blankets, candlesticks, snuffboxes, etc. A special museum finally had to be built to house all this indiscriminate Georgiana.

There were, of course, many compensating features. Not all his hobbies were as excessive as his collecting or as bloody as his hunting. At his favorite residence, the estate and castle of Konopisht in Bohemia, he established a model farm, and grew roses that became the envy of the world's horticulturalists. Aloof he might be, but those who did manage to break through his reserve, such as the German Emperor for one, were genuinely devoted to him. Few might love him, but even fewer would impugn his intelligence, ability, determination, and courage. Harsh he might appear, but much of his harshness may have been no more than a mask he felt his position forced him to wear.

As for his unpopularity, the affair of his marriage was to gain him a fair amount of public sympathy, even though that marriage never noticeably altered his disposition.

A Courting Deception Uncovered

In the early nineties, rumors abounded in Vienna society that Franz Ferdinand was paying court to one of the daughters of Archduke Friedrich and Archduchess Isabella in Pressburg. He was known to be a frequent traveler between Vienna and Pressburg, and sometimes visited the archducal family as often as twice a week. Archduchess Isabella, self-important and ambitious, was vastly pleased at the prospect of becoming mother-in-law to the future Emperor.

One evening, after Franz Ferdinand, who had been playing tennis that day, had left for Vienna, a servant discovered that the Archduke had left his watch behind in the dressing room. He picked it up and took it to Isabella. The watch was somewhat unusual in that it had a large number of trinkets—collected by its owner over the years—strung together in place of the usual watch chain. Curious, the Archduchess examined these trinkets, until she came to a locket designed to hold a miniature portrait.

Expecting, perhaps, to discover which one of her daughters Franz Ferdinand really favored (pretty Marie Christine, the eldest, was generally considered to be his most likely choice), she opened the locket. Instead of being faced with one of her daughters' pictures, she was startled to see a photograph of her lady in waiting, Countess Sophie Chotek. Furiously angry, and in the best tradition of old-fashioned melodrama, she discharged her lady in waiting on the spot, forcing her to leave the archducal house that same evening.

Countess Sophie Chotek von Chotkova und Wognin was a handsome, proud, and tall woman, with dark hair, dark flashing eyes, and a great deal of vital energy. Her family was of Czech origin. Her father had been a diplomat, who had gone on to serve as chief equerry at the Imperial Court in Vienna. There was little money.

Franz Ferdinand may first have met Sophie as early as 1888 at a dance in Prague. Seeing her again during a number of social occasions, he finally fell very much in love with her. The attention paid to Archduke Friedrich's daughter had been nothing but a cover for being with Sophie. During the days the lovers were separated from each other, letters were carried from Vienna to Pressburg and back by his trusted valet and later major domo, Franz Janaczek. (When last heard of a few years ago, Janaczek, then eighty-nine, was still in the family's employ, serving Franz Ferdinand's eldest son. Duke Maximilian of Hohenberg.) For almost a year, until the incident of the forgotten watch, the deception worked very well indeed.

Unfortunately, the disappointed Archduchess was not the only person to take offense at the affair. In the spring of 1899, after having been reassured by his physician that his health was good, and that there was little or no danger of his giving tuberculosis to his future wife or children, Franz Ferdinand decided to marry Sophie. The decision brought on a bitter battle with Court, society, and Emperor, which Franz Ferdinand never fully won.

CHAPTER II

Emperor and Nephew

The Court Objects

Marriage, the Emperor and his advisers felt, was out of the question. The Choteks were an ancient and noble Bohemian family, but Habsburg house law plainly stipulated that a Habsburg could marry none but an eligible partner. The definition of eligibility was descent either from the House of Habsburg, or from a detailed list of families that included all the ruling dynasties of Europe and a number of princely though no longer sovereign houses. The Choteks could claim neither.

A Habsburg unhappy over this might request the approval of the Emperor as head of the family to enter into a morganatic marriage. In such a marriage, the wife did not assume her husband's rank, and the children could not claim the titles, privileges, and offices of the line of Habsburg-Lorraine. Several Habsburgs had done so, but never a successor to the throne, and the Emperor was wholly unwilling to approve a morganatic marriage in this case.

16

Franz Joseph was far from being a heartless or arrogant
man. Many bourgeois as well as nobles had served him and
the state (although the former, if able, would very soon
have a knighthood conferred on them; old Austria compared perhaps only to Great Britain in the amount of social
nobility that it offered). He was, however, a firm believer
in tradition and the law's observance. Equally profound
was his conviction that while an increasingly democratic
society might blur old class distinctions, the monarchy was
not a class but a divinely ordained institution above all
groups and classes. Private happiness, therefore, ought in
the Emperor's view always to give way to the higher dynas-
tic duties of a Habsburg.

But if Franz Joseph was stubborn in withholding his approval of the marriage, so was his nephew in demanding it.
None of the Court's emissaries could dissuade him from his
resolve. When the Emperor sent the urbane Dr. Marschall,
Franz Ferdinand's old tutor, to explain the obstacles to marrying Sophie, the only result was that Marschall forever after was out of favor with Franz Ferdinand and years later
saw his expected appointment as Prince Archbishop of Vienna blocked by his former pupil.

The most honorable course for Franz Ferdinand to follow—the Duke of Windsor took it not quite four decades
later—would have been to make a clear choice between inclination and duty, either marrying Sophie and retiring to
private life, or giving up Sophie and keeping his rights to
the throne. But he was resolved, whatever the cost, both to
marry her and to remain the Heir Apparent.

"I beg Your Excellency," he wrote to the Prime Minister,
von Koerber, whom he was trying to enlist in his aid early
in 1900, "to make His Majesty show me some pity, for I have
reached the very limit of my physical and moral strength,

and am no longer responsible for anything!" "Your Excellency is aware," he wrote in another note, "of my unshakable intention; it is now a question of my life, my existence, and my future."

In his oral entreaties to the Prime Minister he was, if anything, even more desperate. Renouncing the throne, he argued, was impossible; to do so would be a violation of divine law. To give up Sophie was equally unthinkable. Should the Emperor persist in his opposition, he might go mad or shoot himself, or else, as he told Koerber in a somewhat calmer mood, he would simply wait and delay the marriage until old Franz Joseph was dead, even though he would be a man without happiness until then.

Matters might have been settled more easily had relations between Emperor and nephew been better. But there never had been much affection between them. The prospect of an audience with the Emperor would put Franz Ferdinand in a state of nervous agitation; afterwards, he would frequently flee Vienna and remain away from the city as long as he could. Franz Joseph, for his part, was no more eager to receive his impetuous nephew. ("I saw him on this occasion only," the Emperor, with his usual understatement, was relieved to write to a close friend after meeting Franz Ferdinand at a military parade, "since he went on to Semlin at 2 o'clock to shoot eagles on the Lower Danube. I was rather glad that there was no chance for an argument.")

Strained relations between crown prince and monarch are, of course, nothing new or surprising. The one, understandably, is as eager to assume power as the other is to remain alive and retain it. What was involved here was something else. Franz Joseph and Franz Ferdinand represented not just different generations, but different worlds. All that the nephew lacked the uncle possessed: balance, popularity, quiet authority.

Franz Joseph

His venerable age and the length of his reign alone were enough to make him the symbol of tradition and glory. Nearly seventy at the time of the marriage controversy, and ruler of Austria-Hungary since the revolutionary year of 1848, Franz Joseph was the quintessential Emperor, the last perhaps that Europe has seen. He was also a gentleman.

His working day began at four o'clock in the morning and did not end until eight or so at night. His needs and desires were almost Spartan in their simplicity. Yet in every public word and gesture, Franz Joseph was the monarch. No one left an audience with him without knowing that he had been face to face with an Emperor.

Unlike Franz Ferdinand, the Emperor knew how to control his feelings. He had had more than his share of personal sorrows. His brother, Maximilian, had been stood up against a wall and shot in Mexico. His only son, Rudolf, had ended violently at Mayerling. His wife, the beautiful and kind Elizabeth of Bavaria, had been murdered by a half-demented Italian anarchist in 1898. Franz Joseph kept his tears to himself. Private emotions were for private occasions.

The same sense of dignity which imposed this reserve sometimes showed up in an observance of formality and decorum that might have been considered old-fashioned at Queen Victoria's Court. There was, for example, the matter of how archducal babies were to be saluted.

Living in the Hofburg, the Emperor's Vienna residence, were several Habsburg relatives prodigiously blessed with children. Regulations prescribed that every time one of the children passed through the courtyard, the guards had to salute by presenting arms, sounding the drums, and lowering the flag. Since most of the children were far too young to understand the meaning of this performance—some of them still wore diapers—the salute would usually be acknowledged by a nod from their tutor or by a bow from a pleased if somewhat startled nurse. Finally, against his own better judgment, an aide suggested to Franz Joseph that the regulations be changed, and that only those archdukes and duchesses who had been declared of age be saluted in this fashion. Franz Joseph was very much annoyed. The idea, he said, was a slight against the dynasty; things were to remain as they had always been; and he never wished to hear such a proposal again.

The Emperor knew very well that times were changing. "He said," Theodore Roosevelt recorded of an audience with him during the ex-President's world tour in 1910, "that he had been particularly interested in seeing me because he was the last representative of the old system, whereas I embodied the new movement, the movement of the present and future, and that he had wished to see me so as to know how the prominent exponent of that movement thought and felt." However, while he might have a look at the century's odd new men, for himself he wished to live as he always had. Only after being asked repeatedly did he at last permit the addition of several automobiles to the royal coaches, but he himself would hardly ever use these new inventions, and he could never be persuaded to enter an elevator. For almost seventy years, the story went, he spent every summer vacation in the resort town of Ischl, where he visited the same old friends, ordered the same fiacre for his use, and gave the coachman the same tip each year.

What mattered of course was that behind these externals lay the qualities of the true gentleman: good manners, kindness, generosity, and fairness. He could be very stern; indeed more than one visitor was disconcerted to see how much displeasure he could convey by no more than the hard and long glance of his pale blue eyes. But he would no more lose his temper than use a harsh word. Every order issued by Franz Joseph, Emperor of Austria and Apostolic King of Hungary—and there were many orders each day—began with the words "I request."

Unlike Franz Ferdinand again, he knew the meaning of generosity. Shortly before the World War, Franz Ferdinand proposed that his advisor on foreign affairs, Count Ottokar Czernin, be appointed to Austria's upper house. Relations between uncle and nephew were still far from being cordial, and there were a great many rumors that the men around Franz Ferdinand were conspiring against the Emperor. As the Prime Minister mentioned Czernin's name, Franz Joseph hesitated for a moment, and then said: "Oh yes, he's the man who is to become foreign minister after I am dead. Yes, he should be in the Upper House and learn something about the job."

A good Catholic himself, he had no use for intolerance of other faiths. "His Empire was too large," a contemporary observer has written, "the nations and religions were too many to allow him to feel or show any likes or dislikes in this connection. He was used to being blessed by Catholic bishops, Protestant ministers, Jewish rabbis, Greek-Orthodox popes, and Mohammedan muftis and imams; he met all of them with the same friendliness and respect."

Set he might be in his ways, but they were good ways. Unwilling he might be—in contrast to Franz Ferdinand—to deal with the new problems of racialism and nationalism which threatened to break up his monarchy. Yet ironically, it was the respect his person evoked which chiefly held the Austrian Empire together. When, after a rule that had lasted for sixty-eight years, he closed his eyes in 1916 at the age of eighty-six, his death all but meant that of Austria-Hungary too.

Renunciation and Marriage

None of his qualities made it any easier for Franz Joseph to sympathize with his nephew's predicament. What finally forced him to change his stand in the summer of 1900 were reasons of state. Pope Leo XIII, Emperor Wilhelm of Germany, and Tsar Nicholas all had interceded in Franz Ferdinand's behalf. Softly saying "was I not to be spared even this?" Franz Joseph gave his reluctant approval to a morganatic marriage.

On June 28, 1900, in the presence of the Emperor, all archdukes, the principal ministers of the monarchy, the Cardinal Prince Archbishop of Vienna, and the Primate of Hungary, Franz Ferdinand took the following written oath in the Secret Council Chamber of the Vienna Hofburg:

> Our marriage with the Countess Chotek is not an eligible but a morganatic marriage, and is to be considered as such for now and all time; in consequence whereof neither Our wife nor the issue to be hoped for with God's blessing from this Our marriage, nor their descendants, will possess or be entitled to claim those rights, titles, armorial bearings, privileges, etc., that belong to the eligible wives and to the issue of Archdukes from eligible marriages. And in particular We

again recognize and declare that inasmuch as the issue from Our aforesaid marriage and their descendants are not members of the most high Archhouse, they possess no right to succeed to the Throne.

Three days after the oath of renunciation, Franz Ferdinand and Sophie Chotek were married in the chapel of Reichsstadt castle in Bohemia. Almost the entire Chotek family attended the wedding. The only Habsburgs to come were Franz Ferdinand's stepmother, Maria Theresia, and her two daughters. No other members of the Imperial House attended; even his brothers stayed away.

Franz Joseph sent a telegram conferring the title of a Princess of Hohenberg upon Sophie. Nine years later, he raised her in rank to a Duchess, with the right of being addressed as "Highness."

The Emperor never again mentioned the marriage question in his nephew's presence, and tried his best to be kind to Sophie at their occasional meetings. The most uncharitable known remark he ever made about her was contained in a private letter to the motherly Katharina Schratt, his friend of many years' standing: "At 7:30 I went to the city," he wrote three months after the marriage, "where I stayed until 4:30 and saw several people, including my nephew Franz. At my invitation, he brought his wife. Things went quite well; she was natural and modest, but does not look quite young any more."

Despite the Emperor's attitude, Franz Ferdinand and Sophie were exposed to a great many slights at Court. Court protocol seemed inflexible. Sophie was not allowed to accompany her husband in the royal carriage with its golden spokes, nor could she sit by his side in the Burgtheater's royal box. At court dinners, the youngest archduchess would be placed above her at the table. At court balls, Franz Ferdinand might lead the procession, but Sophie would be forced to leave his side and appear behind the last princess of royal blood.

Very slowly, these galling reminders of her morganatic status were being dropped, particularly after she had been received with the honors due to an archduchess at several foreign courts. Wilhelm II, during the archducal couple's visit to Potsdam in 1909, had ingeniously solved the seating problem by placing his guests at several small and separate tables.

But by the time Vienna was ready to follow the example set by foreign monarchs, Franz Ferdinand and Sophie had largely withdrawn from court functions. It was not much of a sacrifice. The Archduke had never got along well with his Habsburg relatives, and his home life with Sophie was one of supreme happiness.

"Soph is a treasure, I am indescribably happy," he wrote a week after the wedding to his stepmother, "She looks after me so much, I am doing wonderfully. I am so healthy and much less nervous. I feel as though I had been born again."

The birth of their children confirmed them in their affection. First there was Sophie, born in 1901, then Maximilian in 1902, and Ernst in 1904. A fourth child died stillborn. Franz Ferdinand was the fondest of fathers; his day began and ended by looking in on his children. Rumors abounded that he and Sophie harbored hidden ambitions for their future, and that he planned to have the renunciation oath annulled upon Franz Joseph's death. He himself denied this. "The Habsburg crown," he wrote to a supporter, "is a crown of thorns, and no one who is not born to it should desire it. A withdrawal of the renunciation will never be considered."

Franz Ferdinand's public character remained as difficult as it had ever been, but his private happiness was true and it was lasting. "You don't know," he confided in a letter to his stepmother in 1904,

> how happy I am with my family, and how I can't thank God enough for all my happiness.
>
> The *most* intelligent thing I've ever done in my life has been the marriage to my Soph. She is everything to me: my wife, my adviser, my doctor, my warner, in a word: my entire happiness. Now, after four years, we love each other as on our first year of marriage, and our happiness has not been marred for a single second.
>
> And our children. They are my whole delight and pride. I sit with them and admire them the whole day because I love them so.

Political Plans

There was much beside his family to keep Franz Ferdinand busy at this time. He was preparing for the day when he would become ruler of an Empire which, as he was well aware, showed every sign of falling apart.

The dual monarchy of Austria-Hungary admittedly was an anachronism. It comprised something like a dozen nationalities and cultures, and the spirit of its government was one of improvisation, compromise, and tolerance. The centers of administration were Vienna and Budapest. Germans and Hungarians predominated in the higher echelons of army and administration, but such careers were by no means closed to the Empire's other nationalities, to Czechs, Italians, and Poles, to Croats, Slovaks, Serbs, Rumanians.

Both politically and economically, the union of Central

and Southeastern Europe which Austria-Hungary provided made a great deal of sense. How much so was discovered after the Empire's willfull destruction in 1919, when it became very clear that none of its successor states were capable of standing by themselves, and all of them at one time or another fell victim to the pressure first of Germany and then of Russia.

But at the turn of the century most of Austria-Hungary's nationalities were tired of the Empire. A multinational state, they felt, was out of keeping with the age. Modern democracy required equal rights for all; modern nationalism required that each nationality form its own nation. Many Poles thus wished to see the establishment of a new Polish state, many Slavs were putting their hopes in Russia, many Magyars wanted an independent Hungary, many Serbs wished to join the neighboring kingdom of Serbia.

Much of the criticism was justified. The monarchy was not perfect, and the concepts on which it rested were doubtlessly obsolete. Old Austria's basic trouble, however, lay not in the suppression of national rights, or in civic inequality. Neither was of an unbearable kind; change might be slow but it was taking place. The basic trouble lay in the mistaken assumption of its rulers that traditions were stronger than passions, and that, fundamentally, men were rational beings who would prefer peace to chaos, and the shelter of Empire to the predictable excesses of modern racialism and nationalism.

Having ruled over Austria for nearly two generations, Franz Joseph was wary of undertaking any major reforms in the structure of the monarchy. Franz Ferdinand felt differently.

In the years that followed his marriage, Franz Ferdinand acquired a good deal of actual power. He was beginning to place several people of his choice in responsible army positions, and he did much to support the expansion of the navy. He also worked on plans for Imperial reform. "I *must* have the nationalities with me," he wrote, "for this is the only salvation for the future."

His early ideas for reform envisaged the substitution of "Dualism" with "Trialism." A third state was to be formed within the frontiers of the monarchy, consisting of the Empire's Southern Slavs—Croats, Slovenes, and Serbs—and power was to be shared more equally between Germans, Hungarians, and Slavs. Later, he apparently became convinced that Trialism was not enough and that nothing short of complete federalism along the lines of the American or Swiss systems could save the state. Presumably this would have provided for a division of the Empire into as many as sixteen autonomous states, linked together by a common ruler: the Emperor. There would also have been a joint foreign policy, joint armed forces, a joint economic system, and a federal parliament elected by the member states in proportion to their population.

It is not entirely clear which of these plans Franz Ferdinand would have put into execution in the event of his succession to the throne. At the time, Trialism received more publicity, but it is likely that in his last years Franz Ferdinand favored federalism. Nor is it certain whether his reforms would have been successful.

Austria-Hungary, wrote a skeptical contemporary observer, was

a broken pot held together with a piece of wire. It might do duty as long as it was treated with due care, but woe if it were exposed to too many hard knocks or got some kick or other. Then it would be liable to fall to pieces.

Autonomy might all too easily lead to independence. Certainly the Hungarians, who were ruling their portion of the Empire with a strong hand, and who had no intention of surrendering any part of it, were incensed over Franz Ferdinand's reported plans. By a feat of gerrymandering of truly heroic proportions, and by other such devices, eight and a half million Magyars were represented in the parliament at Budapest by 392 deputies, and eight million non-Magyars by 21.

Franz Ferdinand bore the Hungarians no greater love than they did him. "Rabble," "Huns," "Asiatics" were some of his epithets for the Magyars. And it is conceivable that Hungarian opposition alone would have been sufficient to wreck any schemes for reform. No one can say of course, for it must also be remembered that Franz Ferdinand was a man of considerable ability and obstinacy, and that he was by no means alone in believing that Austria-Hungary's only choice lay between reform and destruction. What mattered was that in 1913, the chances of success looked favorable enough to make someone in the neighboring kingdom of Serbia decide that Franz Ferdinand should be killed.

CHAPTER III

The Trip to Sarajevo

An Invitation to the Maneuvers

In the late summer of 1913, General Oskar Potiorek, Governor of the Austrian provinces of Bosnia and Herzegovina, invited Franz Ferdinand to the maneuvers of the Fifteenth and Sixteenth Army Corps that were to be held in Bosnia the following June under Potiorek's command. Would the Archduke, he asked, attend in his capacity as Inspector General of the Armed Forces, and set aside a day to let himself be received in the capital of Sarajevo as Heir to the Throne? As for a place to stay during the visit, Potiorek suggested the pretty resort town of Ilidže near Sarajevo.

Franz Ferdinand accepted. It was time for a goodwill trip of this sort; no Habsburg had shown himself in Bosnia since the Emperor's visit of 1910. Besides, it was an opportunity to have Sophie along, and to see that she was received with full honors.

The extent to which thoughts about Sophie influenced

his decision can only be guessed at. It is known, however, that he delayed asking the Emperor's permission to have Sophie come to Ilidže until early in June, 1914, and that when the printed programs of the journey reached the Imperial Palace, there was considerable consternation. The form and design of Sophie's as well as of Franz Ferdinand's program were those reserved for members of the Imperial House. "This is a bit much! What are we coming to!" said Franz Joseph's venerable aide, Count Paar, as he looked at Sophie's program. The Emperor, reportedly, was no more pleased, but he had no taste for scenes and simply left for his Ischl vacation a few days early in order to avoid his nephew.

If Franz Ferdinand's reasons for accepting the invitation were not entirely straightforward, neither were General Potiorek's for extending it. There was more involved for him than the usual display of royal pageantry with which, since the days of the first Egyptian dynasty, kings and princes have at certain intervals entertained and impressed their subjects. The truth was that General Potiorek had recently run into a great deal of trouble with a restive Bosnian population, and that he was eager for some visible evidence of Franz Ferdinand's support.

Occupation and Annexation

The story is told in Bosnia that when God created the earth, He carried two sacks, one full of earth, the other full of stones. As he was passing over what was to become Bosnia and Herzegovina, the sack of stones burst and all its contents came crashing down.

The accident's results still show. There is a good deal more wild and mountainous terrain in Bosnia than there is arable land, and to make one's living from the Bosnian soil seems always to have meant a life of want and hardship. God's sack, however, must have contained something else besides rocks, for the country is rich in mineral resources —coal, iron, silver—and in vast, fairy tale forests, where bears and wolves, chamoix and deer, wild boar and lynx can be found to this day. The country's rivers are full of fish, and toward the Southern Coast, oranges, lemons, plums, olives, grapes, and figs grow.

Such pleasures of the region, but even more its strategic location between the Black Sea and the Adriatic had invited conquest, in turn, from Illyrians, Romans, Byzantines, Serbians, and Magyars, until in the fifteenth century, the Turks had come, apparently to stay. But by the nineteenth century, Bosnia's Turkish overlord had become "the sick man of Europe," and the vast holdings of the Ottoman Empire were beginning to crumble. In Bosnia and Herzegovina, armed insurrection against Turkish rule erupted in 1874, which was soon joined by the neighboring regions of Bulgaria, Serbia, and Montenegro. The revolt fared badly, until in 1877, the Russians, as the self-appointed protectors of Slavdom, declared war on Turkey, quickly routed the sick man, and forced him to promise independence to Serbia and Rumania, autonomy to Bulgaria, and reforms to Bosnia-Herzegovina.

At this point, the European powers, alarmed at the prospects of a Near East dominated by St. Petersburg, intervened and pressed Russia to submit its Turkish peace terms to an international Congress. In 1878, the Congress met in Berlin, under the chairmanship of Prince Otto von Bismarck, the German Chancellor. The settlement reached presented nearly everyone among the participants with some choice piece of Turkish territory. (Only the Germans took nothing, and the Italians had to be satisfied with some vague promises for the future; "The Italians," said Bismarck, "have such a large appetite and such poor teeth.") The Russians received the Caucasian border town of Kars and the Black Sea Port of Batum, and gained independence for Serbia and Rumania, with a modified sort of autonomy for Bulgaria.

To counteract Russia's gains, Bosnia and Herzegovina— where all the trouble had started—went to Austria-Hungary "to occupy and administer." Nominally, the territory remained Turkish; actually, no one expected the Austrian occupation to be anything but permanent.

In October, 1908, having first bought off the Russians by an ambiguous promise of Austrian support in the question of the Dardanelles, the Austrians proclaimed the outright annexation of Bosnia and Herzegovina. There were several good reasons for this step. Three months earlier, Young Turk reformers had seized power in Constantinople, which raised the alarming possibility that the dissolution of the Ottoman Empire might be coming to a halt, and that the Turks might even ask for the return of their Bosnian property. In Bosnia-Herzegovina the Austrian occupation regime was unpopular, and the need for some sort of representative government obvious. Yet if there were to be any real change, it could be introduced far more easily if Franz Joseph were able to act as sovereign, rather than as the temporary administrator of someone else's territory.

There also were some good reasons against annexation. Legally, it was a clear violation of the 1878 Treaty of Berlin. Nor did the need to break the treaty seem truly compelling to a good many Austrians. Someone who has had an affair with a woman for thirty years, commented one such critic, and who after all this time suddenly feels the need to legalize the relationship, must strike his friends as more than a bit odd. Franz Ferdinand had definitely been opposed to annexation. "Considering our sad domestic state of affairs," he had written in a hastily penciled note to the Austrian foreign minister in August, "I am, quite generally speaking, against all such displays of strength. In my opinion, only a well-consolidated, strong state can afford such things. . . ."

In spite of Franz Ferdinand's misgivings, international reaction to annexation was nonviolent. The great powers, while annoyed, in the end were satisfied when Austria paid a large cash compensation to the Turks. Not so the Serbians. In Belgrade, large and angry crowds filled the streets, shouted "Down With Austria!," and demanded action. The Serbian government called up the reserves, and the parliament voted the necessary credits for war. Only when the Russians frankly warned Serbia that they did not intend to support them in a war over Bosnia did the Belgrade government draw back. Serbia never forgave or forgot the annexation, however.

The reason for Serbia's pique was not that Bosnia suffered misery and oppression under Austrian rule. The quality of Austrian administration was generally competent and certainly far superior to that of the Turks. The Austrians, in their slow way, did all the things which the conscientious colonial administrator is prone to do, even if it seldom seems to endear him to those he administers. They built roads and railways; they provided material prosperity and orderly government; and, with the grant of a constitution in 1910, they prepared the way for full autonomy.

What caused the anger in Belgrade was that Serbia coveted Bosnia and Herzegovina for itself. Strong groups within the kingdom wished to create a Greater Serbia which, with Serbia itself as a nucleus, would comprise the Austrian provinces of Bosnia, Herzegovina, Slavonia, and Croatia, parts of Turkish-held Macedonia, and the independent principality of Montenegro. Their argument was that ethnically, Serbs, Bosnians, Croats, Slovenes, and Montenegrines were closely related, and should be considered one people—the South Slavs, or Yugoslavs. Pan-Serb agitation received a new and strong impetus with the First Balkan War of 1912, in which Greece, Bulgaria and Serbia joined forces to detach Macedonia from Turkey. The allies' victories over the Turks aroused a great deal of enthusiasm for the Serbian cause in Austria's South Slav provinces, even though Bulgaria, in the Second Balkan War, was to see its recent associates turn into enemies in a fight over the Macedonian spoils.

The Death of a Hero

With the spirited support of Serbia, a fair amount of unrest developed in Bosnia, particularly among those who were young enough to have had no experience or recollection of Turkish rule. In 1913, in the wake of Serbia's Balkan War victories, anti-Austrian agitation became so virulent that Governor Potiorek saw himself forced to impose press censorship and to suspend parliament temporarily.

The population of Bosnia and Herzegovina at that time numbered just under two million. Of that total, over 40 per cent were of the Serb-Orthodox faith—a church that was and is closely related to the Greek-Orthodox; over 30 per cent were Moslems; and not quite 25 per cent were Roman Catholics. The remainder were mostly Jews and Protestants. Race and religion were nearly synonymous. Most of the Serb-Orthodox were Serbs—"Serb" being a racial or ethnic designation, which referred to any member of this Slavic group whether or not he was a citizen of Serbia, as distinct from "Serbian," which was a national designation referring to a citizen of the Kingdom of Serbia. The Moslems were either Turks or Serbs. The Roman Catholics were mostly Croats.

By and large, Bosnia's Serbs were in favor of union with Serbia. The Croats were divided: some wanted Serb-Croat union; others declined the Serbian offer of racial brotherhood and preferred to remain within the Empire. The Moslems were largely loyal to Austria.

The agitation took two principal forms. One was to use existing legal organizations as covers for illegal activities. The other was to work through an underground organization that called itself *Mlada Bosna*—"Young Bosnia"—supported by and patterned after a secret Serbian terrorist organization known as the Black Hand. Its basic structure was that of various individual "circles," between which contact was maintained by special intermediaries. Each circle kept its membership small, so that a *Mlada Bosna* member could reveal no more than the names of a very few associates in case of arrest. Members were recruited mainly from among high-school and college students and the poorer peasants. All of *Mlada Bosna's* key members also belonged to the Belgrade Black Hand.

The guiding spirit behind *Mlada Bosna* was a young man named Vladimir Gaćinović. The son of a Serb-Orthodox priest in Herzegovina, he had studied theology for a while, but had changed his field when he discovered the writings of the Russian anarchists. His favorite among them was Bakunin, who held that the way to achieve a free and happy society was to assassinate the proper number of kings, presidents, and grand dukes.

During the annexation crisis, Gaćinović left Bosnia for Belgrade, vainly hoping that there would be war and that he might find a chance to bear arms against Austria. While in Belgrade, he met many of the men who were to become prominent in the Black Hand, and who thought as he did about Russian anarchism. His finest hour came after he had found a martyr to the cause.

In 1910, during the opening of Parliament in Sarajevo, a Serb from Herzegovina, Bogdan Žerajić, fired five shots at the Austrian governor of Bosnia, General Varešanin. The sixth bullet he used to kill himself. General Varešanin, unhurt but displeased, reportedly stepped over to the blood-spattered Žerajić, kicked him, and called him a "filthy cur." As a final indignity, the would-be assassin's body was buried in the corner of the cemetery reserved for suicides and criminals.

Gaćinović seized the occasion to write a fiery pamphlet entitled "The Death of A Hero" in praise of Žerajić—"a man of action, of strength, of life and virtue, a type such as opens an epoch, proclaims ideas and enlivens suffering and spell-bound hearts." Quoting Žerajić as saying "I leave it to Serbdom to avenge me," Gaćinović ended his eulogy by asking rhetorically: "Young Serbs, will you produce such men?"

Armed with copies of his pamphlet and with other propagandist ammunition, Gaćinović made frequent forays from Serbia into Bosnia to look after the affairs of *Mlada Bosna.* "He speaks," an associate of his has written of this period, "offers encouragement, and disappears again like a shadow, as though the earth had swallowed him, since he forever feels that he is being followed by Austrian agents."

Žerajić did become a hero to many Bosnian Serbs, but the concrete results were disappointing. *Mlada Bosna*'s sister organization in neighboring Croatia did much better, managing to kill a Croat Secretary of Education in 1912, and to wound the Governor the next year. In Bosnia-Herzegovina, however, there were no further assassinations, successful or attempted.

Chlumetz to Ilidže: Portents and Accidents

Franz Ferdinand, early in June, was showing an odd reluctance to attend the Bosnian maneuvers. He saw the Emperor, and suggested that for health reasons, he would just as soon not go. Franz Joseph left the decision up to his nephew. A few days later, Franz Ferdinand's Private Secretary took a phone call from Colonel Bardolff at the Archduke's Military Chancellery. He was very sorry, Bardolff said, but there would have to be a small change on the return trip. The departure from Bosnia would have to be advanced by one hour, else it would be impossible to make the proper train connections.

Franz Ferdinand reacted with unreasonable fury. Angrily tearing up a handkerchief he shouted: "Tell Colonel Bardolff that if he should spoil our taste for the Bosnian trip even more than he has done so far by these daily difficulties and troubles, he can hold the maneuvers by himself. I won't go at all then. He seems to have forgotten that the maneuvers will be over on the morning of the twenty-ninth, and that after that it will be a nonmilitary, private trip, with a lady present who deserves some consideration."

On June 12 and 13, Franz Ferdinand received the German Emperor at his estate of Konopisht in Bohemia. The weather was so perfect, and the park in such lovely summer bloom, that he decided to open it to the public on June 14, the Sunday after Wilhelm's departure. On Wednesday, June 17, accompanied by Sophie, he followed an invitation to go quail hunting at Countess Jella Haugwitz' estate of Namiest. He stayed until June 20, when he left for his other Bohemian castle of Chlumetz. Franz Ferdinand, the Countess later said, had struck her as unusually depressed, and full of forebodings.

Three days later, the archducal couple started on their Bosnian journey. The program provided for their traveling together as far as Vienna only. From there, Franz Ferdinand was to go to Trieste and to cross the Adriatic on the battleship *Viribus Unitis,* while Sophie was to take the land route by way of Budapest.

On the afternoon of Tuesday, June 23, Franz Ferdinand made a present of his gold watch to his valet, the faithful Janaczek, asking him to remain with Sophie and the children in the event that anything should ever happen to him. He and Sophie then took leave from the children, and caught the train to Vienna. At the station, the first of a number of accidents occurred which later enabled several witnesses to claim early premonitions of disaster.

For years, Franz Ferdinand had been using his own special parlor car. As the Vienna express, to which his parlor car had been coupled a few miles out of town, pulled into Chlumetz station, smoke was seen rising from a hotbox. One of the parlor car's journal boxes, it turned out, had become badly overheated. No one could explain the accident. Hotboxes usually occurred only in very old or carelessly attended cars; neither was the case here. The porter in charge, normally the very model of the calm and conscientious official, was a picture of despair. There was nothing left to do, however, but to uncouple the car, and to make room for Franz Ferdinand and Sophie in the first-class compartment that had been reserved for the Archduke's young Chamberlain. "Well, that's a promising beginning for this trip," said Franz Ferdinand.

At seven o'clock that evening, the train arrived at Vienna's Franz Joseph Station. From there, Franz Ferdinand and Sophie drove to Belvedere castle, their official residence in the city. Franz Ferdinand, after a light supper, then went on to the *Südbahnhof* to catch his train to Trieste, while Sophie stayed over until the next morning, June 24.

The Duchess' trip passed without further surprises. She traveled in a less capricious parlor car. There were no official receptions for her anywhere along the route, but at many stations large and curious crowds had turned up for a look. Between the Bosnian border and Ilidže she could see that every station had put out flags in welcome.

On June 25, at 9:20 A.M., she and her party arrived at Ilidže in pouring rain. Station, surrounding buildings, *Kurrestaurant,* and many private houses along the road to the hotel had been decorated with flags and bunting, which now hung limp and sodden. Still, there was a cordial reception for her at the station, and an automobile to take her to the Hotel Bosna, where she and Franz Ferdinand were to stay.

At the Bosna, more receptions followed for the Duchess. When she finally managed to withdraw to her rooms, she found that looking out from her first-floor windows, she had a fine view of the resort's well-kept park, and that the rooms themselves had been provided not only with quantities of flowers, but with elaborately carved, inlaid furniture, Oriental rugs, mosque lamps, a collection of Turkish arms, and other antiques loaned by Sarajevo's best firms—not, perhaps, without the thought of making some sales to the august visitors. Amid this Eastern splendor, she awaited her husband's arrival, which was scheduled for midafternoon.

Franz Ferdinand's trip had not at first run quite so smoothly. He had left on June 23, the evening before Sophie's departure. As he arrived at the *Südbahnhof,* he was met by a disconsolate station-master. The *Südbahndirektion,* the station-master said, had put a parlor car at the Archduke's disposal to replace his own which had broken down at Chlumetz, but he was afraid that the electric wiring system had suddenly failed. In the short time before the train's departure, it was impossible to fix it. Would the Archduke mind very much if the car were to be illuminated with candles?

At nine o'clock, Franz Ferdinand's secretary, who was to accompany Sophie the next day, came to the *Südbahnhof* to receive his last minute instructions. The picture that faced him was a weird one, and he remembered it for a long time afterwards: at the table of the parlor car sat Franz Ferdinand, framed to his right and to his left by burning candles. As the secretary took his leave, Franz Ferdinand said to him: "Good-by then; look after Her Highness, see that everything is all right. Get her there in good shape. What do you think about these lights? Just like in a grave, isn't it? At first my carriage is afire when it pulls into the station, and now this other car does not seem to be in a cooperative mood either. Oh well, take care of yourself. Good-by."

The next morning, at Trieste, Franz Ferdinand was piped aboard the battleship *Viribus Unitis.* On June 25, after an eighteen-hour trip across a calm Adriatic, he boarded the smaller warship *Dalmat* at the mouth of the river Narenta. Aboard the *Dalmat,* he was welcomed by Governor Potiorek and his staff, who had traveled to the Adriatic coast to meet their visitor. Preceded by the revenue cutter *Zadar,* the archducal party traveled up the river to the small town of Metković, where a special train to Ilidže was awaiting them. Large and good-natured crowds had taken up positions on both banks of the Narenta for the entire length of the trip. Flags and brightly colored rugs decorated most house fronts, and in several places triumphal arches had been erected. In every town salutes were fired as the *Dalmat* steamed by, while the crowds waved, cheered, or ran along the river bank to keep up with the ship's progress. Some men in the crowd, dressed in native costume, sent exuberant shots into the air from their long-barreled guns.

At Metković, Franz Ferdinand left the *Dalmat,* and after a brief reception by the local authorities entered his train. At Mostar, the next station, there was a two-hour stopover for a more elaborate reception. Mostar was the capital of Herzegovina, a strikingly Oriental and sunny city of about 16,000, its mosques and whitewashed houses surrounded by pine, cypress, and laurel trees.

At the station, Mostar's mayor, all of the town's leading dignitaries, and a band had assembled to greet Franz Ferdinand. The mayor made the sort of brief but flowery address we seem to have lost both the taste and the talent for today:

> While the rays of that sun still warm us that shone on us through the Most Serene visit of His Imperial and Royal Apostolic Majesty [the mayor said; the reference was to Franz Joseph's trip in 1910] a new proof of the highest Imperial favor, the presence of Your Imperial and Royal Highness in our midst, brings happiness to us.
>
> I most humbly thank Your Royal Highness for the gracious visit being paid to our city and I pray that God may grant health and a long and happy life to Your Royal and Imperial

Highness and Your August House. I also beg Your Royal and Imperial Highness to be gracious enough to lay at the steps of the greatest of thrones the feelings of our filial love for, and our devotion and unshakable loyalty to, the exalted person of our beloved Emperor.

I welcome Your Royal Highness among us, in our rocky Herzegovina. Hurrah!

Franz Ferdinand replied in a similar vein, ending with a sentence spoken in Croat: "Will you, Mr. Mayor, convey my most cordial salute to the inhabitants of this beautiful city, in whose development I take the most sincere interest."

At 10:30 A.M., after a tour of Mostar, the archducal party boarded the train again, and arrived in Ilidže, as scheduled, at three. A bright sun had been shining in Mostar, but in Ilidže it was still raining steadily. Despite the bad weather, a large crowd had gathered in front of the station. As the train moved into the station, the sound of commands to the waiting guard of honor could be heard, and the garrison band struck up Haydn's graceful national anthem, "God Save Francis, Our Emperor. . . ."

Franz Ferdinand, alighting, was greeted by a number of military dignitaries, passed the guard of honor in review; found a friendly word for everyone who had come to welcome him, and then proceeded to the hotel to join Sophie. He was in excellent spirits, and later in the afternoon he and Sophie decided to take an unscheduled shopping trip into Sarajevo, where they came face to face with one of their assassins.

CHAPTER IV

The Conspirators

Bomb, Crucifix, and Dagger: Narodna Odbrana
and Ujedinjenje ili Smrt

On October 8, 1908, two days after Austria's annexation of Bosnia and Herzegovina, a number of men met in Belgrade to found a secret organization which they named the *Narodna Odbrana*—"National Defense." Among those present or represented at the meeting were the Serbian Foreign Minister, Milovan Milovanović, and a number of other ranking ministers, officials, and generals. General Bozo Jankosić of the Serbian Army, a kindly looking man with a flowing white beard, was elected president.

The purpose of the *Narodna Odbrana* was to enlist and train partisans, for a possible war against Austria, to carry on anti-Austrian propaganda in Serbia and abroad, and to enlist reliable spies and saboteurs in the Austrian provinces Serbia meant to annex. The *Narodna Odbrana's* work was beautifully organized and it was effective. It soon had agents in every important Bosnian locality—informants, propagandists, and relay men along an underground railway that was used to smuggle fugitives from Bosnia into Serbia, and propaganda material, weapons, and conspirators from Serbia into Bosnia.

In the spring of 1909, the irritated Austrians pressed the Serbian government to put a stop to these activities. Serbia, having been deserted by Russia during the annexation crisis, stood very much alone at that time, and the *Narodna Odbrana* decided to transform itself into a primarily cultural organization that would concentrate on education and propaganda at home rather than on espionage and violence abroad.

While the *Narodna Odbrana* never became the precise Serbian equivalent of a Rotary Club or a Great Books Seminar, it did in subsequent years largely abandon revolutionary action. It therefore became desirable to replace it with a new terrorist organization. The new group's charter members were ten Serbian partisan leaders and army officers. Several had played a part in the Serbian revolution of 1903, when they had been among those who had forced their way into the royal palace, shot and killed King Alexander Obrenović, Queen Draga, the queen's brothers, and a number of cabinet ministers, and proclaimed Peter Karageorgević the new king. On May 9, 1911, the ten finally adopted the written statutes for a secret organization which they christened *Ujedinjenje ili Smrt*, "Union or Death," but which became better known as the "Black Hand."

Black Hand membership very soon stood at about 300. Many of the early joiners were veterans of the regicide of 1903. Most were army officers, but there also was a fair sprinkling of diplomats, lawyers, journalists, university professors, and others. By 1914, it is possible that membership was up to about 2,500. More would have joined had they been admitted, but the Black Hand consistently chose to remain an elite organization. This was particularly true of its operations outside Serbia, where absolute secrecy and loyalty were essential. Total Black Hand membership in Bosnia-Herzegovina, for example, may never have exceeded thirty.

The professed aim of the Black Hand was the creation, by means of violence, of a Greater Serbia. "This organization," read the first two articles of its statutes, "was created in order to realize the national ideal, the unification of all Serbs. . . . This organization prefers terrorist action to cultural activities; it will therefore remain secret."

To achieve its aim, the Black Hand used methods of organization that combined the paraphernalia of Masonic ritual with the practical efficiency of a mail order catalogue. At the bottom of the organizational pyramid was a large number of compact groups of from three to five members each. Above them were several district committees; above these a single Central Committee at Belgrade. The top of the pyramid consisted of a ten-member, policy making Central Executive Committee. Members' names were known to a very few people only; in general, groups were referred to by Roman, and individual members by Arabic code numerals.

In those Austrian and Turkish territories which the Black Hand meant to join to Serbia, and where it operated as well as in Serbia proper, the basic group was often larger, and had more freedom of action. "Major revolutionary action, however," the statutes prescribed, "shall be made dependent upon the approval of the Central Committee in Belgrade." Representatives from all of the "unredeemed territories" had a place in the Central Committee; the representative from Bosnia-Herzegovina was a Gaćinović, the panegyrist of Žerajić.

Initiation of new members took place in a darkened room, lighted by a single candle. In the center of the room stood a table covered with a black cloth, on which were displayed a dagger, a revolver, and a crucifix. After listening to a brief speech on the Black Hand's aims and rules, and on the dangers to which anyone joining it exposed himself, each candidate was asked if he was ready to swear the initiation oath. As he replied that he was, a cloaked, masked man—a member of a higher group—silently entered from an adjoining room. In the presence of the masked man, the candidate then pronounced the following oath:

> I, ***, in joining the organization "Union or Death," swear by the Sun that warms me, by the Earth that nourishes me, before God, by the blood of my ancestors, on my honor and on my life, that I will from this moment until my death be faithful to the laws of this organization; and that I will always be ready to make any sacrifice for it.
>
> I swear before God, on my honor and on my life, that I will execute all missions and commands without question.
>
> I swear before God, on my honor and on my life, that I will take all the secrets of this organization into my grave with me.
>
> May God and my comrades in the organization be my judges if, knowingly or not, I should ever violate this oath.

Afterwards the masked stranger shook hands with the novices and, still without uttering a word, left the room. Each new member then wrote out and signed a copy of the oath, which went to the Central Committee in Belgrade, and received his code number and the password or recognition signal of the moment.

The Black Hand's seal was in keeping with the spirit of the oath. The center showed a clenched fist holding an unfurled flag bearing a skull and crossbones. To the left of the flag were a dagger, a bomb, and a bottle of poison. Around it ran the legend *Ujedinjenje ili Smrt*—"Union or Death."

Communications between Central Committee and local groups were seldon put in writing, although sometimes a code advertisement might be placed in a reputable Belgrade daily read mostly by business people. Financing was by membership dues and by occasional collections among nonmembers. Discipline was maintained by having each member act as an informer—"all members are obliged to observe . . . the behavior of comrades known to them"— and by threatening death to anyone who revealed Black Hand secrets.

The organization's principal activities were the establishment of a school for guerillas and saboteurs, the appointment of frontier officers, and political murders. It is impossible to say precisely how many assassinations the Black Hand sponsored. Much information about the organization came to light at the trial of some of its leaders in 1917, but on this particular subject little has been revealed. It is probable, however, that the Black Hand was involved in an unsuccessful attempt to kill Emperor Franz Joseph in 1911, and it seems certain that in 1912 it aided in a Croat terrorist's gun plot against the governor of Croatia which missed the intended victim, but killed a bystander and a policeman.

The guerilla academy was established in 1911, in an out-of-the-way village near the ancient Orthodox bishopric of Niš. Here students, the majority of whom came from Bosnia and Herzegovina, received instruction in shooting, bomb-throwing, bridge-blowing, espionage, and related skills. Many of them had been recruited by the border officers, the most valuable single group of members, perhaps, of the Black Hand.

By an arrangement between the Black Hand and the Serbian General Staff, there were appointed, as officers in charge of a half dozen crucial border stations facing Austria and Turkey, Black Hand members who, in addition to their more conventional duties, were entrusted with espionage and subversion. To the War Ministry, these frontier officers were responsible for co-ordinating espionage activities in those sections of Austrian and Turkish territory that lay across their respective posts. To the Black Hand, they were responsible for sponsoring and organizing revolutionary activities in the same areas, and for serving as links in the underground railway originally established by the *Narodna Odbrana*, and now taken over by the Black Hand.

Other things which the Black Hand borrowed from the *Narodna Odbrana* were its prestige and name. The frontier officers did nothing to counteract the general assumption that the group they were secretly representing was the *Narodna Odbrana*, and with few exceptions enrolled their collaborators across the border in that organization rather than in the Black Hand.

It all worked out to a neat bit of camouflage. Should an agent be caught, the Austrian police might possibly make him admit a connection with the *Narodna Odbrana*, but he would be unable to say anything about the Black Hand, since he was quite genuinely ignorant of its existence. The Austrians, who had found out a good deal about the activities of the *Narodna Odbrana*, thus knew next to nothing about those of the Black Hand, and mistakenly continued to attribute most of the subversion in Bosnia to the older organization.

rchduke Franz Ferdinand of Austria-
with his wife, Sophie, Duchess of
nberg, and their three children:
millian, Ernst, and Sophie.

2. Franz Ferdinand

3. Franz Joseph I, Emperor of Austria
and Apostolic King of Hungary. A photograph taken in 1916, the year of the Emperor's death at the age of 86.

4. Nicola Pašić, Prime Minister of Serbia

5. Colonel Dragutin Dimitrijević, called Apis

6. General Oskar orek, Governor of B and Herzegovina.

ЈЕДНА ЛЕГИТИМАЦИЈА
(У факсимилу)

Врховна Централна Управа Организације УЈединење или Смрт", овим Делегира свога члана Бр.1872. да у Паризу – Француској – образује обласну Управу и спроведе организацију у духу Устава и пословника Организације.

" Резултат доставити познатим путем.

· Photographie du modèle d'une carte de légitimation.

7. A Black Hand document: "Identification (Original) The Central Executive Com of the Organization Union or Death hereby delegates its member No. 1872 with orga a local committee in Paris, France, in the spirit of the constitution and rules of pro of the organization. Results to be reported to the Central Executive Committee th the familiar channels." On the rubber stamp, to the left of the clenched fist holdi flag with a skull and crossbones, note the bomb, the dagger, and the poison bottle. scription around it reads: "Union or Death – Central Executive Committee."

The Belgrade government was in a far better position to know, despite the secrecy that surrounded the Black Hand even in Serbia. At first, there was close cooperation between government and Black Hand. Black Hand members held important positions in army and civil service; the Crown Prince, Alexander, reportedly gave the new organization 26,000 dinars toward starting a newspaper, *The Piémont;* and members of the Black Hand's Central Executive Committee took care to inform selected cabinet members of any major decisions they had taken. Later, relations cooled and even became hostile. Prince Alexander lost much of his enthusiasm when, despite his cash contribution, the Black Hand refused him a position of leadership. More important, in 1914, the government, then headed by Nikola Pašić, engaged in a drawn-out, bitter power struggle with the Black Hand over the question of whether civilian or military control was to have priority in the territories Serbia had annexed during the Balkan Wars.

Despite such friction, the government continued to be rather well informed about what went on in the Black Hand. One likely reason for this was that one of the organization's more trusted members, a man named Milan Ciganović—he was to play a major role in the Sarajevo plot—very probably was a personal agent of Pašić, and had joined the organization primarily to keep the Prime Minister informed of its doings.

Apis

Thirty-seven years of age in 1914, heavy-set and quite bald, with an elegantly upswept moustache and the pleasantest of manners, Colonel Dragutin Dimitrijević was the

Chief of the Intelligence Department in the Serbian General Staff, and the moving spirit behind the Black Hand.

His background and education were the customary ones for the professional army officer: *lycée* in Belgrade, then, at eighteen, the Military Academy. He was a popular student and a brilliant one. He also displayed so much restless activity that his fellow-students at the *lycée* amicably nicknamed him Apis—the Bee—a name that stuck to him for the remainder of his life. He graduated from the Military Academy with such an outstanding record that he went directly into the General Staff.

Even in his youth, Apis was an ardent patriot. To help achieve Serbian greatness, he became a specialist in revolution, conspiracy, and assassination. He was, quite possibly, the foremost European expert in regicide of his time.

He acquired this skill by much experiment and experience. His first effort was still quite clumsy and probably doomed to fail from the start. In 1901, a number of young Serbian officers undertook to remove the autocratic and unpopular King Alexander and his wife Draga, a woman with a dubious past. The plan Apis worked out called for doing the killing at the Queen's Birthday Ball. A few of the officers were to seize Belgrade's two power plants and to shut off the electricity. The others were to attend the Ball, and at the moment the lights went off were to set fire to the curtains, sound a fire alarm, and poison the royal couple during the ensuing confusion.

The poison was secured and successfully tested on a cat; everything else, however, went wrong. The power stations turned out to be so well guarded that the officers could not force their way in. Moreover, the king and queen failed to appear at the ball.

His first setback apparently did not disconcert Apis too

badly, and in the course of pursuing the murder scheme he learned the value of binding conspirators together by fear as well as by common motive. In the winter of 1902, he drafted the following oath, which all the less cautious members of the group readily signed:

Anticipating certain collapse of the state if the existing situation continues for even the shortest time, and blaming for this primarily the King and his paramour Draga Mašin, we swear that we shall murder them and to that effect affix our signatures. In place of these dishonorable individuals, we shall bring to the Serbian throne Peter Karageorgević, grandson of the Leader [a reference to Kara George, the leader of the first Serbian revolt against the Turks in 1804], and the legitimate son of Prince Alexander Karageorgević.

In the spring of 1903, amid indications that the police had discovered the plot, Apis, with the knowledge of one other officer only, destroyed the document. He did not tell anyone else what he had done, so that the other conspirators continued to feel endangered and thus firmly bound by an oath that in reality no longer existed.

Later that year, in June, some of the group stormed the royal palace under cover of night, after much hectic searching found the king and queen, who had been hiding in an alcove behind a secret door of their bedroom, shot them and threw their naked and bloody bodies from the bedroom window into the garden below. In town, the remaining conspirators sought out and killed the others on their liquidation list. Early in the foray, Apis had thrown himself at the palace guard, who opened fire and left him badly wounded. He eventually recovered, but three bullets left from the encounter were never removed from his body.

The new dynasty was grateful to Apis, then a Captain,

and to his fellow conspirators. Parliament thanked him for what he had done, calling him "the savior of the father-land." Promotions, however, did not come unusually fast for so outstanding an officer as Dimitrijević was. One reason may have been that he was as critical of the new regime as he was unwilling to give up his secret position of power.

Apis was held in great regard by his fellow-officers, and, having been appointed Professor of Tactics at the Military Academy, in addition to his general-staff duties, he exercised a profound influence over a large number of students as well. In the years that followed the coup of 1903, Apis, al-ways careful to keep to the background, became a leader in the fight for army reforms, against corruption in govern-ment, and for a Greater Serbia. "Although there was no-thing despotic about him, his suggestions and wishes were treated as commands," a friend of his has written since. "One saw him nowhere, yet one knew that he was doing everything. . . . There was no minister of war who did not have the feeling of having another, invisible minister next to him."

Trips to Germany and Russia taught Apis some new military ideas, and when the Balkan Wars of 1912 and 1913 broke out, the Serbian army's victories owed much to the strategy he had planned. He himself could take no active part in the fighting. Disguised as a simple partisan, he had, just before the beginning of the First Balkan War, made his way into Turkish territory and won over the most powerful of Albanian chieftains to the Serbian cause. He returned from this exploit gravely ill. For a while, his condition was critical. After a specialist was called in from Berlin and diagnosed his disease as Maltese fever, a rare and painful illness, he slowly improved, but he was still far too ill to lead any troops. In June, 1913, when he had quite recovered, he was appointed head of Serbian Intelligence. One of his first acts was to organize a very superior espionage service in Austria-Hungary.

His increasing military responsibilities did not cause Apis to abandon conspiracy and violence. Among other plots, he sent a young enthusiast to Vienna to try his hand at killing Emperor Franz Joseph in 1911, three years later agreed with a Bulgarian revolutionary group to the assassination of Ferdinand of Bulgaria, and during the World War formulated a plot against the King of Greece.

Apis' principal instrument for the organization of political terror was the Black Hand. He had been charter member number six, and, although nominally he was never anything but one among ten on the Central Executive Committee, he very soon became its true leader. Partly this was due to the high rate of attrition among the organization's leadership; of the ten charter members, three died in the Balkan Wars, and one left Belgrade to serve at the Serbian Legation in Athens. But to a much larger degree it was Apis' personal qualities which made him the Black Hand's life and soul.

Personal magnetism, great intelligence, and utter discretion combined to make Apis a wonderful organizer of whatever intrigue he happened to be pursuing at the moment. Brave, incorruptible, modest, vastly patriotic, and totally ruthless, he reminds one of a number of other leaders Europe, and more recently the Middle East, have seen since the French Revolution. It is a line that begins with Robespierre and ends, for the time being, with Colonel Nassar. Apis' weakness—aside from his conviction that patriotic aims left no room for moral scruples—was that for all his immediate political skill, he knew little about the world outside Serbia, and that he had no real sense for what was politically feasible and what, in the long run, was not.

Apis Plans A Murder

The exact dates and circumstances of how Franz Ferdinand's murder was planned—although not the motives, for those are very plain indeed—have never been established with absolute certainty, and probably never will be. The plot's surviving participants have either kept silent or told stories widely at variance with one another, and a written confession left by Apis himself (which was suppressed by a succession of Belgrade governments until its release by Tito's in 1953) is plainly a mixture of truth and untruth. The following account, therefore, can claim no more than that it is based on the most likely among several stories and on the testimony of the more credible among the witnesses, and must remain open to some amount of doubt.

Early in November, 1913, Danilo Ilić, a young newspaper editor and Black Hand member in Sarajevo, crossed the border into Serbia, to look up a frontier officer, Colonel Čedomir Popović. Some revolutionary action, Ilić said, ought to be taken in Bosnia. Popović replied that to him, the time did not seem right for acts of open violence.

The answer did not satisfy Ilić. Would Popović mind if he, Ilić, talked things over with Apis? Popović thought this an excellent idea, gave Ilić money and travel papers for the journey to Belgrade, and asked him to stop by on the way back to tell him what had been decided. Ilić failed to do so, since he chose a different route for his return trip. Popović had reason to believe, however, that what Ilić discussed with Apis was an attempt on Governor Potiorek's life.

At any rate, Apis' chief aide, Major Voja Tankosić, careful as always to cover up any traces that might lead to Serbia, organized a meeting of some trusted Bosnian revolutionaries in France. Early in January, 1914, there came together in the Hôtel-Restaurant St. Jérôme, on the rue St. Jérôme in Toulouse, the pamphleteer Gaćinović and two other Bosnian Black Hand members, Mustafa Golubić and Muhamed Mehmedbašić. Golubić was a law student of twenty-two. Mehmedbašić was a cabinetmaker from Herzegovina, a Moslem in his late twenties, and this account of the Toulouse meeting and its consequences is based largely on the story he himself has told of it.

At the St. Jérôme, according to Mehmedbašić, Gaćinović spoke at some length on the need to arouse Bosnia by acts of terrorism. The three young men then debated who might best be assassinated, mentioning Franz Ferdinand among others, but settling on Potiorek as the most effective victim. The man chosen as the assassin was Mehmedbašić. The weapon he was to use was a poisoned dagger. Gaćinović procured the poison in which to dip the dagger, and Mehmedbašić set out for the return trip to Bosnia.

As his train passed into Austrian territory, he noticed that several policemen were searching the compartments for something. In some panic, he threw the dagger out of the window, and flushed the poison down the toilet. A while later he learned that the police had been after a petty thief.

Mehmedbašić wrote to Gaćinović to report the fiasco and to ask for further instructions. He also looked up Ilić in Sarajevo, to say that he still was ready to assassinate Potiorek. Ilić's answer was to forget about Potiorek. A decision had meanwhile been made, Ilić said, to kill Franz Ferdinand instead.

At what point Apis decided to have Franz Ferdinand

murdered is not clear. That it was Apis, however, who planned the murder is in as little doubt as are his reasons for wanting Franz Ferdinand's death.

Much nonsense has been written about Apis' motives by people intent on vindicating his deed. Franz Ferdinand supposedly was a warmonger. Apis supposedly had found out that the Bosnian maneuvers were nothing but the prelude to an Austrian attack on Serbia. The German Kaiser, during the meeting at Konopisht in June, supposedly had promised Franz Ferdinand his country's help in smashing the Serbian state. The truth was that there had been no such talk at Konopisht, that there was nothing sinister about the Bosnian maneuvers, and that Franz Ferdinand dreaded the thought of war with Serbia since he realized that it would lead to a disastrous war with Serbia's ally Russia. Moreover, as head of Serbian Intelligence, Apis knew very well what was fact and what was rumor.

Apis decided on Franz Ferdinand's assassination not because he thought him a warmonger, but because he feared the Archduke's ideas might bring about the solution of Austria-Hungary's nationality problems by offering major concessions to the monarchy's South Slavs. Greater Serbian agitation needed dissatisfied Serbs in Austria. Franz Ferdinand's schemes for Trialism or Federalism, if they were ever allowed to be put into practice, would mean the collapse of the Yugoslav dream. In fact, the creation of a prosperous, autonomous South Slav state within the Austrian Empire represented an even graver threat than that. Not only might union with Serbia lose its appeal to Austria's Serbs —union with an Austro-Hungarian-Slav federation might well make sense to a great number of people in the kingdom of Serbia some day.

Apis was not alone in being appalled by the prospect. In

a moment of frankness, Prime Minister Nikola Pašić confided to an Italian friend during the war that he had trembled only once for the future of his country—when he had found out about Franz Ferdinand's plan for reorganizing the Austro-Hungarian monarchy.

At about the time of the Toulouse meeting, Apis learned about the Archduke's forthcoming visit to Sarajevo, and he very quickly decided that the killing of Franz Ferdinand would make far greater sense than that of Potiorek. It is unlikely that Apis thought the murder would lead to war with Austria, and it is even less likely that he wanted such a war at that time. He made sure, however, that if the unexpected should happen, Serbia would not have to fight alone.

For some time, Apis had been working in close harmony with the Russian military attaché to Belgrade, Colonel Victor Artamonov. Artamonov had been providing Apis with money to finance his intelligence network in Austria at a time when the Serbian General Staff was short of funds. In return, Apis probably shared some of the information gathered by his agents with Artamonov. Apis now may have told the Russian attaché about the assassination scheme, and asked if Serbia could count on Russian aid in the event of war.

When Artamonov, apparently after consulting with St. Petersburg, reportedly assured him that Russia would stand by Serbia if Austria attacked first, Apis definitely made up his mind to have Franz Ferdinand killed.

CHAPTER V

The Preparations

Coffee Shops and Terrorists

Having decided on the murder, Colonel Dimitrijević preferred to touch few of the actual details himself. Instead, he left the preparations to his principal Black Hand aide, Major Voja Tankosić.

Tankosić was a kindly and gentle man in his private life, who was capable of acting with total ruthlessness wherever his political beliefs were involved. He had played a leading part in the coup of 1903, when he had directed the killing of the queen's two brothers. During the Balkan War, he made a name for himself as a partisan fighter. A close associate of Apis, he was charter member number seven of the Black Hand, and went on to become the commanding officer of its guerilla academy near Niš.

Tankosić had little difficulty in recruiting his assassins. There were, at this time, a great many disaffected young Bosnians in Belgrade. Some were high-school students who had come to Serbia to study. Others had served as partisans in the Balkan Wars, and now had a good deal of time on their hands which they were spending in talking about revolution and Greater Serbia. Most of these youths had little money, although some of the ex-partisans held minor government jobs. Their principal meeting places were several inexpensive Belgrade coffee shops, where for no more than the price of a cup of coffee they could sit and talk for as long as the mood struck them: the *Zlatna Moruna* or Golden Sturgeon; across from it the *Žirovni Venac* or Acorn Garland; and not far from these the *Moruna* or Sturgeon, and the *Zeleni Venac* or Green Garland.

The world of these coffee shops was one of excitement, of restlessness, conspiracy, and good companionship. The partisans, despite the martial beards they often affected, were as a rule only a few years older than the eager high-school juniors and seniors in their audience. They talked endlessly of their recent exploits against Turks and Bulgarians, and of how they were looking forward to fighting the Austrians next. Both groups seemed forever to be living in expectation of some great happening that would change their lives, forever to be plotting wars and violence. Their poverty was sometimes bitter. There might be no food for a day; some of them might sleep in Belgrade's public shelter or in shacks they built themselves of boards and newspapers. It did not matter—it was shared poverty. Beside, they felt themselves to be the vanguard of a different future, of the new Empire of all South Slavs.

From among this group, Tankosić chose his recruits. He chose well: one absolutely trustworthy youth, who had a very definite idea of what the crime he was going to commit was really about, and two relative innocents. Their names were Gavrilo Princip, Nedjelko Čabrinović, and Trifko Grabež.

Grabež was a dark and serious-looking young man of nineteen. He was the son of a Serb-Orthodox priest in Pale, a small town about twelve miles east of Sarajevo. At the age of seventeen, he was expelled from school for striking one of his teachers. He thereupon left Bosnia for Belgrade to continue his schooling, passed through three high-school classes within about a year and a half, and in the spring of 1914 was finishing his junior year.

At his trial, the judge was to express some surprise over the rapidity of Grabež's educational progress in Belgrade, asking "Are our schools better than the Serbian schools, or are Bosnian students being favored?" Grabež gave a curt reply: "The spirit of instruction is different. One does not get five to six hours of Latin, Greek is not taught, and the whole emphasis is different."

Greatly addicted to devising plans for the overthrow of authority, Grabež joined the Black Hand and spent much of his time in the company of the ex-partisans and exiles of the coffee shops. For all his talk of violence, his health was poor; he was probably suffering from consumption even then.

Nedjelko Čabrinović, nineteen like Grabež, and a handsome, black-haired youth, had had a rather more varied career. His father was an Austrian police spy, and relations between father and son were constantly marked by bickering and by outright hostility. His father, Čabrinović claimed at his trial, failed to support him and mistreated him, once locking him up for three days for behaving badly toward a servant. (In 1924, near the tenth anniversary of the Sarajevo crime, Čabrinović's father died a suicide.)

Čabrinović finished the first two years of commercial high school, but he was a poor student, and his father made him leave school at about the age of fourteen. He tried a number of trades, apprenticing himself in turn to a plumber, a carpenter, and a typesetter. He had frequent quarrels with most of his employers, and quit his first job as a printer in anger after some superior struck him. Leaving Bosnia, he made his way to Belgrade, where he found work in a print shop specializing in anarchist literature.

Before long, he became quite ill. Like Grabež, he was probably a consumptive. He returned home to Bosnia for a rest cure, bringing with him a number of anarchist books which he was fond of reading as well as printing, and which his mother, when she discovered them, very promptly burned.

After his condition improved, he went to work for a printer in Sarajevo, took a leading part in a typesetters' strike in 1912, and as a result received an expulsion order from the city for a period of five years. Returning to Belgrade, he began to associate with the young revolutionaries of the coffee shops. When he fell ill again, and when his money ran short, someone introduced him to Major Milan Vasić, Secretary of both the *Narodna Odbrana* and the Black Hand, at the Acorn Garland cafe.

As Čabrinović later told it in court, he happened to have a volume of Maupassant stories with him at the time of their meeting. Vasić took the book away from him, saying that this sort of reading was not for Čabrinović, and gave him some money as well as a batch of Greater Serbian literature. "I don't know how to thank you for your kindness," said Čabrinović. Vasić replied that he could do so by just being a good Serb.

Čabrinović, who had been first a socialist and then an anarchist, became a passionate nationalist in Belgrade, although there is no evidence that he was ever admitted to Black Hand membership. Nor would it seem probable that he was; for, strongly attached to whatever convinctions he held at the moment, and pathetically anxious to make everyone forget that his father was serving the Austrians as a police informer, Čabrinović had a dangerous tendency to be incautious and talkative.

After some more wanderings, which included a trip back to Sarajevo—the five year expulsion order had been commuted to two months—his friends procured a job for him at the Serbian Government Printing Office in Belgrade. It was here that Čabrinović was working early in 1914.

Gavrilo Princip, the third of Tankosić's recruits, and the outstanding one among them, was born in July, 1894, in the village of Oblej, in the wild and mountainous region that separates Bosnia from the Dalmation coast. His father worked as a postman, and Gavrilo was the fourth among nine children, six of whom died in infancy. He attended high school in Sarajevo and Tuzla, but in May, 1912, he left Bosnia for Belgrade, ostensibly in order to continue his education there.

Princip had become an active propagandist for the Greater Serbian cause while still at school in Bosnia, and in Belgrade he quickly found his way to the right coffee shops. He joined the Black Hand, and enrolled in Tankosić's partisan academy. When his turn came to go to the front, however, it was discovered that his health rendered him quite unfit for actual service. The disease he was suffering from very probably was tuberculosis. Slight of build, thin lipped and pale, Princip certainly always seemed to look frail, if not actually ill, and it is difficult to see how anything but his immense strength of will ever got him admitted to the partisan academy.

Having been sent back by Tankosić, Princip spent the next year or so either in Belgrade or near Sarajevo, studying for high school examinations and plotting revolution with a number of friends which included Gaćinović, Grabež, and Čabrinović. His family mailed him a modest sum of money for his support each month, but Princip seldom seemed to have any of it left. Although essentially far from gregarious by nature, he would gladly pay for the meal of some fellow-student poorer than himself, or loan money to his friends, no matter how slim the chances of repayment.

In February, 1914, having spent the winter in the village of Hadžići near Sarajevo, Princip was back in Belgrade, preparing for his final high school examinations, and looking for an opportunity to strike some blow against the Austrians.

The Clean Young Assassins

Certain similarities between Tankosić's three recruits for the murder are striking. They all knew each other. "Princip was my best friend," said Čabrinović at his trial, and Grabež and Princip roomed together for some time in Belgrade. They were of the same age—all were nineteen. They came from poor families, and had spent childhoods that were far from happy, although Princip and Grabež did not dislike their families with Čabrinović's intensity. Legally, they were citizens of Austria-Hungary, ethnically, they were Serbs, and they felt that their loyalty belonged to Serbia, not to Austria.

Aside from their compulsion to commit treason and murder, they really were good and kindly fellows. They shared what they had, and with the possible exception of Čabrinović, they worked and studied hard. They had had little or no trouble with the police. Grabež had been sentenced to two weeks in prison for striking his high-school teacher, and

Čabrinović had been told to leave Sarajevo for his activities in the typesetters' strike, but these two minor offenses apart, they had perfectly clean records.

They were, in fact, remarkably free of bad habits. In some ways, it might even be said that they were excessively serious and moral young men. They had no expensive tastes. They drank sparingly, if at all. They made no bad debts, did not gamble, and we definitely know at least of Princip that he was frightfully shy in the company of women.

Their health was bad. Knowing themselves to be in more or less advanced stages of consumption, they believed that it was all but their duty to sacrifice whatever life they might have left to their cause. At their trial, for example, the following exchange took place between Čabrinović and his defense counsel, Dr. Premužić:

Premužić: "You told me, when we talked about the [newspaper] *Zora,* that you still had some doubts at that moment, and that reading it made an impression on you,"

Čabrinović: "Yes."

Premužić: "I ask the defendant to sum up the contents of the *Zora* article."

Čabrinović: "There was a story in it about a young Serb professor who had killed himself somewhere, and that he had acted foolishly, for by sacrificing himself he could have disposed of at least one of our enemies. Since he had decided to die, he should have killed at least one enemy."

No murderer's motives, of course, are entirely unmixed. Dreams of glory that many a high-school student has dreamed before and since may have helped to drive them on—Žerajić's martyrdom and fame called for imitation. They may have been seriously concerned over the poverty in which the ordinary Bosnian peasant lived, hoping that any sort of change could improve his lot. "People are re-

duced to complete poverty . . . ," said Princip at their
trial. "I am the son of peasants and I know what is happening in the villages. That is why I wanted to take revenge,
and I regret nothing." But since very obviously it was not
Franz Ferdinand who had impoverished Bosnia's peasants,
their overriding motive was a different one—the creation
of a Greater Serbia.

Nominally, Princip, Čabrinović, and Grabež were Serb-
Orthodox by religion. Actually, none of them practiced his
faith. "I am an atheist," said Princip at the trial, and he
might have been speaking for his friends as well. Yet while
they were atheists, they had found a new secular belief for
which they were ready to die with the conviction and fortitude of any religious martyr. One of the most revealing exchanges took place when the President of the Court, Alois
von Curinaldi, questioned Grabež on his faith:

Curinaldi: "Do you believe in God or are you an atheist?"

Grabež: "I am a believer."

Curinaldi: "How can you reconcile your faith with the
destruction of one of God's creatures? You know that as far
as religion is concerned that is a mortal sin."

Grabež: "My faith does not go that far."

Curinaldi: "Your father is a parish priest. What sort of
education did he give you? Did he inculcate any religious
feelings in you?"

Grabež: "He gave me a religious education, within the
framework of Holy Scripture."

Curinaldi: "How did you follow your father's teach-
ings?"

Grabež: "I did as a child, but then, coming into contact
with other people, there were other influences."

Curinaldi: "These young people have no faith?"

Grabež: "Not the faith you are thinking of, but they have a national religion, and that to a high degree."

If the national religion, the advancement of Serbo-Croat union, required Franz Ferdinand's death, they would kill him. It was that simple.

Perhaps not all three realized what Apis' real motives were for wanting Franz Ferdinand killed. Possibly Grabež and Čabrinović thought of him mainly as a potential enemy and oppressor of the Serbs, and only Princip realized fully that Apis had sentenced Franz Ferdinand to death not because the Archduke was hostile to the Slavs but, on the contrary, because he planned reforms that might prove far too attractive to them. At their trial, in order to give the Austrians no clue that might point to Apis and the Black Hand, the three usually took great pains to hide their true motives, and the extent to which they were aware of the reasons for Apis' decision may therefore never be known. What is certain, however, is that none of them felt that what he was about to commit was a crime.

No matter on what grounds, Franz Ferdinand had been declared an enemy of Serbia and of Serbo-Croat union. The Black Hand had decided that he should die. They were merely engaged in carrying out a sentence and killing an enemy. All that was involved, as Princip put it to Curinaldi —and again he might have been the spokesman for the whole group—was the removal of "an evildoer. I meant to do a good deed."

Shooting Lessons and Weapons

Apis had delegated much of the work of organizing the murder to Tankosić. Tankosić, in turn, also avoided direct contacts with the youths as much as he could, and used yet another agent for many of his dealings with them. The go-between was Milan Ciganović, a twenty-six year old native of Bosnia, an early Black Hand member who had served as a partisan under Tankosić against the Bulgarians, and who now held a minor post with the Serbian State Railways. The chain of command that led from Apis to Tankosić to Ciganović to Princip and his two associates was cumbersome, but it had one immense advantage. Should the youths survive their crime, and be arrested by the Austrian police, they might reveal Ciganović's name, and under extremely persistent questioning even Tankosić's, but they could logically stop there, without so much as hinting that they knew of Apis' existence. This was an absolutely essential precaution, for should the Austrians ever discover—and be able to prove—that the man who had organized the murder was Colonel Dimitrijević, Chief of Serbian Intelligence, they would have ample reason to accuse the Belgrade government of complicity, and appear justified in taking the strongest of measures against Serbia.

By April, the three youths had definitely agreed to commit the murder. In May, they practiced shooting. The best shot among them was Princip, which was not too surprising perhaps in view of his having attended the Black Hand's partisan academy two years before.

On May 27, Ciganović gave them the weapons they were to use—four revolvers and six bombs—and some vials of poison. The guns were Belgian automatics of the most recent model. The bombs, manufactured at the Serbian State Arsenal of Kragujevac, were beautifully suited for assassinations. Rectangular in shape, and weighing less than two and a half pounds, they were harmless looking, easy to handle, and compact enough to carry in a coat pocket, being even smaller in size than the revolvers. When Čabrinović

removed his bomb from his pocket on June 28, one spectator thought that he was taking out a pipe.

The bombs may have been among some weapons which
Ciganović had saved from the Balkan Wars; Grabež
claimed at the trial that he saw a whole suitcase full of
bombs in Ciganović's room. The guns were bought by
Dimitrijević.

The poison was cyanide, packed in small vials carefully
wrapped in cotton. After killing the Archduke, the three
were under instructions to shoot themselves, and, should
this prove impossible, they were to commit suicide by swal-
lowing the cyanide.

The Trip to the Border

Since Princip, Čabrinović, and Grabež were to use the
underground route to Bosnia, and since the Austrians
might be expected to have strong security forces on duty
during the Archduke's visit, the three started for Sarajevo
a full four weeks ahead of Franz Ferdinand's arrival at
Ilidže. We do not know for certain whether it was Ciganović, Tankosić, or Apis himself who planned their trip;
what we do know is that it was planned with considerable
attention to detail.

On May 28, Princip and his two friends left Belgrade.
The first part of their trip, from Belgrade to the town of
Šabac, resembled a pleasant excursion, for they traveled by
river boat. At Šabac, a small Serbian border post facing Austria, they went to look for the local frontier officer, Captain
Rada Popović. Finding him—at a local coffee shop playing
cards—they identified themselves by handing him a note
bearing the letters M. C.—Milan Ciganović's initials. The
two letters told Popović all he needed to know; the day be-

fore, he had been to Belgrade and received Apis' instructions.

He left the coffee shop, and took his visitors to the customs house. There he filled out and signed the proper forms indicating that they were customs officials, and hence entitled to free tickets on the Serbian State Railways, and to half-price tickets on the private railways. (Aside from being well-organized, the Sarajevo plot was cheap—there can have been few other murders in which the killers managed to buy tickets at reduced rates to take them to the scene of the crime.) He also gave them a letter to Captain Prvanović, the frontier officer at Loznica, some twenty miles southwest of Šabac. "Try to receive these people and to guide them where you know your way," he wrote.

On their arrival at Loznica, they looked up Prvanović and gave him Popović's letter. The captain picked up his telephone to call one of his sergeants at the frontier and to consult about the best border crossing point, but there was some trouble with the line, and he was unable to get through. He therefore asked the youths to be back the next day.

The three spent the night at a small resort town outside of Loznica. Here they had their first fight. The exultant Čabrinović could not refrain from writing a half dozen post cards to friends. On one card, he quoted these all too apt lines written by the nineteenth-century Serbian leader and national hero Kara George:

> Noble waters of the Drina
> Frontier between Bosnia and Serbia
> Soon will come the time
> When I shall cross you
> To enter faithful Bosnia.

Princip, appalled by Čabrinović's lack of caution, spoke sharply to his friend, and for some time after that refused to exchange another word with him.

The next morning, Saturday, May 30, the three were sitting in a coffee shop at Loznica when a border guard entered and asked them to accompany him to the customs house. There they found the captain and three of his sergeants of the border guard. Whose station, Prvanović asked the sergeants, was the safest one for an undisclosed crossing? The customs guard from Lješnica thought that his was. Lješnica faced a wooded little island in the river Drina that separated Serbia from Austria. One might rest there. Besides, hidden pathways on the island as well as on either bank of the river across from it offered enough protection to make the region one that was greatly favored among the local smugglers. His post, in short, might well be the perfect spot from which to take Princip and Grabež across.

The suggestion was accepted, and the group split up. Princip and Grabež traveled north with the sergeant to try to slip across the border near Lješnica, while Čabrinović— equipped with a letter of introduction from Captain Prvanović—went south, to try his luck at a town called Mali Zvornik.

CHAPTER VI

Pašić

The Prime Minister's Alarm

At about the same time, the Serbian Prime Minister, Nikola Pašić, learned about the plot. Who his informant was is not certain. One guess would be that it was Ciganović, who was rumored to be Pašić's confidential agent in the Black Hand. Another would be that someone in the Serbian police made the discovery. Government and Black Hand were at loggerheads at that period, and either the police or Pašić's own agents must have been on special guard against any unusual Black Hand activity.

Pašić went into conference with the Minister of the Interior, Stojan Protić, and several other cabinet members. Serbia was not ready for a major war—the Balkan Wars were still far too recent—and Pašić had no desire to run the risk of conflict with Austria at that particular moment. The decision reached, therefore, was to prevent Franz Ferdinand's murder by the simple device of stopping the assassins.

Protić sent the necessary orders to the frontier authorities along the Drina not to let Princip, Grabež, and Čabrinović pass. In theory, the frontier officers came under the Minister of the Interior's authority; their involvement with Black Hand work was something that, in theory again, was no part of their official functions—which were those of guarding the borders rather than of smuggling assassins across them. The frontier officers, however, sent word that it was too late for any effective action. The three youths, their message went, already had crossed into Austria. Whether this was true, or whether the frontier officers had chosen to follow Apis' rather than Protić's orders is a matter of conjecture again, since the precise date on which the Minister's instructions went out has never been revealed.

An Inadequate Warning

A truly unenviable dilemma now confronted Pašić. He had two main courses of action open to him. One was to consider that he had done his duty by trying to stop the assassins at the border, and to let further events take their own course. The other was to prevent the murder by giving the Austrians the facts about the plot.

If he did nothing, and the assassins succeeded, he would have to share some of the guilt for Franz Ferdinand's death. Worse, if the assassins confessed their Belgrade connections, Serbia would face some very embarrassing Austrian questions and demands, and the possibility of war.

If, on the other hand, he revealed the plot to the Austrians, he might well find himself the next victim marked for assassination by the Black Hand. Pašić was no coward, but there were other dangers involved as well. Telling the Austrians the facts would mean admitting the extent to which the Serbian government was aware of, and had tolerated, those subversive activities which it always disclaimed. Beside, a parliamentary election was coming up in Serbia that summer. Many Serbian voters would consider the assassins heroes not murderers. Should it ever become known that Pašić had delivered these youths and their Bosnian helpers to the Austrian police, he might just as soon announce his retirement from politics and save himself the bother of an election campaign.

Finding himself in this quandary, Pašić chose a course of action very much in keeping with his character. A liberal at home, and a pan-Serb abroad. Pašić owed the many years he had spent in office to his considerable popularity, to his shrewdness, and to his immense political skill, which included the exercise of great caution in critical situations. Pašić was the owner of a magnificent, flowing white beard; "the beard will manage all right" was a phrase often heard among his supporters when matters looked dangerous or hopeless. He frequently did.

From the regicide of 1903 until his death in 1926, it was Pašić who, with few interruptions, held power in Serbia. Yet, significantly enough, Pašić had taken pains to avoid making any advance commitments to the regicides, and at the height of the crisis, he simply could not be found anywhere in Belgrade. Or there was the story—very likely apocryphal—told about an interview he supposedly gave to a foreign correspondent. As he was talking to the journalist, his wife entered the room. Pašić rose, and introduced her as Jeanne Pašić. After the journalist had left, Mme. Pašić angrily turned to her husband. Why, she asked him, had he introduced her by that name; surely he must remember that her name was Georgina. Pašić's supposed reply was that he had some excellent reasons. Very probably, he said, the correspondent would mention the meeting with the prime minister's wife. If his article should prove politically embarrassing, one could always deny his entire account by saying that Pašić could not possibly have introduced his wife under the name of Jeanne, when everyone knew that it was Georgina.

Pašić now decided that what he would do was to warn the Austrians through the Serbian Minister in Vienna, but to make the warning neither formal nor specific. This form of warning, if extremely well handled, had the advantage that, without giving too many of the facts away, it might be sufficient to absolve him from any further responsibility for what would happen to both Franz Ferdinand and the would-be assassins. The trouble with it was that it probably was too clever by far, and that it definitely was badly handled.

The Serbian Minister to Vienna was a pan-Serb named Jovan Jovanović, whose extremist views were so well known that the Austrians had on several occasions hinted to Belgrade that they would not mind at all if he were to be recalled. The Court snubbed him, and the Foreign Minister, Count Berchtold, greatly preferred not to receive him. A practice therefore developed by which Jovanović would have most of his dealings not with the Foreign Minister, but with the Minister of Finance, Bilinski, with whom he got along much more easily. It was an unusual arrangement, but old Austria abounded in unusual arrangements. Beside, it made some sense in this case, since administratively, Bosnia and Herzegovina came under the jurisdiction of Bilinski's Ministry.

Pašić's instruction to alert the Austrians, and yet to do so in an innocuous manner, severely taxed Jovanović's diplomatic ingenuity. He was, at that time, the Black Hand's choice for the Foreign Ministry in the event that Pašić's government should be overthrown, and he could make no disclosure that contained even the slightest risk of putting the Austrians on that organization's trail. Nor could he afford to create the impression that his government was trying to intimidate the Austrians to the point of making Franz Ferdinand abandon his Bosnian trip.

Late in May or early in June, Jovanović called Bilinski's secretary to say that he would like to see the Minister some time. There was no hurry about it, he added, and the appointment was set for a date several days later.

On June 5, Jovanović had his interview with Bilinski. What he was about to tell him, Jovanović said, was purely on his personal initiative. (The use of the phrase "personal initiative" is a time-honored and useful diplomatic practice. Translated into nondiplomatic language, its meaning is roughly that the person using it is speaking in the name of his government—no diplomat who wishes to remain one ever makes truly private suggestions involving policy to a foreign government—but that, if so desired, no official cognizance need be taken of his words. In this fashion, should his proposals be accepted, nothing has been lost. Should they be disregarded, the rejection will cause his home government no loss of prestige, since for the record, they had never been made in the first place.)

He had heard, Jovanović said, that the Bosnian maneuvers were to be held along the River Drina, and that Franz Ferdinand was to be in personal charge. (Both assumptions were incorrect. Franz Ferdinand was a guest at the maneuvers, the commanding general being Potiorek, and the location of the maneuvers was about fifty miles west of the Drina, and thus at a safe distance from the Serbian border.) He then, according to his own report, told Bilinski: "If that is true, I can assure Your Excellency that this will cause much discontent among the Serbs, who will consider it a provocative gesture. Maneuvers, under such circumstances, are a dangerous thing. Some young Serb might put a live rather than a blank cartridge in his gun, and fire it. That bullet might hit the man who provoked him. Therefore it might be good and reasonable if Archduke Franz Ferdinand were not to go to Sarajevo, and if the maneuvers were to take place neither on St. Vitus' Day [June 28] nor in Bosnia."

Bilinski, presumably unfamiliar with the meaning of the phrase "personal initiative," and far from guessing that he was being warned about an actual assassination plot, tried to reassure Jovanović. No, he said, he really could not believe that the maneuvers would have such an effect. According to his information, things had been quite peaceful in Bosnia recently. As the frustrated Jovanović took his leave the kindly Bilinski tried to humor him. "Let us hope nothing does happen," he said.

Back at the Serbian Legation, Jovanović confessed to the military attaché that he was worried; Bilinski had not seemed at all impressed by his warning. Nor is it possible to see how he could have been. On the basis of quite inaccurate premises, and in the vaguest of terms, Jovanović had warned him not so much of an assassination plot as against holding the Bosnian maneuvers—which certainly were none of the Finance Minister's business. Nor was Franz Ferdinand's trip any of Bilinski's concern. Even though Bosnia and Herzegovina were under the jurisdiction of his Ministry, Franz Ferdinand was visiting the region in his capacity as Inspector General of the Armed Forces, so that all arrangements for the trip became the responsibilty of General Potiorek, as the ranking military figure. Bilinski's Ministry, in fact, didn't even receive a copy of the travel program.

Despite his misgivings, Jovanović did not take the matter up again in plainer terms either with Bilinski or with anyone else in Vienna. Bilinski, for his part, attached so little importance to Jovanović's remarks that while he may have repeated them in an equally casual manner to Berchtold —there is sharp contradiction between the witnesses involved whether he informed the Foreign Minister at all, and no document mentioning any Serbian warning has been found in the archives of the Austrian Foreign Ministry—he did not consider it necessary to report the conversation to either the Emperor or to Franz Ferdinand. Europe was a very large step closer to the World War.

The Black Hand Votes Against Apis

A more promising attempt to halt the assassination came from an unexpected quarter. On June 14, 1914, Apis called a meeting of the Black Hand's Central Executive Committee in Belgrade. So far, only he, Tankosić, Ciganović, and perhaps one or two other Black Hand members had been involved in planning the murder. Apis now informed the entire Central Committee of the plot against Franz Ferdinand.

It must have been a memorable meeting. Apis' influence had long dominated the Black Hand. The Committee members were not exactly squeamish—many of them had been among the regicides of 1903, and all of them were satisfied that the pan-Serb aim justified violence. Yet when confronted with this bald plan for killing the Austrian Heir to the Throne, they sobered, for it was plain that they might be inviting war.

A long and violent debate ensued. Apis stubbornly defended his position. The opposition, equally vocal, was stronger; at the end, a large majority voted against Apis' plan.

Apis gave in. He would call the assassination off, he promised the Committee. The promise was without meaning. Apis later assured one member of the Committee that he had indeed sent an emissary out after the assassins to dissuade them from their deed, but that they had refused. This story constitutes the sole evidence that Apis so much as tried to carry out the Committee's vote.

CHAPTER VII

Crossing the Drina

Čabrinović's Journey

FRONTIER OFFICER
LOZNICA DISTRICT
Official No.:

Dear Sunić:

Please help this boy cross the border from Mali Zvornik with his passport. It should be safer, Jakovljević can accompany him.

In case Sunić should not be in Mali Zvornik, this letter is addressed to Mr. Milan Jakovljević.

Regards,
Prvan

Bearing this letter from the helpful Captain Prvanović, Čabrinović arrived at the town of Mali Zvornik, on the Serbian side of the border, on May 30. Sunić, chief of the customs office, was in fact absent, so Čabrinović looked up Jakovljević, a local teacher and one of the agents along the underground railway.

Jakovljević took Čabrinović to the Serbian frontier post, where he asked a guard to make the proper exit notations in Čabrinović's passport. Actually, the travel documents Čabrinović was carrying were not his own, but Grabež's. The two had traded passports before separating at Loznica; Čabrinović's name was too well known to the Austrian police as that of a troublemaker and hence might cause suspicion.

While the Serbian guard busied himself with the travel papers, Čabrinović and his companion went to have a cup of coffee. When they had finished, they strolled back and picked up the passport. The two of them then walked to the neighboring town of Zvornik, which was on the Austrian side of the border. Čabrinović, still using Grabež's name, registered at the Austrian frontier post, exchanging a few words of small talk with the guard on duty.

Having completed these formalities, they walked into town, and Jakovljević introduced Čabrinović to a man named Dakić, who was Secretary to the mayor of Zvornik and the next agent along the underground route to his side of the border.

Dakić took Čabrinović to dinner, found him a place to stay overnight, and the next morning, May 31, told him where and when the mail coach for Tuzla was leaving. Čabrinović, setting out on foot, caught the coach a short distance out of town, and soon arrived in Tuzla. Tuzla was a small industrial town on the way to Sarajevo, about twenty-five miles east of Zvornik, where the three youths had agreed to meet again if they succeeded in crossing the border. At Tuzla, Čabrinović settled down to wait for his friends, whose trip meanwhile was going much less smoothly than his had.

Gavrilo Princip (right) in Belgrade. Seated with him on a park bench is Trifko Grabež extreme left. The man between them may be Milan Ciganović.

Gavrilo Princip in
following his ar-

10. Danilo Ilić

11. Trifko Grabež

12. Vaso Čubrilović

13. Cvijetko Popović

14. Miško Jovanović

15. Veljko Čubrilović

Border-guards and Smugglers: Princip and Grabež Cross the Frontier

Grbić, the sergeant of the Serbian border guard whom Captain Prvanović had assigned as a guide to Princip and Grabež, took his charges to his post at Lješnica. He saw to it that they were given a place to sleep at the Lješnica border guards' barracks, and the next morning, May 31, he ferried them across the Drina to Isaković Island. Isaković, while still Serbian territory, was situated next to the Austrian frontier, and on the side facing Austria the river was narrow and shallow enough to be traversed on foot.

On the island, the three travelers went to a local inn and waited for a peasant with the euphonious name of Mićo Mičić to turn up. Mičić was a young farmer who lived on the Austrian side of the border. As he told the Court later, he was in the habit of making frequent trips to the island to drink Serbian plum brandy, and "to dance and have fun with the girls."

Mičić, disappointingly, did not come that day, and the three spent the night in the innkeeper's house. The next day, when Mičić did drop in, Sergeant Grbić told him how he might help. "These are two students," he explained. "They're from Sarajevo; they want to go to Tuzla." Mičić was ready to be of assistance. He would go, he said, and fetch a car for Princip and Grabež. The sergeant told him that he had not quite understood him. "They'll have to pass secretly; they have no passports." Mičić, said Grbić, was to go back and fetch his friend Jakov Milović.

While Mičić probably was no smuggler—at least not a professional one—Milović, a farmer in his forties from another nearby village, definitely was. In addition to smuggling for profit, he acted as a courier and guide on the underground railway, either for reasons of conviction, or because the Serbian border guards closed their eyes to his smuggling activities in return for these other services.

Milović was in no hurry to comply with Grbić's request. "Later maybe; I can't do it now," he said, and went to have a look at his corn field near the border.

Mičić returned to the island to report to Grbić. "Jakov is coming," he said reassuringly. In court later, this prompted a surprised question from the judge. Whenever the trip was being mentioned during the trial, Princip and Grabež were thoughtful enough to try to clear the great many people who had aided them along the route by saying that they had threatened them with dire reprisals if they refused to help or if they disclosed what they had seen. Mičić told a similar story in court. Grbić, he said, had warned him that if he valued his life, he must say nothing about their meeting. Here the judge interrupted. Why, he asked Mičić, had he voluntarily gone back to join the travelers on the island after hearing such threats? Mičić had an obvious answer: "I returned. I had not finished my brandy."

At three o'clock in the afternoon, Milović turned up at the inn, and at dusk, the party left the island. They walked quietly and in single file, at a distance of about twenty feet from one another. Milović, who looked like the smuggler that he was, led the way. Mičić followed. Then came the two students. At one point, Mičić wordlessly dropped out and left for his home. No one spoke. It had been raining hard that day, and the pathways they were using were muddy as well as rough, but it was essential that they avoid the main roads. Princip and Grabež had to pay close attention in order not to stumble, but Milović seemed to be familiar with every part of the wooded terrain through which they were passing, and they met neither Austrian border guards nor policemen. In court later, Milović could not hide his professional pride. He could have taken them across undetected even if it had been daytime, he said.

After walking for some time, they reached Milović's house, and took a brief rest. They were safely inside Austrian territory now, but they were still a good twenty-five miles from Tuzla. Still guided by Milović, they started on their way again, but it was beginning to rain so hard and to get so dark that they decided to stop and spend the night in a deserted cottage near the edge of the woods, not far from the house they had just left.

The Underground Railway: Continuing On to Priboj

In the morning, they walked on until they came to a farm owned by Obren Milošević, a friend of Milović's. (Novelists are fortunate; they can invent obviously different names for their characters and thus spare their readers much confusion. In a historical narrative like this, one can only record that the names of Princip's and Grabež's successive guides were Mičić, Milović, and Milošević, and hope.) At Milošević's farm, they had some coffee and asked to be given bags to carry their weapons in. They had been hiding them under their clothing while crossing the border, but they found this too uncomfortable to do for long. Milošević obliged, and found them some pieces of cloth for wrapping the weapons as well as the bags they had asked for.

At the trial, Milošević played the role of the simple-minded Balkan peasant to the hilt. He had had no idea, he said, what the youths were about, and pleaded innocent— the actual exchange going like this:

Judge: "Are you guilty?"

Milošević: "God willing, no."

When one lawyer asked whether he had not thought it strange to have two young students turn up at his farm with bombs and guns, his reply went: "How could I think that? If intelligent people, people with an education, act like that, how can I, a simple fellow, find fault with it? Sir, I thought they were government officials."

Accompanied now by Milošević as well as Milović, who were carrying the arms, the two presumed government officials walked through the woods for nearly four hours until they reached the outskirts of the small town of Priboj. They stopped frequently on the way, to make sure they were not being seen, and once, when they noticed the imprints of heavy boots on the soft and muddy soil, they hid for a while, since they feared that the imprints had been made by the police.

Outside Priboj they hid again, in a meadow behind a thicket, while their two guides went to fetch the local agent on the underground route, Veljko Čubrilović, a young school teacher. Čubrilović was riding to a funeral in a nearby village with the Priboj parish priest, but the peasants managed to intercept him. Milović took him aside, and told him about his two charges. Čubrilović made his excuses to the priest. The water really was too high for him to go on, he said. The priest laughed, and called him a coward, and rode on alone.

Princip and Grabež went out into the road as they saw their guides return with Čubrilović. They explained who they were, and asked Čubrilović to arrange for their transportation to Tuzla. Turning to Milović and Milošević— no longer needed as guides now—they gave them some money for their trouble, and let them take their departure.

Čubrilović put the arms in his saddlebag, and, while being told about the purpose of the trip, took Princip and Grabež to the house of a prosperous old farmer he knew named Mitar Kerović.

On reaching Kerović's house, however, Grabež, who felt exhausted and miserable after all the walking he had done, wasted no time in pulling off his shoes and falling into bed.

Sitting around the living-room table with Kerović and his three sons, Princip and Čubrilović meanwhile were discussing the safest way to reach Tuzla. The farmer's youngest son, Nedjo, had recently hurt his hand with an axe, and Čubrilović had an inspiration. "Let Nedjo go to Tuzla today before the wound gets worse," he suggested. "That way, they can go with him."

Nedjo's eldest brother shrugged his shoulders. He did not mind the idea, but who, he wanted to know, would pay for the cart?

Čubrilović reassured him: "The cart will be paid for."

The matter settled, the men began to talk about some coming local elections, and about the saddlebag which Čubrilović had brought in with him. Čubrilović had been reluctant to touch the bombs at first, but Princip and Grabež had eased his fears by telling him that the bombs could not explode until the caps were unscrewed, and the bombs themselves were knocked against some hard object. The school teacher was drinking glass after glass of plum brandy now, and feeling boastful.

"Do you know who these people are?" he asked the Kerovićes. "They're going to Sarajevo to throw bombs and kill the Archduke who is going to come there."

Crossing over to the bed where he had placed his saddlebag, Čubrilović took out a bomb and displayed it to his hosts. Princip joined him, and demonstrated how to unscrew and throw the bomb. For good measure, he also brought out a revolver for the company to admire.

This, no doubt, was the ugliest aspect of the assassins' trip: hiding from the police and needing helpers, they left behind them a terrible trail of people whom they had implicated in their deed. The Kerovićes were truly simple peasants. In court, for example, all of them were vague about such basic facts as their own ages. "How old are you," the judge asked one of the sons, himself the father of five children. "I don't know," came the answer. "My father should know." Semiliterate, their interest in international affairs was negligible, and their information about the aims of pan-Serbism small. (Their vagueness, incidentally, extended to certain other personal matters as well. "Were you drunk that night," the judge asked old Mr. Kerović. Kerović, an impressive figure of a Bosnian farmer with prominent cheekbones, a large hooked nose, and a splendid white walrus moustache, admitted that he had been. Just how much, the judge wanted to know, had he had to drink? Kerović: "When I drink, I don't keep count. I drink as much as I can." His defense counsel tried to interfere. Had he really forgotten how much he had had? Kerović, petulantly: "I don't know. I take my flask and drink what I can.")

Yet for all their lack of sophistication, Mitar Kerović and every one of his sons, along with many others, later found themselves arraigned in court on the two capital charges of treason and of being accessories to murder as a result of Princip's and Grabež's visit. Very possibly, the way one of the Kerovićes tried to plead, while unusual, was truthful enough:

Judge: "Are you guilty?"

Jovo Kerović: "I don't know. How should I know?"

The Underground Railway: The Last Stage

Late that night, June 2, at about eleven o'clock, Princip and Grabež left the house. Nedjo and a friend of his carried the weapons, and all four got into the cart. Grabež had recovered a bit, but still did not feel very talkative. It had stopped raining, and the night was beautiful and clear —so clear, in fact, that the young men were concerned that they might be seen by some passing police patrol.

Still, Grabež and Princip managed to get some sleep, while Nedjo and his friend did the driving. At one village along the way there was a police barracks, and thus some definite danger. Princip and Grabež knew about it, however, since they had brought a special map with them from Belgrade, showing the location of every police barracks in Bosnia. They therefore left the cart before reaching the village, walked around it, and re-entered the cart at a safe distance, whereupon they went to sleep again.

Arriving at the outskirts of Tuzla early the next morning, the two students got out, and went to wash themselves in a nearby river. Princip's clothes were covered with mud and dirt after the walk through the woods and the ride in the peasants' cart. Not wishing to run the risk of being arrested on a vagrancy charge at this point, he bought a new pair of trousers. Having washed and changed, he and Grabež had some breakfast at a coffee shop in town, sitting at different tables and pretending not to know each other.

Their drivers, meanwhile, had gone on into Tuzla with the weapons to see Miško Jovanović, a distant relative of Veljo Čubrilović, the Priboj agent on the underground route. Jovanović was a middle-aged and eminently respectable businessman in Tuzla. He was a director of a local bank, the president of a school board, a member at the Serb-

Orthodox Episcopal Council, and, among his unlisted activities, the local agent on the underground railway. He lived in a building which housed Tuzla's cinema—of which he was the manager—his private apartments, and a Serb reading and club room.

Nedjo and his friend gave Jovanović the weapons and a note from Čubrilović reading "Miško, receive these people," adding that the people mentioned in the note would meet him in the Serb reading-room at nine that morning. Nedjo then went on to the hospital to have his injured hand looked after, while Jovanović took the guns and bombs and placed them in his hall closet. Later, he began to worry whether this was a good hiding place; his wife kept some of her kitchen utensils in there, and might stumble against them. He got out an old box, put the arms inside, and took it upstairs to the attic, where he hid it behind some bricks. He still felt far from pleased about having the arms in his house, however.

Punctually at nine, he met Princip and Grabež in the reading-room, and hopefully asked them if they would not like to pick up their arms. The boys declined—they were in the country illegally, and controls around Sarajevo were bound to be extremely strict in view of Franz Ferdinand's expected arrival. Would Jovanović be kind enough to take the weapons to Sarajevo for them?

It now was their host's turn to say no. He could not take the risk, Jovanović said, but he was willing to keep the weapons for them for a few days. Princip agreed. Someone would come by, he promised, identify himself by showing Jovanović a pack of *Stefanija* cigarettes, and pick up the arms.

Princip and Grabež then took their leave, and joined Čabrinović who, having reached Tuzla three days ahead of his friends, had been waiting for them in town so that they could travel the rest of the way to Sarajevo together. They found Čabrinović slightly worried. The day before, he had gone to a restaurant to eat lunch, and there had run into a detective he knew from Sarajevo. They had talked about Čabrinović's family. He saw his father quite often, the detective said, and everybody was doing very well. Čabrinović grew careless, and mentioned that he had been to Belgrade. The detective became interested. "How is life there?" he asked. "Not so good," complained Čabrinović with some presence of mind. "Wages are low and life is expensive. If you want a fairly decent meal, it costs you a dinar and a half, if you're satisfied with less, it costs you a dinar."

The detective went on to eat his lunch, pleased presumably at the low cost of living in Bosnia, and apparently suspecting nothing. Čabrinović also had had the bad luck to be seen by another official who knew him, however, and he suggested to his two friends that they all leave as soon as possible.

The same day, therefore, the three young men took the train to Sarajevo. Entering their compartment, they met an old friend—the detective who had been Čabrinović's luncheon companion. Princip took one good look at the guileless policeman, and decided that he need not worry about him.

Čabrinović and the detective made some small talk. Things were busy these days in Sarajevo, the detective volunteered. The city was expecting the arrival of none less than the Austrian Heir to the Throne. When was he going to be there, asked Čabrinović, and the detective obliged him with the date.

On their arrival in Sarajevo that evening, June 3, the

three friends separated—Grabež to go to his home town of Pale, Čabrinović to live with his family in Sarajevo, and Princip to stay with a friend of his in town. Quite possibly, the whole conspiratorial apparatus of their journey from Belgrade to Sarajevo had been a needless bit of romantic folderol. All of them were Austrian subjects; had they returned to Bosnia as peaceful travelers, there was no legal reason why anyone should have stopped them at the frontier. They would have been left with the problem of procuring the weapons, but these could either have been bought in Bosnia, or been smuggled in for them from Serbia. Whether necessary or not, however, the decision had been made to travel by the Black Hand's underground railway, and, as their trip proved, that route was working to perfection.

CHAPTER VIII

Waiting

Ilić's Parallel Action: Mehmedbašić

The friend in whose house Princip stayed at Sarajevo was Danilo Ilić, a twenty-three year old fellow-revolutionary. Ilić was a rather tall and good-looking young man, with calm blue eyes and a pale and sensitive face that suggested the poet. He had attended the State Teachers' College in Sarajevo on an Austrian government scholarship, had taught school briefly at a small town in Eastern Bosnia, but had fallen ill and resigned. He returned home to recuperate at the house of his widowed mother, and when his health improved worked at a local bank for about half a year.

In 1913, he went to Belgrade. A leader of the local Bosnian revolutionary organization *Mlada Bosna,* and an old and close personal friend of Gaćinović—the pamphleteer and apologist for the would-be murderer Žerajić —Ilić had no difficulty in finding his way to the right coffee shops. He also joined the Black Hand, and won the confidence of Apis.

When his illness recurred, he went back to Sarajevo. For a while, he found employment as a proofreader, and then became an editor of a local Serb paper. He drew no regular salary, but was paid for whatever articles he contributed. He was the owner of a house that brought him a modest amount of rent each month, but his combined income as a landlord and a journalist was not enough to live on, and it proved necessary for Ilić's mother to pay many of his bills. It also is possible that he received an occasional gift of money from the Black Hand. If so, Belgrade's money was well spent, for Ilić possessed a very considerable influence over the young students of his acquaintance, and proved to be a generally able and discreet organizer of secret activities.

While the preparations for the murder were being made in Belgrade, Ilić had been corresponding with Princip. When Princip wrote him around Easter, 1914, that the assassination had definitely been decided on, Ilić set about recruiting three local youths who were to join in the crime.

One of Ilić's recruits was Muhamed Mehmedbašić, whose attempt to kill Governor Potiorek that January had failed before it started when Mehmedbašić had panicked and rid himself of both poison and dagger as his train was crossing the Austrian border. Ilić now wrote him a letter—Mehmedbašić was living in Herzegovina—and asked him to come to the provincial capital of Mostar, to discuss an important matter. It is not likely that Ilić had many illusions about Mehmedbašić's reliability after this earlier fiasco, but he was needed for the political effects which his participation in the murder would create. Mehmedbašić was a Moslem; all the other conspirators were Serbs. If the

Austrians were to arrest none but Serbs, people might say that theirs obviously was the only disaffected group. The name Muhamed Mehmedbašić, on the other hand, the plotters hoped, might create the impression of more general discontent. They must have been gravely disappointed that no likely Croat assassin was in sight to join their group.

Franz Ferdinand, Ilić told Mehmedbašić when they met at Mostar, was going to visit Sarajevo in June, and Belgrade was in favor of killing him rather than Potiorek first. The bombs and guns would be provided by Belgrade, Ilić added. Was Mehmedbašić willing to take part in the murder?

Mehmedbašić said that he was, but that he had one objection. At Toulouse, he had definitely promised Gaćinović to kill Potiorek, he said, and he would like to get Gaćinović's consent to the change of plan.

They wrote a joint letter to Gaćinović, who, fully informed about the scheme against Franz Ferdinand, sent a quick and succinct reply: "Forward Lions." Mehmedbašić promised Ilić that he could count on him.

Two More Assassins Are Recruited

Ilić also enlisted two recruits in Sarajevo. He first talked to a friend of his from the State Teachers' College named Lazar Djukić. Djukić once had mentioned in front of Ilić that if only the arms could be procured, one ought to kill Franz Ferdinand when he came to Sarajevo. Ilić now gave Djukić the good news that the arms were available. Was he willing to be one of the assassins?

Djukić, confronted with a concrete scheme for murder, lost his enthusiasm and begged off. He volunteered, however, to introduce Ilić to a friend of his who, he said, would probably be pleased to take his place. The friend was

Vaso Čubrilović, a seventeen-year-old Sarajevo high-school
sophomore and a brother of Veljko Čubrilović, the Priboj
agent on the underground route who had helped Princip
and Grabež on their trip. Čubrilović not only agreed to
take part in the plot, but when Ilić mentioned that he
needed one more assassin, said that he thought he knew
just the right person, and that he would gladly talk to him
about it.

The fellow he had in mind was a friend, Cvijetko
Popović, a brilliant high-school student of eighteen.
Popović immediately declared his readiness, and Ilić's
Sarajevo group was complete.

Whether the two had any inkling of why Apis wanted
the Archduke dead is extremely doubtful. Their answers
in court certainly do not suggest it, but rather reflect the
phraseology of political pamphlets read avidly and understood imperfectly.

Why, the presiding judge, von Curinaldi, asked Popović,
had he wished for Franz Ferdinand's death? "He possessed
influence," said Popović. Curinaldi asked Popović to elaborate. Just what did he think of the Archduke?

Popović: "I had the impression that he liked us other
Slavs better than the Magyars. I heard that when he came
to Budapest, he only stayed for an hour."

Curinaldi: "Is that really your conviction?"

Popović: "Yes."

Curinaldi: "In that case, should you not have wanted
him to stay alive in the interest of the Slavs?"

Popović: ". . . Through him, I wanted to revenge myself
on those groups who oppress the Slavs . . . . I thought that
such vengeance would be an effective warning to the ruling
circles."

Čubrilović's answers showed a similar spirit. What ethnic

group did Čubrilović feel he belonged to, Curinaldi wanted to know at one point. Did he consider himself a Serb or a Croat?

Čubrilović: "I am a Serbo-Croat."

Curinaldi: "What does that term mean?"

Čubrilović: "It means that I don't consider myself solely a Serb, but that I must work for Croatia as well as for Serbia."

Curinaldi: "Are you a nationalist?"

Čubrilović: "Yes."

Curinaldi: "What does that mean?"

Čubrilović: "It means that one must fight to have our people arrive at their proper stage of development."

But whether Popović and Čubrilović truly understood the motives of the deed they were about to participate in was a matter of minor importance to Ilić. The less they knew, in fact, the better. The recruitment of Mehmed-bašić, Čubrilović, and Popović would seem to have served the main purpose not of increasing the group's effectiveness, but of making the crime look like a local affair. If arrests were made, and it turned out that all the assassins had recently come to Bosnia from Belgrade, it would be blatantly obvious that the plot had been organized across the border. Since this was the very last impression that Apis wished to create, the appearance on the scene of some extras who had never been to Serbia was essential.

In all, it was an arrangement that showed a touch of genius. The boys sent from Belgrade were trained in shooting and bomb-throwing, and should be able to carry off their parts well on June 28. If arrested, they could be expected to reveal nothing to the police, since at least two of the three were trusted Black Hand members. The boys from Sarajevo might not be of much help to Princip,

Čabrinović, and Grabež, but they would deflect attention from Apis. Under interrogation they were unlikely to talk either—for the simple reason that they did not know very much.

Ilić Picks Up the Weapons

On Sunday, June 14, a week and a half after his friends' arrival in Sarajevo, Ilić rang the bell of Miško Jovanović's house in Tuzla. Jovanović was in his study, and his wife ushered the young man in. Ilić identified himself by taking out the pack of *Stefanija* cigarettes. Jovanović, impatient to be rid of the bothersome weapons, wasted few words. "How are you going to carry them," he asked. "One can't put six bombs and four revolvers into one's pocket."

Ilić had an unpleasant surprise for Jovanović. No one knew him in Tuzla, he said, and there always was the chance that the police might stop and search him. Would Jovanović therefore be kind enough to wrap the arms in a harmless looking package, and take them to a train station past Tuzla, where Ilić would pick them up from him.

Jovanović had no choice. He would meet Ilić in Doboj the next day, he promised. Doboj was a town about thirty-five miles northeast of Tuzla. Jovanović owned some lumber there, and needed workmen to make it up into crossbars for rails, so that he had a good excuse for the trip.

After Ilić had left, Jovanović thought briefly of having his servant go to Doboj in his stead, but not wanting to get the man into trouble, he rejected the temptation. He climbed up to the attic, put the weapons he had hidden there into a sugar carton, wrapped the carton in white paper, and tied it securely with some string. It was about the last sensible thing he was to do about the arms.

Early the next morning, he took the train to Doboj, accompanied, it so happened, by his sister-in-law, who had no idea what the package he was carrying contained. At the Tuzla station, he hopefully if cautiously looked around for Ilić, but could see him nowhere. Nor was he able to find him on the train. Arriving at Doboj, the rattled Jovanović simply set down the box in the second-class waiting-room, put his overcoat on top of it, and accompanied his sister-in-law out of the station. He returned to the waiting-room, still could detect no trace of Ilić, and went to the shop of a tailor he knew in town. The tailor himself unfortunately was out, and only the young apprentice was in the store. Jovanović casually asked the boy to keep an eye on his package and his overcoat, and left to see a business associate of his about getting some workmen for the lumber. An hour or so later, he returned to the tailor shop. He found the tailor in, and the two men sat down to talk about local affairs. Shortly before the next train from Tuzla was due, Jovanović rose, and asked the tailor a favor. "If you are going to have lunch before I get back," he said, "please don't close your shop, for a man will come to whom I must give back a box."

At the station, Jovanović was relieved to see Ilić getting out of the train. He walked to the tailor's with him, found the store empty but the door open, gave him the package of arms he had left there, and took his leave to have lunch.

Ilić, still exercising the sort of precaution that showed the spirit of conspiratorial play-acting rather than that of common sense, took an express train to within two stations of Sarajevo, changed to the local train, got out at a stop on the outskirts of Sarajevo, took the streetcar as far as the city's cathedral, walked the rest of the way home, and hid the weapons under a couch in his room. If Ilić had simply picked up the arms from Jovanović, and taken them back on the next direct train to Sarajevo, there is no conceivable reason why he should have run into any trouble. This way, the arms had been left entirely unattended twice—once in the Doboj waiting-room and once at the tailor shop—and guarded by a quite possibly curious young tailor's apprentice for a whole hour. Beside, by traveling as circuitously as he did, Ilić had been seen by considerably more people than he would have been had he taken the obvious and easy route. If all went well in the end, it was in spite of Ilić's arrangements, not because of them.

The Unconspiratorial Conspirators

Trying to attract as little police attention to themselves as possible, the conspirators took pains to lead conspicuously carefree and bohemian lives during the weeks they spent waiting in Sarajevo. Princip even went out with some girls. When the friends met, which was rarely, it was at night. As June 28 drew closer, Ilić in particular grew worried that the police might be on their trail, and urged caution.

We know relatively few details about the activities of the conspirators in this period, and we can only assume that they followed the usual occupations and pastimes of high-school students on their summer vacation—which, after all, most of them were. Čabrinović had some fleeting thoughts about abandoning the murder scheme. His family had been so kind to him when they first saw him again that he felt like making his peace with the world and starting afresh, but soon there were new scenes with his father when he stayed out too late at night, and the mood passed.

Aside from Čabrinović, none of the youths appears to have had any qualms of conscience. What they were about to do, they assured themselves, was a great and noble act, not a murder. "Sentimentality," Wallace Stevens has written, "is the failure of feeling." Their single-mindedness very possibly was the failure of youth. At its root was a deep and genuine idealism that was stronger than any fears or doubts—the same kind of idealism which, far from evil in its essence, has gone into so many bad causes in this century.

If anyone among them showed some torment it was Princip. He was living in Ilić's modest, whitewashed house in a quiet sidestreet near the Oriental bazaar, and he had much leisure for thought and worry. Principal among them was that people would misunderstand the motives of his deed. What he really regretted, he confided to a friend of his as they were walking along the Quay one evening, was that there had not been enough time to pass his high-school graduating examination in Belgrade. Now people might say that his had simply been the case of a poor high-school student who had failed to graduate, and who had taken out his disappointment in violence. Perhaps because of this fear, Princip spent some of the last free days of his life with his school books.

Another thought that bothered him was that Sarajevo might not be a worthy location for his sacrifice. Along with many of his revolutionary friends, he had no fondness for large cities, and despised what he thought of as the morality of the market place. Sarajevo—Austrianized, busy Sarajevo—was not a city he loved. "If I could stuff Sarajevo into a matchbox," he told his friend that same evening, "I would set it afire."

But all these were minor, and usually unspoken, doubts.

Princip, Grabež, and Ilić unhesitatingly agreed upon some of the last advance preparations for the trip when they got together and arranged precisely what station along Franz Ferdinand's route each assassin was to occupy on June 28. Princip also had the unplanned good luck to catch a glimpse of their intended victims some days in advance of the murder.

CHAPTER IX

Maneuvers

A Shopping Trip to Sarajevo

"Be greeted, our hope!" wrote one of Sarajevo's Croat newspapers on June 25, in welcome of Franz Ferdinand. "Hail to you!" exclaimed another, which like every paper in town was putting out a special edition in honor of the Archduke's arrival. "Be Greeted, Illustrious Prince!" chimed in a Moslem headline writer. The Serbian papers were somewhat more guarded. One filled its whole front page with a picture of Franz Ferdinand, but hinted editorially that it might be well if the Heir to the Throne were to become "the noble spokesman before the illustrious crown for the justified wishes and needs of the Serb people in our fatherland." But even this editorial ended with a "Hail to the Heir Apparent."

The journalistic enthusiasm may have been a good deal too fulsome, but the archducal visit obviously was a cheerful and exciting event in the life of the city. Franz Ferdinand, too, for all his original misgivings, was beginning to enjoy the trip. The *objets d'art* with which the local dealers had crammed his rooms at the Hotel Bosna in Ilidže apparently whetted his collector's appetite. In the afternoon of June 25, the day of his arrival in Bosnia, he and the Duchess decided on the spur of the moment to take an unscheduled shopping trip into Sarajevo.

At five o'clock, they left Ilidže by car, and drove to the store of the town's leading furniture and antique dealer, where they spent more than an hour looking at silks, rugs, inlay and metal work, and made a great many purchases. While they were shopping, word spread that they were in town, and a crowd collected in front of the store. It soon became so large that it filled the entire street. When the archducal couple emerged, everyone pressed around, acclaiming the visitors with shouts of "Živio!"— the Serbo-Croat exclamation of cheer and welcome.

Franz Ferdinand and Sophie were anxious to have a look at a few of the stalls at the famous Oriental bazaar. The bazaar was a wonderful place, with all the color, noise, and life of the medieval markets of the East. The expert could find some very beautiful and wholly handmade things here, although the ordinary tourist was cautioned by a dry word of warning in his Baedeker to the effect that "many of the so-called Oriental goods are of Austrian make."

As Franz Ferdinand and Sophie were trying to make their way to the bazaar, they found their path all but barred by the enthusiastic crowd. The officers in the Archduke's entourage slowly had to pave a way through the mass of people for the visitors from Vienna, who were smilingly acknowledging the many cheers with which they were being greeted from all sides. When, their shopping finished, they finally re-entered their car, there were more cheers, and the archducal couple returned to Ilidže well pleased with the results of their surprise visit.

Something they did not know, and never were to learn, was that one member of the crowd outside the shop was Gavrilo Princip. He managed to get so close to Franz Ferdinand that they were almost face to face, but he held himself in check and did not shoot. Plans plainly provided for Sunday, June 28, as the day of the murder, with a large group of assassins, not one single individual, committing the deed, and Princip was a disciplined revolutionary. What he did do was to fix the Archduke's features clearly in his mind, so there would be no mistake on Sunday, and to tell his friends about the meeting later that evening.

Čabrinović, incidentally, was less favored by luck. That same day, he put on his best clothes and traveled to Ilidže to get a look at his victims. He thought that he was being recognized by a Moslem detective near the hotel, however, devoted all his energies to losing him, and went back to Sarajevo without having seen either Franz Ferdinand or Sophie. The detective, who had in fact recognized Čabrinović, telephoned police headquarters, and reported the meeting. The answer he supposedly received from Dr. Gerde, Sarajevo's Chief of Police, was to leave Čabrinović alone. Čabrinović's record was clear at the time, and Gerde apparently associated the boy's name with that of his father, the Austrian police spy.

The Maneuvers

Franz Ferdinand spent the next two days attending the army maneuvers about ten miles west of Ilidže. The major part of the terrain consisted of naked, jagged rocks, creating an impression of utter desolation, but at several points there were magnificent views across the river Ivan below, and occasional meadows and woods in the ravines reminded the visitor of Swiss Alpine scenery. Roads were few and poor, and there was little shelter. It was a logical area for the maneuvers, for many of the border regions of the Austro-Hungarian Empire consisted of just such rough mountain terrain.

About 22,000 troops took part, with Bosnia's Fifteenth Army Corps drawn up against Croatia's Sixteenth Corps. The over-all command lay in the hands of Bosnia's Governor and Franz Ferdinand's host, General Potiorek.

On both mornings, Franz Ferdinand left Ilidže for the maneuver area by special train before six. At the nearest station, horses were waiting for him, and he and his party rode on from there on horseback to join the troops. The weather was terrible, and visibility low. Rain, hail, and even snow were falling, and only occasionally did some cold gust of wind provide a break in the fog. The maneuvers were going extremely well, however. Troop training had obviously been good, and both Army Corps executed their movements with skill and precision despite terrain and weather. Franz Ferdinand, no amateur in military matters, was liberal with his praise for the troops and Potiorek.

He did not complain about the hardships. In fact, there was one reason why they might have pleased him. Twenty policemen had been assigned to him during the maneuvers to look after his personal safety. They did not have an easy time of it. With his strong dislike for bodyguards, he was forever trying to lose them by riding off in the most unexpected directions and by never telling them in advance where he was going next. He was often successful; what with the rocky terrain and the fog, the poor policemen were hard put indeed to keep him in their sight. Just how easy it would have been for an assassin to take a shot at him during the maneuvers—given the Archduke's casual attitude toward security and Potiorek's inadequate measures to guard him—was shown by two incidents.

On the first day of the maneuvers, a man was seen to come running after the Archduke's car. No one intercepted him. Franz Ferdinand, catching sight of him, had the car stopped. The man turned out to be a peddler from Austria, and the amused Archduke bought some postcards and medals from him. The peddler, thanking his customer, mentioned that he knew the Archduke well; he made it a practice, he said, to attend all the maneuvers, and thus had seen him often.

Another time a civilian suddenly jumped out of the bushes, holding a long, black tube. For a moment, everyone sat rigid with fright or surprise. Then a police officer, who had managed to stay close to Franz Ferdinand by putting on an umpire's badge so that the Archduke would not know who he was, managed to catch the man by the collar. Franz Ferdinand, laughing out loud, stopped the false umpire. "But that's the court photographer," he called. "Do let go of him; that's his business! These people have to live too, after all!"

Early in the afternoon of Friday, June 27, a bugler of the guard blew retreat, signaling the end of the maneuvers. Franz Ferdinand, after a final review of the troops, issued the following directive to indicate his satisfaction with what he had seen:

> I have had an opportunity during the past two days to observe a large part of the XVth and XVIth Army Corps under unfavorable weather conditions and on sometimes difficult terrain.

I had been convinced that I would find nothing but the best, and my expectations were fully confirmed by the outstanding performances of all officers and men. I shall report this to His Majesty the Emperor, our beloved Commander-in-Chief, and in the name of the Service I express my cordial thanks and fullest appreciation to His Excellency, the Inspector of the Army [General Potiorek], and to all generals, officers and men of both Corps, who have again been proving themselves in the events of the recent past.

This directive is to be communicated to all men in their respective mother tongues immediately.

ARCHDUKE FRANZ, GENERAL OF THE CAVALRY.

The promised report to the Emperor went out at four o'clock that same afternoon. "The state of the troops," Franz Ferdinand said in his telegram to his uncle, "their training and performance have been excellent and beyond all praise. Morale is excellent; they have been trained well and show great ability. There were almost no sick calls." He added a few personal words. "Everyone well and in good spirits," he wired. "Tomorrow I shall visit Sarajevo and leave in the evening."

Farewell Dinner in Ilidže

Not only had the maneuvers been a success, but both Franz Ferdinand and Sophie had been having a very pleasant stay. While the Archduke was attending the maneuvers, Sophie was paying official visits to schools, orphanages, and churches in Sarajevo. She was given a cordial reception wherever she went, and in turn was gracious and kind herself. The schedule worked out for her was haphazard at times; at some places, she turned up as much as two or three hours late. On the other hand, some of the arrangements

showed an endearing kind of forethought. In the Augus-
tinian convent school, for example, after acknowledging the
teachers' speeches of welcome, listening to the childrens'
choir, and receiving her bouquet of roses, she had gifts for
all of the school's pupils—pictures of the archducal family
for the older group, and, for the younger group, candy.

On her return to Ilidže on both afternoons, she went for
brief strolls in the park with her husband in spite of the
poor weather, and watched the bear cubs that were kept
there. In honor of the visitors, the cubs were released from
their cage, whereupon two of them promptly escaped, and
had to be recaptured by their harried keeper.

On the first two days, Sophie and Franz Ferdinand had
dinner in the company of all the members of their entourage, and the atmosphere at the table was pleasant and free.
Baron Conrad, the Chief of the General Staff, who was
among those invited, and who on some previous occasions
had exchanged sharp words with Franz Ferdinand, later
recalled that he almost had the feeling of being at a relaxed
family dinner. Franz Ferdinand's health seemed good
again, Conrad thought, and both he and Sophie were their
most charming selves. They talked about the maneuvers,
their impressions of Bosnia, the German Emperor's recent
visit with the Archduke at Konopischt and his praise for
the gardens there, and about Franz Ferdinand's plans to
attend autumn maneuvers in Germany, to which he as well
as Conrad had been invited. The company remained
together for some time after dinner, talking easily and
comfortably. One of the things that contributed to the
archducal couple's happy mood was a telephone call received by Sophie one night, saying that her eldest son,
Maximilian, had just passed his high-school examinations

with distinction. Visibly pleased, the proud parents accepted everyone's congratulations.

On Saturday, June 27, dinner was a more formal affair. It was to be their last night in Bosnia, and all of Sarajevo's dignitaries had been invited. The windows of the hotel's dining-room, where the court dinner was being held, were kept open, and through them, the sounds of music being played by the Sarajevo garrison band on the lawn below drifted in. They were rendering a pleasant if unstartling program: Schumann's "Träumerei," a phantasy on "La Bohême," a Lehár medley, "The Blue Danube." Nor did the menu offer any surprises. From soufflé to lamb to filet of beef to roast goose to salad and fruit, it was all good, solid banquet fare, although the French wines were followed by two of the Empire's specialties: a local wine from Mostar, and a Tokay from Hungary.

Sophie was the only woman present. Placed between the Serb-Orthodox and the Roman-Catholic Archbishops of Sarajevo, she was capably presiding over the dinner together with her husband, who sat across from her between the President of Bosnia's Parliament and General Potiorek. When dinner was finished, the Archduke and the Duchess rose, and held court for a while near their respective ends of the table. Among the guests who came to pay their respect to Sophie was Dr. Josip Sunarić, a leader of Bosnia's Croats, and a Vice-President of Parliament. He had warned Potiorek against the Bosnian trip when he first heard about it, since he thought that some local Serbs might be in an ugly mood, and that the visitors faced definite danger. When Sophie caught sight of him, she took a few steps toward him, and, as Sunarić recalled it later, said with a radiant smile on her face: "Dear Dr. Sunarić, you were wrong after all; things don't always turn out the way you say they will. Everywhere we have gone here we have been greeted with so much friendliness—and by every last Serb, too—with so much cordiality and unsimulated warmth, that we are very happy about it!"

"Your Highness, I pray to God that when I have the honor tomorrow night of seeing you again, you can repeat those words to me. I shall breathe easier then, a great deal easier."

Shortly afterwards, most of the guests took their leave, but a smaller group, consisting largely of the members of Franz Ferdinand's entourage, remained until midnight. Franz Ferdinand, while still in excellent spirits, made a remark to the effect that he was glad the trip was over. Someone thereupon suggested that Franz Ferdinand cancel the next day's visit to Sarajevo, and return to Vienna directly. It was not a wholly unreasonable suggestion. The Archduke was fond of making impulsive changes in his travel schedules, and the program for June 28 was a very slight one. Following a stop at the town's military camp, he was to drive through Sarajevo for a brief reception at the City Hall in the morning, spend the next hour at the National Museum, and go on to the Governor's residence for a farewell luncheon at 12:30. Nothing was planned for the afternoon, but according to the program, the archducal party was not to leave Ilidže until nine o'clock in the evening.

Franz Ferdinand seemed tempted to agree with the suggestion that he cut his visit short, until some of the military aides spoke up. Potiorek's adjutant reasonably pointed out that to cancel the visit would be interpreted as a slight to the population of Sarajevo, who were expecting the Archduke on Sunday. Some of the Archduke's aides, rightly again, added that it would be an open insult to General Potiorek as well, and Franz Ferdinand, who apparently did not care too much one way or the other, decided that it would be wisest to keep to the original schedule. Archduke Franz Ferdinand, heir to the throne of Austria, was going to be in Sarajevo on the morning of June 28, 1914.

The Assassins' Last Party

The assassins, meanwhile, were making their last-minute preparation. Sometime during the week, Ilić went to Belgrade to receive his final instructions from Dimitrijević. Precisely what was said between them we do not know. On Ilić's return, he summoned Mehmedbašić to Sarajevo. On Saturday, June 27, he introduced him to Princip at a Sarajevo café as "Mehmedbašić, who tomorrow is to be with us," and the three of them signed a post card to their common friend Gaćinović who was living in Switzerland at the time.

Also on Saturday, Ilić met Popović and Čubrilović, his Sarajevo recruits, at a Turkish coffee shop. He walked to a nearby park with them, and gave each of them a bomb, a pistol and ammunition, and their portion of poison. He showed them how to load and shoot the guns, and how to throw the bombs. Firing off two practice shots with Popović's gun, he said: "Anyone getting this bullet, he's done for."

Princip, at about the same time, looked up Čabrinović, handed him his cyanide, and told him where his post for the assassination was going to be. He asked him to stay there and nowhere else, since each of the conspirators had his definitely assigned station. For reasons that are not clear, Čabrinović was to be given no gun; all that any of the defendants would say about it in court later was that "that was the way things were organized." Princip assured him, however, that he would receive his bomb the next morning, and so he did. Sometime that day, Princip also went out to the cemetary, and left a wreath on the grave of Žerajić.

In the evening, several members of Sarajevo's illegal *Mlada Bosna* group met for a party at Semiz's inn. Semiz's really was a wine shop rather than an inn, a small place with a few simple tables and chairs, and a great many casks and barrels standing about. It was dark inside Semiz's even during the daytime, for only a single window admitted the light. Through it, one could see the Lateiner Bridge, Princip's station for the assassination. (The Lateiner Bridge will no longer be found on a Sarajevo street map under that name; its current name is Princip Bridge.)

Just which of the assassins attended the party we do not know, although it appears certain that Princip was there. The boys sang and drank red wine. Their judgment on wine, incidentally, had much in common with that of the Hotel Bosna's *sommelier* who had chosen a local wine from Mostar to follow the Bordeaux and the Burgandy at Franz Ferdinand's court dinner in Ilidže that evening—the reason they liked to meet at Semiz's was the good Mostar wine sold there.

Despite the wine and the singing, Princip was in a dark mood, and very much occupied with his own thoughts. He even surprised a friend by drinking down a glass of wine in one gulp. A friend managed to cheer him up by telling some jokes, and the group soon was happily cursing the Austrians amid more songs and laughter.

When the group broke up, the mood was an easy one. Princip, who did not feel like going to sleep yet, joined two of his friends in the street, and walked to their home with them. In the darkness outside their house, he embraced them, and told them to go in immediately, lest they be seen with him.

The next morning at eight, Ilić joined Čabrinović and Grabež at the same Turkish coffee shop where he had met his Sarajevo recruits the day before. He handed a bomb to Čabrinović, and bomb and revolver to Grabež. All the assassins now had their arms and knew their stations. Everything was ready for the murder of Franz Ferdinand.

CHAPTER X

Čabrinović

Upon Saint Vitus' Day

Saint Vitus' Day, June 28, 1389. The Turks, after a murderous battle, have defeated the Serbian army at Kossovo, or Blackbirds' Field, in the plains of Southern Serbia. The Prince of the Serbs, Lazar, is a captive of the Turks. One of his men, Miloš Obilić, smuggles himself into the Turkish camp, finds the Sultan, Murad I, and strikes him dead. In reprisal, the Sultan's son, Bayazid, has his captured enemy Lazar brought out and beheaded. The battle of Blackbirds' Field on Saint Vitus' Day 1389 means the end of the medieval Serbian Empire. Serbia, henceforth, becomes a vassal state of Turkey. A whole cycle of legends, folk songs, and ballads gathers around the battle, and each year, the Serbs commemorate June 28 as a day of national mourning.

Autumn, 1912. In the First Balkan War, the armies of the small kingdom of Serbia, wholly independent again since the end of the nineteenth century, have badly defeated those of the Turkish Empire. Blackbirds' Field has been recaptured from the Turks, and the humiliation of the defeat of 1389 finally wiped out.

Saint Vitus' Day, June 28, 1914. The date has been chosen for Franz Ferdinand's visit to Sarajevo purely by accident, but in the streets of the city stand seven youths ready to strike at Serbia's new enemy, Austria, and to sacrifice Franz Ferdinand, and possibly themselves, for the cause of creating a new Serbian Empire.

To the City Hall

Early on Sunday morning, June 28, Franz Ferdinand called in his Chamberlain, Baron Morsey, to dictate two telegrams. One was addressed to his Private Secretary at Chlumetz Castle, the other to his three children. "Papa and Mamma," the telegram to his children read, were well, and looked forward to being with them again on Tuesday.

At nine o'clock, having finished his dictation, he and Sophie attended mass together in a room at the hotel that had been specially prepared for the purpose. The room was oppressively warm, and smelled of too many flowers. After mass, they walked to the Ilidže station, accompanied by their retinues. From there, a special train, departing at 9:25, took them to Sarajevo. At the Sarajevo station, General Potiorek was waiting for the archducal party.

Their first stop in town was the Philipović army camp, located opposite the railroad station, where they were formally welcomed by Sarajevo's commanding general, Michael von Appel. Following a very brief review of the troops, the archducal party, at about ten o'clock, got into their cars to drive up the city's broadest avenue, the Appel Quay, to the City Hall for the Mayor's reception.

The procession which now started out from Philipović camp numbered six cars in all. In the first car sat Fehim Effendi Čurčić, the Mayor of Sarajevo, and Dr. Gerde, the city's Commissioner of Police. The second automobile, a high-sided gray touring car flying the black and yellow Habsburg pennant, held the most distinguished of the visitors, and the car's top was rolled back in order to allow the crowds a good view of its occupants. In front, next to the driver, sat Franz Count Harrach, the owner of the car, and a member of the Austro-Hungarian Voluntary Automobile Corps. In back, on the left, sat Franz Ferdinand, dressed in his general's uniform, and wearing all his decorations. At his side was Sophie, in a billowing white dress and a very large hat, and across from them, on the folding seat, sat Governor Potiorek. The next car's passengers were Countess Lanjus, Sophie's lady in waiting; Colonel Carl von Bardolff, the head of Franz Ferdinand's military chancellery; Lieutenant Colonel Merizzi, General Potiorek's chief adjutant; and the car's owner, Count Boos-Waldeck. In the two automobiles that followed traveled various other members of Franz Ferdinand's staff and of the Bosnian administration; the six and last automobile was empty, to be used as a reserve car in case of accident.

In contrast to the previous week's cold and rain, the day had opened with splendid summer weather. At the Mayor's suggestion, a great many citizens had decorated their houses and stores with flags, flowers, and oriental rugs. The decorations were particularly colorful along the official route, and in numerous windows one could see pictures of Franz Ferdinand. The visit was an exciting and festive event for Sarajevo. ("Because of the great amount of material," the *Sarajevoer Tagblatt* apologized on June 27, amid all the stories about the previous day's maneuvers and about Sunday's program, "today's installment of our novel [*Typhoon,* by Heinz E'Monts] had to be omitted.") The sidewalks were full of people cheering Franz Ferdinand and Sophie as they were passing by. There was an occasional policeman and secret service agent among them, but no lines of soldiers or police had been formed to hold back the crowds.

Security arrangements, in fact, were startlingly casual. Many spectators still had a vivid memory of how differently things had been handled during the Emperor's visit to Sarajevo in 1910. On that occasion, all the soldiers of the Sarajevo garrison had been called out to line the streets through which Franz Joseph was to pass, and his route had been so chosen that nowhere was there enough room for dangerously large crowds to assemble. Over two hundred suspects were placed under police arrest for the duration of the Imperial visit, and a number of other citizens were told not to leave their houses.

This time, while thousands of troops were in the region for maneuvers, the city was declared off-limits to them for the duration of Franz Ferdinand's and Sophie's visit. Only one full infantry battalion and five smaller units—not more than a few hundred men in all—remained in town. Of this number, most were busy with various military duties, and only the infantry battalion and part of one infantry company were available at their barracks in case of emergency. Precautionary arrests apparently numbered thirty-five. All security arrangements lay in the hands of a police force that comprised no more than a hundred and twenty men, including uniformed policemen and plainclothes detectives.

There were several reasons for the contrast between 1910 and 1914. The strict security measures taken during his visit had not escaped Franz Joseph, and he was quite plainly displeased with them. Throwing a bad fright into some of the local dignitaries accompanying him, he sometimes disregarded the careful advance arrangements to walk right through the crowds, and when he took his leave, everyone noticed the coolness of manner with which he treated the responsible head of the civil administration. Nor was it possible in 1914 to make large-scale arrests without showing very good cause, since a new Constitution had meanwhile been introduced.

There were other reasons as well. Franz Ferdinand was a man of great personal bravery who disliked the presence of secret service men. Nor can he have been anxious to have a cordon of troops between the crowd and himself. After all, the visit's purpose was to give people a glimpse of their future Emperor. Perfect security was next to impossible to achieve in Bosnia; underneath the voluminous dresses of the Moslem women, for example, almost any sort of arms might be hidden, and the police, instructed to show every sign of respect for Moslem sensibilities, would have to hesitate very much before making a body search. Finally, even the tightest of security precautions normally are useless in the case of assassins truly willing to sacrifice their own lives.

But these are speculations. The fact remains that while there were many reasons for not equaling the precautions taken in 1910, none were good enough. In the summer of 1914, Austrian authorities were as aware of the existence of secret societies as they were of the fact that there was a sizable number of young men in Bosnia who thought the uses of violence were sweet. And it was Potiorek, as Inspector of the Army and Governor of Bosnia, who bore the ultimate responsibility for whatever arrangements the police made or failed to make. Potiorek, although several people later claimed that they had plainly warned him, apparently felt that the presence of the troops during maneuvers was sufficient protection, and ignored the fact that the concluding day's visit to Sarajevo was to be a civilian and not a military one—Franz Ferdinand was to be received as Heir to the Throne, not as Inspector General. In the end there were far too few policemen guarding Franz Ferdinand's route to the City Hall.

Aided by the lax security, the seven assassins, mingling with the crowds, had all safely taken up their positions along the Appel Quay. The first post, near the building of the Austro-Hungarian Bank by the Čumurja Bridge, was that of Mehmedbašić, the one Moslem among the conspirators. A few steps from him, also on the side of the river, and across from the Teachers' College, stood Čabrinović, the printer. A bit further up in the direction of the City Hall were Ilić's two Sarajevo recruits, Čubrilović and Popović. Near the next bridge, the Lateiner Bridge, stood Princip, and the final post was that of his friend Grabež, who had come with him from Belgrade on the underground route. Grabež was impatiently pacing up and down the Quay, to find the best vantage point from which to shoot. Ilić, the organizer of the Sarajevo group, had no fixed post of his own, but moved between the other six assassins, to keep their spirits up and to see that all was well.

He paused to stop by Mehmedbašić, and said softly: "Be strong, be brave." Not much later, at barely a quarter past ten in the morning, the procession of cars was approaching, and Mehmedbašić's opportunity to be strong and brave had come. As the second car, in which Franz Ferdinand was riding, drew up to eye level, Mehmedbašić froze, and did nothing. His apology later was that he thought he could see a policeman stepping up behind him at the precise moment the cars were passing by. If he were to bring his bomb out, he said his quick reasoning went, the policeman would seize him by the arm, the whole plot would be revealed, and all the remaining conspirators would be prevented from taking action. While he was still pursuing these thoughts, he said, the Archduke's car was gone, and with it his opportunity to do his part.

The next conspirator whom Franz Ferdinand had to pass was Čabrinović. As the cars slowly drove by him among the cheers of the crowd, Čabrinović, the unstable, boastful ex-anarchist, ex-socialist, ex-strike leader, about whom even his friends had their reservations, suddenly proved how calm his nerves could be under pressure. He pulled out his bomb, took careful aim, and hurled it straight at Franz Ferdinand's car.

Čabrinović

On the morning of June 28, Nedjelko Čabrinović took leave from his family. He gave twenty crowns, most of the money he owned, to his grandmother, of whom he was very fond, and who had occasionally helped him out with gifts of money in the past. She was reluctant to accept the unexpected present at first, saying that she wished to keep only half of it, but her grandson insisted. He had five crowns left, and gave those to his sister. He was going on a long trip, he told her, from which he would never return.

Alone, Čabrinović wept. He was seized by a sudden surge of affection for his father. His father, he thought, had treated him badly, and had given him a miserable education, and yet he could feel fondness and pity for him now. What made him saddest, however, was the thought of being separated forever from his sister and his grandmother.

He left the house, and accompanied by a friend, went to a photographer's shop where, shortly after nine o'clock, he asked to have his picture taken, "so that," as he explained at his trial later, "a memory would remain behind me." Dressed rather formally in a dark suit, a white shirt with a stiff round collar, and high button shoes, he posed sitting on the side of a low armchair. In his left hand, he held a copy of Sarajevo's nationalist Serb paper, *Srpska Riječ*, and in his right inside coat pocket he carried his bomb, which was to show up as a slight bulge in the finished portrait. To prevent the police from seizing the pictures afterwards, he gave the photographer a false name and an equally false address in another city. When they had left the shop, he asked his friend to send two prints to that address, but to give four others to his grandmother.

He said goodby to his friend, and walked to the Appel Quay to take up his post. To attract no attention to himself, he casually walked up and down the Quay. Catching sight of a boy he knew, a mentally retarded mute, he asked him to join him, since he thought it wiser not to be seen alone. It was sunny and warm on the river side where he was strolling, but he was careful to keep his coat tightly buttoned, so that he would not risk dropping the bomb.

Most of the spectators stood on the other side of the street, where there was shade and protection from the sun. Among them was a doctor who had come to the capital with his daughter for the Archduke's visit. Watching Čabrinović on the sunny side of the street, his dark coat buttoned, and his left hand inside his coat pocket as though he was holding something, the doctor thought that there was something odd about him. "What's this young man doing there?" he wondered aloud, addressing his question to two acquaintances with him.

A short while later, at a quarter past ten, the cars came into sight. As they approached, Čabrinović's excitement mounted. He stepped away from the crowd as far as possible in order not to hurt any bystanders, and drew the bomb out of his pocket. He let the first car pass him, and struck the bomb's percussion cap against a lantern post. The doctor across the street, who was still watching him, thought that he was taking out and emptying a pipe. The doctor turned to his companions in disbelief and asked: "Do you suppose he's going to light his pipe as the Heir to the Throne is passing?"

His friends were not listening. "Look!" one of them called out. "There he is! Call 'Hurrah!' Three times and loud!"

Others around him also felt it proper to shout hurrah. As they did so, and craned their necks for a look at their august visitors, Čabrinović raised his right arm, took careful aim at Franz Ferdinand's general's helmet with its green feathers, and threw the bomb. As he was letting go of it, he thought he could see Franz Ferdinand turn around and fix him with a cold and steady look.

In the car, just a moment before, General Potiorek had been pointing out a new army barracks to Franz Ferdinand. Count Harrach, the car's owner, who was sitting next to the driver in front, had heard the detonating sound made by Čabrinović's knocking off the cap of the bomb. His instinctive reaction was to think that a tire had blown out. Irony in his voice, he called to the chauffeur: "Bravo. Now we'll have to stop."

The driver, more quick-witted than Harrach, also had heard the sharp, cracking sound, and had seen a black object hurling through the air. Rather than following the Count's instructions and stopping, he did precisely the right thing under the circumstances, pressed down on the accelerator, and drove on at full speed.

As a result, the bomb did not land where it was intended to. Instead, it passed behind Sophie's back—she was sitting on the right, and thus on the side closest to Čabrinović. Franz Ferdinand, sitting next to her, who had also seen the object that came flying at them, raised his hand to protect his wife. With this motion, he deflected the bomb, which fell onto the resilient, folded back roof of the touring car, and bounced off into the street, where it exploded with a detonation that seemed as loud as a cannon shot and filled the air with debris and smoke.

The crowd, excited, began to push and shove, some to have a closer look at what had happened, others—and there were more of them—to get away from the scene as fast as they could. Two women fainted.

The lead car, bearing the mayor, at first continued on its way, and so did Franz Ferdinand's. In the few moments before the bomb exploded, the Archduke did not know what the object he had seen coming at him was, and failed to realize that it had bounced off into the street. Instead, he thought that it had come to rest between himself and Sophie inside the car. He decided to say nothing about it, in order not to frighten his wife.

Turning around at the sound of the explosion, he saw the confusion in the street. He also saw that the car which had been following behind his had come to a stop, and that some of its occupants were getting out. He ordered the driver of his car to stop too. Several members of his entourage were jumping out of their cars and rushing up to his, to find out if anything had happened to him or to Sophie. They saw that the Archduke was completely unhurt, although Sophie's face bore a slight scratch from a flying splinter. The car itself had suffered damage from three bomb fragments. One had dented the gas tank, the second was lodged in the trunk compartment, and a third was stuck in the folding roof. The damage was so slight, however, and there was so much other excitement, that no one even noticed it until much later.

The bomb had worked its real harm elsewhere. There were no dead; but about a dozen spectators were injured, none of them seriously. The worst had been reserved for the automobile following immediately behind Franz Ferdinand's. The car's owner, Count Boos-Waldeck, was hit by several bomb splinters, but he was not doing badly. One of his passengers, however, was bleeding profusely from a wound he had received in the back of his head. He was Lieutenant Colonel Erik von Merizzi, Potiorek's adjutant, who had advised against canceling the Sarajevo visit the night before. Countess Lanjus, Sophie's lady in waiting, who was sitting next to him, although herself hit by a small splinter, was attempting to still the flow of blood by calmly holding a handkerchief to Merizzi's wound. The gash seemed an ugly one, but fortunately, Franz Ferdinand's physician, Dr. Fischer, had been riding in the next car. He had a quick look at the wound, and ordered the Colonel taken to the office of a nearby physician.

The car itself, which had borne the brunt of the explosion, was stalled, and the remaining occupants had to transfer to the fifth and last automobile, which was in better condition than the fourth car directly behind them. The owner of the fourth car, Lieutenant Egger, discovered to his relief that while small fragments of the bomb had pierced his cap and shattered his windshield, he was unhurt, and his car still in running order.

For the civilian wounded, effective help soon materialized with the arrival on the scene of General Appel, Sarajevo's commanding general, who had greeted Franz Ferdinand at the Philipović army camp earlier that morning. He was not a member of the archducal party, but had followed behind the procession on the way to his office, which was located just off the Quay. He took a look at the destruction, and put through a telephone call to the garrison hospital. The doctor in charge, Major Arnstein, quickly responded to his summons, and hurried to the Appel Quay accompanied by three army surgeons. Two of the doctors gave first aid to the injured spectators, while Arnstein and one of the surgeons examined Merizzi, and ordered an ambulance to take him to the hospital for further treatment.

The Arrest

Having thrown his bomb, Čabrinović swallowed the cyanide he was carrying, and jumped into the river Miljačka which faced the quay, and which was low at this time of year. At least four men scrambled in after him. (When they appeared on the witness stand during his trial, Čabrinović got indignant over their statements that they had jumped in behind him. "I was the only one to have jumped into the river," he said. "All the others made their way down.") Two of his pursuers came from among the spectators—one was a shopkeeper, the other a barber—and the two others were a policeman and a plainclothes detective. The barber struck Čabrinović, who was lying sprawled out in the river bed, and the shopkeeper kicked at his left hand. The barber, still irate, drew a gun, and had to be restrained from shooting Čabrinović by the policeman, who pointed out that the police would want to interrogate the young man first.

Together, they made their way up the river bank, and led Čabrinović to the police station. Baron Morsey, Franz Ferdinand's Second Chamberlain, having assured himself that the Archduke was unhurt, joined the group, his saber drawn, and walked along as far as the next bridge, the Lateiner Bridge. Here, they passed by Gavrilo Princip. As they did so, the idea briefly flitted through Princip's mind that he might shoot Čabrinovič, and then himself, and that it would all be over then. Just as quickly, he rejected the thought.

At the police station, the detective who had made the arrest began to interrogate his suspect. The poison Čabrinović had taken had failed to have any fatal effect, but he was in pain from it and from the jump, and he was weary. "Leave me in peace and I will tell you everything," he said to the detective.

The detective tried to take him up on his offer. "From whom did you get the bomb?" he asked.

"From our organization."

"Which organization?"

"I'll tell you later."

"Do you have accomplices?"

But having almost said too much already, Čabrinović refused to answer, and would say no more.

Back at the Appel Quay meanwhile, Franz Ferdinand showed himself more interested in the fate of the victims than in that of his would-be assassin. Having made sure that all the wounded were properly cared for, he said, "Come on, the fellow is insane; let us go on with our program," and the procession started on its way toward the City Hall again.

Past Four Assassins

A few steps from the scene stood Vaso Čubrilović, at seventeen the youngest of the conspirators. He could see the bomb being hurled, and threw himself aside to escape its impact. What he did next is not wholly clear. Several witnesses at the trial testified to having heard an explosive sound reminiscent of a pistol shot at about the time Čabrinović threw his bomb, some stating that they heard this sound before the explosion, others insisting that it came afterward. Čubrilović himself, before his arrest, told several friends that he had fired a shot at Franz Ferdinand. During his trial, however, he changed his story, and denied having shot at the Archduke. His gun, when recovered by the police, was found to be fully loaded. It would therefore seem most likely that Čubrilović did nothing, and that the shotlike sound heard by the witnesses preceded the explosion, and was caused by Čabrinović knocking off the cap of his bomb against the lantern post.

The next would-be assassin, Cvijetko Popović, who had been standing in the shade across the street, no longer was at his post as the cars started up again. Hearing the bomb explode, he left his station and hid his bomb behind a box in the basement of a building a few yards away. In court later, he was frank and to the point about the motives for his inaction. "I lost courage," he said.

His defection left two more assassins, Princip and Grabež.

At eight that morning, Princip had taken his bomb and his revolver, and left Ilić's house where he had been staying since his return to Sarajevo. He walked around the city park for a while, stopping to talk with two students of his acquaintance. Neither of them had any suspicions of what Princip was about to do; one of them, in fact, was the son of the district attorney who later was to lead the prosecution in the trial of Princip and his accomplices.

The two boys were anxious to spend the rest of the morning with Princip, but after a while he excused himself and left them to take up his post at the Lateiner Bridge. When he heard the explosion, he felt certain that it was one of the conspirators who had acted, although he was not sure which one of them. The crowd was running toward the spot, and Princip allowed himself to be drawn along. He saw that the cars had stopped, and a feeling of triumph and relief came over him. Their mission, he thought, had been successfully accomplished.

Seeing Čabrinović being led away and the cars starting up a few minutes later, he realized how wrong his first impression had been. He brought out neither his bomb nor his revolver, however. Everything seemed to be happening much too fast for him, and while he could clearly see Sophie, he was unable to make out Franz Ferdinand. He walked back toward the Lateiner Bridge, overhearing some spectators say that the attempt against the Heir Apparent had failed. Wondering what there remained for him to do, Princip crossed the street, thinking that he should find another station for himself, since the Archduke's itinerary called for his return down the Appel Quay after the City Hall reception.

Trifko Grabež—whose nineteenth birthday this was—meanwhile paced up and down between the Lateiner Bridge and the Kaiser Bridge, looking for Princip. Their plan of action, he testified in court later, called for his throwing a bomb as the cars were approaching, and for Princip to shoot Franz Ferdinand in the ensuing confusion. He did not see Princip anywhere near the appointed spot at the Lateiner Bridge, however. He made his way through the crowds toward the City Hall, frequently crossing from one side of the Quay to the other, but he still could not find Princip. Perhaps, he thought, the police have arrested him.

For a while, Grabež remained on the Kaiser Bridge, near the spot where Žerajić had tried to kill the Austrian Governor in 1910. Too impatient to remain in any one spot for too long, he returned to the Lateiner Bridge. Looking around, he felt convinced that he could see two detectives staring at him, and quickly decided to walk back to the City Hall. By this time, the streets were thronged and he was able to get no farther than the Kaiser Bridge, since too many spectators blocked his way. A few minutes later, he heard a bomb explode, but could see nothing of what had happened. No cars were coming by, and Grabež was beginning to hope that the attempt had succeeded.

Suddenly, however, he caught sight of the official procession coming toward him. Hearing no more shots or explosions, Grabež thought that all his friends must have been arrested. He was on his way back to the Lateiner Bridge when the Archduke's car passed him. He could see that Franz Ferdinand was alive. Grabež did nothing. The crowd, he told a friend before his arrest, was pressing him in so tightly that he was unable to pull out his bomb. To the police, he gave a different explanation, saying that at the decisive moment he lacked the necessary fortitude.

Whatever his motives, Grabež let the cars pass, but stayed near the Kaiser Bridge, in order to wait—like Princip standing below him—for the Archduke and his party to return from the City Hall.

CHAPTER XI

Princip

"Our Hearts Are Full of Happiness"

Outside the City Hall, a massive structure built in the heavy and graceless pseudo-Moorish manner favored in that region around the turn of the century for ministries, railway stations, and other public buildings, the entire city administration was waiting for the archducal party to arrive. At a quarter past ten, they heard the sound of a heavy detonation—Čabrinović's bomb. There was some discussion about what might have caused the explosion, and the concensus of opinion was that it must have been an unscheduled cannon shot fired to salute the visitors.

Almost as soon as they saw the cars draw up, the city fathers learned differently. The fezzed Mayor, Fehim Effendi Čurčić, stepped out of his car, preparing, as arranged, to launch into his speech of welcome. The Archduke followed, but the shock of what he had just gone through seemed suddenly to catch up with him. Unable to control his temper, he stopped the startled Čurčić before he could begin. "Mr. Mayor," he said, "one comes here for a visit and is received with bombs! It is outrageous!" Trying to calm himself, he went on after a pause, "All right, now you may speak."

The Mayor did, and considering the circumstances, his speech could not have been much more inappropriate.

Your Royal and Imperial Highness! [said the Mayor, addressing the irate Franz Ferdinand] Your Highness! [this to address Sophie]

Our hearts are full of happiness over the most gracious visit with which Your Highnesses are pleased to honor our capital city of Sarajevo, and I consider myself happy that Your Highnesses can read in our faces the feelings of our love and devotion, of our unshakable loyalty, and of our obedience to His Majesty our Emperor and King, and to the Most Serene Dynasty of Habsburg-Lorraine. . . .

All the citizens of the capital city of Sarajevo find that their souls are filled with happiness, [no one has recorded the Mayor's having stumbled over this or the following passages] and they most enthusiastically greet Your Highnesses' most illustrious visit with the most cordial of welcomes, deeply convinced that this stay in our beloved city of Sarajevo will ever increase Your Highnesses' most gracious interest in our progress and well-being, and ever fortify our own most profound gratitude and loyalty, a loyalty that shall dwell immutably in our hearts, and that shall grow forever.

In this enthusiasm, we call out from our hearts to Your Highnesses:

Welcome! Long live our beloved and most exalted guests: His Royal and Imperial Highness, the Most Serene Archduke Heir Apparent Franz Ferdinand, and Her Highness, Duchess Sophie!

God maintain His Royal and Imperial Apostolic Majesty, Our Most Gracious Lord Franz Joseph I, Emperor and King!

Franz Ferdinand, stepping forward to give his reply, showed that he was more skillful in coping with an unexpected situation, and was able to think of at least a few appropriate extemporaneous words:

> It gives me special pleasure [said the still shaken Archduke] to accept the assurances of your unshakable loyalty and affection for His Majesty, our Most Gracious Emperor and King. I thank you cordially, Mr. Mayor, for the resounding ovations with which the population received me and my wife, the more so since I see in them an expression of pleasure over the failure of the assassination attempt.
>
> To my sincere satisfaction, I was in the fortunate position of convincing myself personally, during this brief stay in your midst, of the satisfying development of this magnificent region, in the prosperity of which I have always taken the most lively interest.

So far, the Archduke had spoken in German. He now changed to Serbo-Croatian to finish his speech:

> May I ask you [he said to the Mayor] to give my cordial greetings to the inhabitants of this beautiful capital city, and assure you of my unchanged regard and favor.

Both speeches had been given in front of the City Hall. The crowd shouted its applause, and Franz Ferdinand tried very hard to show a smiling face. Everyone entered the City Hall, Sophie to go upstairs to receive a delegation of the town's Moslem ladies, while Franz Ferdinand and his entourage remained in the vestibule downstairs.

Count Harrach's Protection

Once inside, the first thing Franz Ferdinand did was to draft a telegram to the Emperor. Fearing that exaggerated news stories of Čabrinović's attempt might appear in the press, he sent Franz Joseph a brief and reassuring account of what had happened.

There had meanwhile been a telephone call from the garrison hospital to the City Hall, saying that Merizzi's wounds were slight, and that he was in no danger. Franz Ferdinand discussed the welcome piece of news with the assembled officials, and announced his intention of visiting Merizzi at the hospital. He also asked if the bomb-thrower had been arrested. When told that he had been, his temper flared again. "Just watch it," he said, "instead of rendering the fellow harmless they will be truly Austrian about it and give him the medal of merit."

The discussion next turned to the most crucial topic of all—what was to be done about the remaining program for the day? Plans called for an hour's visit to the National Museum before going to the farewell lunch at the Governor's Residence, the Konak, but to drive through the crowded and narrow streets of the old city after having just escaped one bomb was obviously inadvisable. Potiorek said that he considered another attack unlikely, and Dr. Gerde, the Commissioner of Police, who joined the group just as Potiorek was saying this, agreed. Even so, Potiorek suggested canceling the visit to the museum. Instead, he said, the Archduke might consider going directly to lunch, or returning to Ilidže by driving down the Appel Quay at high speed.

No, Franz Ferdinand said, he did not wish to do either, for he definitely intended to visit Merizzi at the hospital.

Afterwards, they might go to the museum by a roundabout route.

Here Baron Rumerskirch, Franz Ferdinand's Chamberlain, interrupted with a sensible question. Where was the hospital, he asked Potiorek. Could one reach it without passing through the city?

Yes, said Potiorek, all one has to do is to drive straight down the Appel Quay.

One of the members of Franz Ferdinand's retinue still felt uneasy. Would it not be better, he asked, to change the day's plans very radically? Why not stay at the City Hall until two companies of troops could be brought into town, and orders issued to evacuate the streets?

Potiorek said No, the troops weren't in proper uniform to be lining the streets.

The suggestion was dropped. They would drive along the Appel Quay to the hospital, visit Merizzi, and go on to the museum.

Colonel Bardolff, the Chief of Franz Ferdinand's Military Chancellery, and one of the few who kept a clear head during the discussion, thought of summing up the new arrangements, and of asking the Commissioner of Police to repeat them. Gerde, without really listening, said "Yes, yes, certainly," and rushed away. No one, apparently, stopped to give the necessary new instructions to the driver of Franz Ferdinand's car.

Potiorek and Gerde had not only made an ill-considered decision; they had also bungled one of its most essential details. In mitigation, it might be said that both were acting under a strain. Potiorek, who had been riding in Franz Ferdinand's car, and had just avoided being torn apart by an assassin's bomb through a sheer piece of luck, must still have been badly scared. Gerde, whose police force had not been watchful enough to prevent the occurrence, must have been a thoroughly worried man at that moment. Merizzi, Potiorek's aide who might normally have been expected to make sure that the driver received his changed instructions, was in the hospital. Also, it should seem all but unimaginable that one assassination attempt might be followed by any others on one and the same day. "Do you think that Sarajevo is full of assassins?" was the rhetorical question which Potiorek reportedly asked a member of Franz Ferdinand's entourage who was suggesting greater caution.

Having decided on the new route, Franz Ferdinand—apparently willing to take chances for himself, but reluctant to do so where his wife's safety was involved—asked Baron Morsey to drive Sophie either directly to the Governor's residence or to Ilidže, and to take along a soldier of the guard for added protection. Morsey went upstairs, but found the reception of Moslem ladies still in progress. Since the ladies had unveiled their faces for the Duchess, no man was allowed to enter, and Morsey had to wait outside the door.

The reception was proving something of a strain on Sophie. She was plainly suffering from the aftereffects of the assassination attempt, and was extraordinarily quiet at first. She soon regained control of herself, however. Talking about her children, she pointed to a little Turkish girl in the room, and said, "You see, this girl is just about as tall as my Sophie." A little later, she expressed some worry. "We have never left our children alone for this long," she said.

When the reception was over, and she emerged from the room, Morsey helped her into her coat and told her about the Archduke's request. The Duchess, in a manner that was at once friendly and determined, refused. She said: "As long as the Archduke shows himself in public today I will not leave him." By way of reply, Baron Morsey bowed.

Downstairs, Franz Ferdinand himself asked his wife to change her mind, but she remained firm, saying, according to one report, "No Franz, I am going with you."

At the foot of the City Hall steps, the cars drew up to take everyone to the hospital. Their order was the same as on the way in, with the Mayor's car in the lead again.

There was to be one difference in the seating arrangements, however. Count Harrach opened the door of his car and helped the Duchess into it. When Franz Ferdinand and Potiorek were seated too, Harrach, instead of taking his former place by the driver's side, stepped onto the left running board, to shield the Archduke and the Duchess with his body. Harrach's choice of the left rather than the right running board probably was an instinctive one. Standing there, he would be away from the side closest to the curb, but he would be acting as a shield against the river side of the Quay, which was where Čabrinović had hurled his bomb from that morning. The Archduke laughed, and told Harrach not to bother, but the Count insisted. Harrach's gesture was a wonderfully Austrian one—kind, impulsive, brave, chivalrous, and ineffectual.

As the cars drove by, the crowds broke into loud cheers, and the gratified Archduke turned to Harrach to comment on the warmth of the reception. But once again, the crowd contained assassins.

By the first bridge past the City Hall, the Kaiser Bridge, stood Trifko Grabež. He had stationed himself there after his failure to do his part earlier in the morning, thinking—as he said in court later—that he might have another chance to kill the Archduke if the cars were to cross the Kaiser

Bridge to drive to the Konak. Instead, he watched them go straight down the Appel Quay, and did nothing.

At least two of his accomplices also had remained near the Appel Quay, hoping for a second chance, and crossing the street from the river side to be closer to the returning cars. One was Vaso Čubrilović. The other was Gavrilo Princip.

Princip

After Čabrinović's arrest, Princip had left his post on the Lateiner Bridge, and walked across to the shady side of the street. He felt that there were too many people for comfort on the Quay, and took a few steps down Franz Joseph Street, Sarajevo's principal shopping center, stopping outside the spacious and elegant food shop of Moritz Schiller. Here, the crowd was not quite so dense, and the solicitous Mr. Schiller even found room to set down a chair on the sidewalk for one of his lady customers.

A friend of Princip's, Mihailo Pušara, passed by, and asked Princip whether he had seen the bomb attack. Princip thought it wisest not to react to the question. Pušara, still sociable, asked if Princip had any news from a certain friend of theirs. As Princip was answering him, they heard loud cries of *Živio*, and saw the first two cars turn into their street.

Franz Ferdinand's chauffeur, not knowing that the day's plans had been changed, had simply followed the Mayor's car in front of him. The driver of that car—either because he, too, was unfamiliar with the new program, or because the Mayor was confused on who was to go to the museum and who was to call on Merizzi at the hospital—had followed the exact route mapped out for the museum visit, and made a right turn into Franz Joseph Street.

General Potiorek, realizing the mistake, immediately leaned toward the driver and called: "What is this? This is the wrong way! We're supposed to take the Appel Quay!"

The driver put his foot on the brake, and began to back up. The maneuver put the car straight in line with Princip. Princip stepped forward, drew his gun, and at a distance of not more than five feet, fired twice. Harrach, standing on the left running board away from the curb, offered no obstacle, and one bullet pierced Franz Ferdinand's neck, while the other entered Sophie's abdomen.

"I aimed at the Archduke . . . ," Princip told the investigating judge during his first interrogation shortly afterwards. "I do not remember what I thought at that moment. I only know that I fired twice, or perhaps several times, without knowing whether I had hit or missed. . . ."

Potiorek, who had happened to look straight at Princip's face during the shooting, was surprised at the weak detonation made by the gun's going off. Turning his attention to Franz Ferdinand and Sophie, he had the impression that the shots had missed their mark, for both continued to sit upright. He thought it wiser to cancel the hospital visit under the circumstances, however, and called to the chauffeur to back up and to drive across the Lateiner Bridge to the Konak.

All the cars behind had come to a halt, and their occupants scurried out to see if their help was needed. Their first impression, like Potiorek's, was that no one had been seriously hurt, but to be on the safe side, Major Hüttenbrenner hurried off in search of a doctor. Lieutenant Grein, the owner of the last car, and Baron Morsey ran past them, and threw themselves into the melee around Princip.

The Arrest

Having fired at his two victims, Princip turned the gun on himself, intending to commit suicide with a third shot. A spectator standing behind him, a man named Ante Velić, saw what he was doing, threw himself forward, and seized Princip's right arm. Seconds later, the mob had closed in on them.

A policeman tried to arrest Princip, but too many people barred his way. A Catholic student of theology, Danilo Pušić, grabbed Princip by the collar. Princip twisted free, but Pušić caught hold of him again. For a moment, Pušić thought of strangling him, but then, as he told it later, he thought of his Eternal Judge, and rejected the temptation.

For a while, everything was utter confusion. Grein and Morsey drew their sabers and struck out at Princip, who still held his automatic. Dozens of hands seemed to reach out to seize him, but could not twist the gun away from him, for Princip had put his gun hand between his knees. Suddenly the furious Morsey saw the automatic, still black with smoke, coming up, aiming—or so it seemed—straight at his dress uniform trousers, and circling twice before it disappeared again.

Morsey continued his saber thrusts at Princip. One of the blows caught the hand with which the dogged Pušić was holding Princip. Pušić, to his immense relief, noticed that the saber apparently had not been sharpened for a long time.

Some sensible soul shouted: "Don't kill him!" Someone less kindly disposed struck Morsey several powerful blows on the back of his helmet with an iron bar. Morsey thrashed about with his saber and shouted: "I'll kill whoever touches me!" Spying a man at his side who looked like a police officer, Morsey pointed his saber at Princip and called: "Arrest him!" Voices from the crowd yelled: "Go away!"

A young Moslem detective, Smail Spahović, had in fact been standing about ten feet away from Princip on Franz Joseph Street with instructions to watch the crowds rather than the cars. He had heard the shots, of course, but had been unable to make out who had fired them. He now pressed through the mob, and managed to seize Princip.

He was ill rewarded for his efforts. From somewhere, a fist shot out and dealt him a powerful blow in the stomach. Princip, who had gained some ground, followed up this punishment by raising his gun and bringing it down again on Spahović's head, unappreciative of the fact that the policeman was rescuing him from a lynching.

Finally Spahović, together with the chief of his squad who had come to his aid, succeeded in dragging Princip away. Spahović's stomach hurt furiously from the blow, and on reaching the Appel Quay, he asked another policeman to take over.

Sometime during all this commotion, Princip managed to take the cyanide out of his pocket and swallow it.

Just as in Čabrinović's case, the poison was ineffective. All it did was to cause him a severe stomach pain and much vomiting. The poison given them by their Belgrade employers had been too old. The consequences of this bit of negligence were truly momentous. Had Čabrinović's and Princip's suicide attempts succeeded—both of them did take their poison—the Austrians might have remained entirely in the dark about the background of the crime, in which case, there would very likely have been no Austro-Serbian crisis, and hence no World War, in 1914.

As Princip was being led away, his bomb slipped from him. Pušić, the theology student who had been the first to lay hands on Princip, saw it lying in the street, and called a warning to a policeman. Another spectator had seen it too, and while not wholly sure what the black, boxlike object was, shouted: "Watch out! Don't step on the bomb!" Hearing him, some people panicked, while others were too excited to care, and the police, arriving in strength now, had a far from easy time clearing the scene.

Princip, meanwhile, had arrived at the police first-aid post. He was in a pitiable state—disheveled, vomiting, and bleeding from several cuts on his head.

The Trip to the Konak

On the way to the Governor's Residence across the river, it became apparent how wrong Potiorek's initial optimism had been, and how seriously Franz Ferdinand and Sophie had been hurt. As the car was reversing to cross the Lateiner Bridge, a thin streak of blood shot from the Archduke's mouth onto Count Harrach's right cheek. Harrach, still on the left running board, had been bending over Franz Ferdinand. He drew out a handkerchief to still the gushing blood.

The Duchess, seeing this, called: "For Heaven's sake! What happened to you?" and sank from her seat, her face falling between her huband's knees.

Harrach, not realizing that she had been hit, thought that she had fainted. Potiorek, sitting opposite her, reached over and tried to help her to sit up. He, too, thought that she was suffering from nothing worse than shock.

Only her husband seemed to have an instinct for what was happening. Turning to his wife despite the bullet in his neck, Franz Ferdinand pleaded: "*Sopherl! Sopherl! Sterbe nicht! Bleibe am Leben für unsere Kinder!*—Sophie dear! Sophie dear! Don't die! Stay alive for our children!"

Having said this, he seemed about to sag down himself. His plumed general's hat, which had made him an easily recognized target for Princip's bullets, fell off; many of its green feathers later were found all over the car's floor. Count Harrach seized the Archduke by the uniform collar to hold him up. He asked: *"Leiden Eure Kaiserliche Hoheit sehr?*—Is Your Imperial Highness suffering very badly?"

"Es ist nichts—It is nothing," said the Archduke in a weak but audible voice. He seemed to be losing consciousness, but, his voice growing steadily weaker, he repeated the phrase *"es ist nichts"* perhaps six or seven times more.

A rattle began to issue from his throat, which subsided as the car drew up in front of the Konak. Two or three doctors, summoned by Major von Hüttenbrenner, were already waiting for them. Four more were to arrive a few minutes later from the garrison hospital, in response to an urgent telephone call made by Major Höger.

Several aides converged on the car, lifted up Sophie and Franz Ferdinand, and carried them inside the Governor's Residence. Crossing the vestibule, they carried them up one flight of stairs, gently placing Sophie on the bed of Potiorek's bedroom, and Franz Ferdinand on a couch in the adjoining study.

The Death of Sophie

Assisted by Countess Lanjus and Colonel von Bardolff, Dr. Wolfgang of the garrison hospital—who not two hours before had given first aid to the spectators wounded by Čabrinović's bomb—began to examine Sophie. Lieutenant Grein and Major Höger meanwhile rushed out in search of a bottle of ether.

It did not take Dr. Wolfgang long to discover that Sophie was beyond medical aid. By the time Höger returned with his ether, the doctor had found the death-wound, a small, dark red spot in the region of Sophie's right groin.

Princip's bullet, passing through the car door and the upholstery of the seat, had entered Sophie's stomach, where, after opening her stomach artery, it came to rest. She had died from internal bleeding; presumably, she was no longer alive as she was being carried into the Konak. Her worried question, after Princip's shots, about her husband had been her last words.

Countess Lanjus, her lady in waiting, closed Sophie's eyes. Quickly, someone found flowers to place on her body —the bouquet given her by the little girl during the morning's City Hall reception, and flowers taken from the decoration of the Konak's dining room table, set for the luncheon that was to have been given in her and Franz Ferdinand's honor at noon.

"His Highness' Sufferings Are Over"

As soon as he realized that Sophie was dead, Colonel von Bardolff hurried into the next room, to see if there was anything he could do for Franz Ferdinand. Here he found Dr. Payer, a regimental surgeon who had administered first aid to Čabrinović's victims with Dr. Wolfgang that morning. With Dr. Payer were four other doctors, summoned by Höger from the garrison hospital, where they had been treating the wounded Merizzi—Dr. Arnstein, Dr. Pollaco, Dr. Hochmann, and Franz Ferdinand's personal physician, Dr. Fischer.

The Archduke was lying on an ottoman, over which a tablet proclaimed that Emperor Franz Joseph had stayed and worked in that room during his visit in 1910. He was in a deep coma. His breathing was barely audible, and his heartbeat and pulse were faint. Blood flowed from his neck and mouth.

To help Dr. Payer, several aides were trying to undress Franz Ferdinand, but they could not manage to open the clasp on his general's sash. At this moment, Baron Morsey entered. He had walked to the Governor's Residence after his slightly quixotic attempt to assist in Princip's arrest, and he had raced up the stairs when a very pale Lieutenant Grein told him at the door of the Konak that Sophie was dead, and Franz Ferdinand badly wounded. In a flash, Morsey recalled how early that morning, the Archduke had proudly shown him the new and elaborate clasp holding his sash together. Making an effort to remember exactly how the clasp had worked, he tried to undo it, but in his excitement he had no more luck than the others. Hastily, he took out a pen knife, and cut away at the sash, throwing the blood-soaked pieces far into the room behind him.

Someone cut open the Archduke's shirt with a pair of scissors, and hands reached out to help him up into a sitting position. As Franz Ferdinand's back was being raised, blood spurted into Morsey's face and onto the yellow cuffs of his uniform. For a few moments, Franz Ferdinand seemed to be feeling better with the blood flowing freely, and his breathing became more audible. Major von Hütten-brenner, suddenly regaining hope, rushed out of the room for some ether.

Dr. Payer, however, remained pessimistic. We'll be lucky, he said softly, if we get him to the garrison hospital alive.

Baron Morsey knelt down by the Archduke's side, and asked him if he had any message for his children. Franz

Ferdinand could no longer reply. His lips, Morsey saw, were stiffening.

At about 11:00 A.M., within a quarter of an hour of Sophie's death, Dr. Payer said: "No more human aid can be given here. His Highness' sufferings are over."

One by one, the men present came forward, and kissed Franz Ferdinand's hand. Baron Rumerskirch, his Chamberlain, closed the dead Archduke's eyes.

Like Sophie, Franz Ferdinand had died from internal bleeding. Princip's bullet had pierced his jugular vein, and come to rest in his spine. Dr. Payer had briefly contemplated an emergency operation right at the Konak, but with the bullet lodged where it was, the doctors' opinion was that an operation would mean certain death.

Two priests, called when there no longer was a doubt that the murder victims were beyond medical aid, gave Franz Ferdinand and Sophie absolution *in extremis,* and performed the last unction. One, dressed in his brown friar's cowl, was the head of the Franciscan establishments in Bosnia, Brother Mihačević. The other was the Jesuit Father Puntigam, now a teacher in Sarajevo, who, it so happened, had once been confessor to the Archduke.

The bodies of Franz Ferdinand and Sophie were placed on two metal bedsteads next to one another as on temporary biers. More clergymen arrived to say prayers for the dead— Archbishop Stadler of Sarajevo, a military chaplain from the garrison, and several of the town's priests.

Downstairs, in the Konak's banquet room, the table set for the now canceled lunch in honor of the visitors from Vienna had meanwhile been hastily cleared of china, silver, and linen, so that it might serve as a work table for Potiorek, Rumerskirch, and their staffs. For several hours, they sat there, drafting a formal protocol of the morning's events,

16. The Reception in Mostar on the way to Sarajevo, June 25, 1914. On the right, in light coat and with plumed helmet, Franz Ferdinand. Half hidden behind him, Governor Potiorek. In the center, Franz Ferdinand's Chamberlain, Baron Rumerskirch.

At the maneuvers: z Ferdinand (third left) and his Staff in Bosnian mountains, 27, 1914.

18. Leaving the City Hall June 28, 1914. Sophie and Franz Ferdinand descend the steps and approach the waiting car.

19. A few minutes before the assassination, the departure from City Hall. Franz F
nand, in plumed helmet, has taken his seat in the car on the left, with Sophie to his r
On the running board, to protect the couple stands Count Harrach.

20. After the assassination, Princip's arrest.

21. After the assassinat
Franz Ferdinand's bloodied
torn uniform coat.

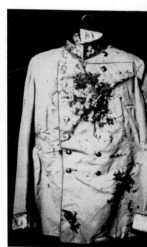

dispatching reports to Vienna on the crime and on the results of Princip's and Čabrinović's first interrogations, asking the Emperor's instructions, issuing orders. Only when the most urgent work was finished did they remember to have a light lunch served.

The most painful message of all was sent by Baron Morsey. It contained the news of the assassination, and was addressed to Dr. Stanowsky, the tutor of Franz Ferdinand's and Sophie's three children.

CHAPTER XII

Riots and Sympathy

"A Decent Member of Bourgeois Society"

The news of Franz Ferdinand's and Sophie's death spread fast through Sarajevo. In the evening, the first sporadic anti-Serb demonstrations took place. They sufficiently alarmed Dr. Gerde, Sarajevo's Commissioner of Police, to make him put in a request for troops. The Commanding General, von Appel, replied to Gerde's appeal by sending two infantry companies into town. The demonstrators' mood was still pacific, however, and, as Appel reported later, the troops were soon able to return to their barracks "without being forced to take any action."

It was not long before they were needed again, for at about 9:30 the next morning, Monday, June 29, the storm broke, as mobs of Croats and Moslems went on a rampage against the city's Serbs. To the London *Times'* shocked correspondent, the mob seemed made up "of the lowest elements, particularly in the Moslem quarter," and an Austrian observer agreed that it consisted of the "work-shy riffraff from town and country." One equally appalled correspondent from Vienna, however, reported having seen "many very well dressed ladies and gentlemen" among them as well.

Carrying black-draped flags and pictures of the Emperor, Franz Ferdinand, and Sophie, singing the national anthem, and shouting *Živio* for the Empire and the Habsburgs, one large mob proceeded to the place of the assassination, where they knelt and prayed for the salvation of the souls of Princip's two victims. After listening to patriotic speeches, they proceeded to the Sarajevo Cathedral, where they said more prayers for the dead. Many wept.

The same mob then went on to assault whatever Serbs they could lay their hands on, to smash Serb property, to loot and pillage. By early afternoon, there was hardly an undamaged Serb school, club, house, or store left in Sarajevo. The mob broke into Sarajevo's best hotel, the "Europe," which belonged to a prominent Serb, and left it a shambles. They attacked and demolished the offices of the city's two Serb newspapers. They broke the windows of the Serb-Orthodox Metropolitan's Palace. The Metropolitan—he had been one of the guests of honor at Franz Ferdinand's state banquet in Ilidže two days before—suffered cuts on his left hand from pieces of glass as he stood behind a window of his palace watching the mob.

At eleven o'clock in the morning, the civilian authorities, apparently aware that Sarajevo's small police force was no match for the demonstrators, asked that troops be held in readiness. An hour later, as the riots continued unabated, General von Appel decided to take matters into his own hands, and to restore order. Governor Potiorek seems to have been paralyzed into inaction at this time; the day before, too, it had been Appel and not Potiorek who had

had the presence of mind to order the troops back from the maneuver area into town. He took no exception to the Commanding General's measure, however, and in less than four hours three battalions and one squadron of troops, assisted by the police, had cleared the streets of demonstrators without having had to fire a single shot.

A few determined hooligans tried to go on rioting for a while longer, but the proclamation of martial law which Potiorek issued at four o'clock in the afternoon effectively cooled their ardor. All inns, read the proclamation, were to close at 8:00 P.M., and coffee shops and "first-class hotels" at ten. No more than three people were allowed to walk together in the street, all public assemblies were banned, and young people under fifteen were made subject to a 7:00 P.M. curfew. Violators of these orders were threatened with penalties that ranged from light prison sentences to death.

Fifty persons had been wounded in the day's rioting, some of them severely. One man had been killed. (He was not a Serb, but a member of the mob killed by a Serb in self-defense.) Rough estimates of property destroyed ran as high as five million crowns, or about one million dollars at the then rate of exchange. "Sarajevo," reported the correspondent of the conservative Vienna *Reichspost* on June 30, "looks like the scene of a pogrom today."

Actually, the physical destruction was not quite as bad as originally feared. In some ways, business even profited from the events of June 28 and 29—the murder and the riots were serving as a grisly form of vacation attraction. For several days, numbers of tourists descended on Sarajevo, to look at the spot from which Čabrinović had thrown his bomb, at Schiller's food store in front of which Princip had fired his fatal shots, and at the smashed windows and broken furniture left by the rioting mob, taking many a photograph of all these scenes.

Only the earliest visitors, however, found many traces of the rioting. A Russian diplomat, sent to Sarajevo by his government on a fact-finding mission a week and a half after the crime, reported back that nearly all of the damage had been repaired, that the shops were open, the streetcars full, and traffic heavy. On the surface, at least, everything had returned to normal.

Beneath it, tension did not disappear that easily. "To the Esteemed Citizens, Officials, and Military Personnel of Sarajevo," ran one sad advertisement in the pro-government *Sarajevoer Tagblatt* on July 4, which was signed by "Several [anonymous] Citizens of Sarajevo." Five days before, the advertisement read, the inn belonging to one Kosta Kontos had been completely demolished, on the mistaken assumption that Kontos was a Serb. This was not so—the innkeeper was a Greek. Moreover, he had always been entirely loyal to the monarchy.

> Since this error has caused him great material damage [the advertisement continued], he asks his honored customers for their continued confidence, declaring most emphatically that he always has been, and always will be, a decent member of bourgeois society, and a respecter of the laws of Austria-Hungary, the orders of the authorities, and civic order.
>
> He is still in business and would like to continue in business. He asks all his friends and customers for their fair understanding, confidence, and patronage. . . .

Collecting for a Monument

Over Potiorek's objections, Minister of Finance Bilinski, the Governor's superior as the head of the entire civil administration of Bosnia-Herzegovina, indignantly ordered the compensation of Sarajevo's "peaceful citizens" for the damages they had suffered. They were to be paid from government funds, Bilinski wired, and the administration was not to take refuge in pleading *force majeure*.

Potiorek, while willing enough to use relief funds to extend emergency aid to any Serb needing such aid as a result of the riots, opposed any full-scale compensation. By their blatantly obvious lack of sympathy for Franz Ferdinand and Sophie, he argued, they had done much to bring the day's violence on themselves.

A bitterly reproachful exchange of letters between Bilinski and Potiorek ensued. Bilinski, who had always favored a conciliatory policy toward Bosnia's Serbs, asked that "the old course" be maintained. Potiorek did not see things that way. The Minister, after guardedly blaming Potiorek for the insufficient security precautions taken to protect the Archduke, added some harsh words about the "riot and plunder" that had followed, " in the face of which the police proved helpless." Potiorek, stung by both charges, denied that the demonstrations had been that bad, or the police that remiss in their duties.

But at any rate, the riots were over, and there was time for some more worthy expression of sympathy for the murdered Archduke and Duchess. On June 29, the presiding officers of Bosnia's parliament issued a statement condemning the deed and the pan-Serb agitation behind it. Many messages of condolence from Bosnia began to arrive at the Imperial Chancellery in Vienna. (Just how sincere these were is another matter. One, for example, was signed by Miško Jovanović, the cinema manager in Tuzla who had helped Princip and Čabrinović on the underground route from Belgrade, and had hidden their bombs and guns for them.)

A local newspaper sponsored a collection to erect a monument on the place of the murder. The list of contributions, published every day, at times makes strange reading. The Serb-Orthodox Metropolitan, hurt in the rioting, sent 200 crowns, the largest contribution that day. Lazar Djukić, who, while refusing to take part in the assassination himself, had recruited Vaso Čubrilović for it, contributed one crown, or not quite 25 cents. Dr. Gerde, whose police force had proved unable to prevent the murder, offered 50 crowns.

"Hail to the Gun of Princip"

The news of Princip's crime caused world-wide shock, even though few people yet guessed what its eventual consequences were going to be. Telegrams and letters of condolence poured into Vienna as soon as the murders became known. Many European courts went into mourning. King George V commanded the British court to wear mourning for one week beginning June 28; Tsar Nicholas II of Russia ordered twelve days' court mourning in memory of Franz Ferdinand.

Kaiser Wilhelm of Germany and President Wilson of the United States were of the same mind when it came to expressing their sympathies for the murdered couple. The German Emperor, recalling his recent visit to Konopisht, sent a telegram to Franz Ferdinand's children which read:

> We can hardly find words to tell you children how our hearts bleed, thinking of you and of your indescribable misery. Only two weeks ago we spent such lovely hours with

your parents, and now we hear of this terrible sadness that you must suffer. May God protect you and give you the strength to bear this blow. The blessing of the parents reaches beyond the grave.

The President of the United States sent the following telegram of condolence to Emperor Franz Joseph:

THE WHITE HOUSE
Washington, June 29, 1914
Deeply shocked at the atrocious murder of His Imperial and Royal Highness Archduke Francis Ferdinand and Consort at an assassin's hands, I extend to Your Majesty, to the Imperial and Royal family, and to the Government of Austria-Hungary the sincere condolences of the Government and people of the United States and an expression of my own profound sympathy.

WOODROW WILSON

And yet, behind several of these professions of sympathy there lay a good deal of relief. The horror over the crime was genuine enough, and a widespread initial impression that the assassination had been organized by anarchists may have caused a personal enough feeling of involvement at many a royal and presidential residence. On the other hand, Franz Ferdinand's political plans had created much fear and worry, either because of their apparent vagueness or because, as in some countries, they seemed to make him look like a potential future enemy. Franz Ferdinand never had had a good press in his lifetime, and there were few people who truly mourned him now.

The crime was a terrible one, of course, the Italian Foreign Minister told one ambassador in a startlingly wrong prediction, "but world peace will not be any worse off."

The Italian press, reported the British Ambassador in Rome to London, was vociferous in denouncing the crime, yet "it is obvious that people generally have regarded the elimination of the late Archduke as almost providential." In France and Russia, the feeling was very much the same. The prevailing mood was best summed up perhaps by the eminently unsentimental King Nicholas of Montenegro. According to "an absolutely reliable but secret source," wrote the French Minister, the King "does not approve the action itself, . . . but he is delighted with the result."

Several journalists, unhampered by governmental responsibilities, could afford to be even blunter in their comments. Not all, however, went as far as an Italian editor named Benito Mussolini—then a Socialist—who some months after the event wrote: "Hail to the gun of Princip and to the bomb of Čabrinović!"

Serbian Condolences

In Serbia, a majority of the people probably felt the same way about Franz Ferdinand's disappearance from the scene, but the government took immediate measures to prevent them from giving voice to their sentiments.

The news of Princip's crime reached Belgrade on Sunday afternoon. The Russian Minister, upon hearing it, reportedly expressed what must have been the fears of many a responsible Serbian politician at that moment. "In heaven's name!" he said. "Let us hope he is not a Serbian." Kaiser Wilhelm's comment, when he read about the Minister's remark, was unkind. "After all," wrote the Emperor, "he would have known!"

General Bozo Janković, the president of the now innocuous *Narodna Odbrana* and a member of Pašić's cabinet, at about the same time was saying very much the same thing to a Hungarian official. That afternoon, Janković was on a train headed for the Adriatic coast with his family for a summer vacation, and hence found himself on Austro-Hungarian territory. As the train sped toward the Croatian capital of Zagreb, two friends hastily entered his compartment, and asked him to step into the corridor with them for a minute. Lowering their voices, they told him that the train was full of Austrian officials—word had just been received at the last station that Franz Ferdinand and Sophie had been murdered in Sarajevo!

The General went pale. He had attended the meeting in which Pašić had told of having learned about the plot, and in which the fruitless decision had been reached to stop the assassins at the border. He therefore must have had a fair idea of what the news meant, even though the *Narodna Odbrana* was not a direct accessory to the crime.

After a few moments of near panic, Janković recovered his composure. Let us stay in our compartments, he told his two friends, and pretend ignorance.

Having arrived at his destination, the Adriatic port city of Fiume, he hired a fiacre to take him to the Hungarian Prefect. Expressing his regrets over the morning's unfortunate occurrence, he asked whether there was any definite information yet about the assassin's identity. Janković already had some thoughts on the subject, but he wanted to make sure.

The assassin, the Prefect said, was a Serb, meaning that he was a Serb ethnically and linguistically, but not a Serbian by nationality.

"Since I had learned before that the assassin was a Bosnian," Janković has recalled the scene, "and since he [the Prefect] confirmed this, I replied that it was a relief to me, a Serbian cabinet minister, that the assassin at least was an Austro-Hungarian and not a Serbian national."

In Belgrade itself, the news of the murder had created a sensation. Some citizens expressed their delight over the day's events, but the prevailing mood at first was one of utter surprise rather than of pleasure. To prevent private feelings of approval from erupting into demonstrations in honor of Princip, and to indicate the government's shock, the quick-thinking Minister of the Interior ordered all theaters, coffee shops, and other places of assembly to close at 10:00 P.M. The Belgrade police followed this up by banning all public concerts, dances, and other amusements.

The next morning, the government newspaper carried an editorial condemning the deed. Most other Belgrade newspapers wrote in a similar vein, although some pointed out that it had been a mistake on Franz Ferdinand's part to choose Saint Vitus' Day, a day so full of historic associations to any Serb, for his visit to Sarajevo.

Only *The Piémont,* the organ of the Black Hand, called Princip a "young martyr," and wrote that the real culprits were the Austrians themselves, who had provoked the murder by creating an insufferable state of affairs in Bosnia. The Serbian police promptly seized the issue.

The government also conveyed its formal sympathies to the Austrians. Pašić himself was on an election campaign in the provinces, but in his place the Minister of Justice and the Secretary General of the Foreign Ministry called at the Austrian Legation on Monday. The call embarrassed everybody concerned.

The Austrian Minister was absent too from Belgrade at that time, and they were received by the chargé d'affaires instead. The chargé, Wilhelm Ritter von Storck, while not yet possessing any concrete evidence about the murder that pointed to Belgrade, was profoundly convinced that the agitation for a Greater Serbia which the government had either tolerated or sponsored for so long was ultimately responsible for Franz Ferdinand's and Sophie's deaths. For years, Storck wrote to Vienna, these people had sowed hatred; they had now reaped murder. Storck was one of those Austrians who believed that only strong action against Serbia could save the Empire. "Serbia must learn to fear us again," he bluntly advised his superiors in Vienna two days after Sarajevo, "otherwise our old border regions, and not just the annexed provinces, will be in danger."

His manner in acknowledging his Serbian visitors' condolences was, as he himself reported it, "reserved but correct," incapable as he was of forgetting his suspicions about the crime's true origins. As more Serbian dignitaries called —the King's Cabinet Secretary, the Royal Chamberlain, the Crown Prince—he grew to dislike his job even more. "I was unable to utter much more than the usual thank-you phrases," he admitted in his dispatch to Vienna.

When he reported the announcement of a week's court mourning the next day, he added that the gesture struck him as another piece of hypocrisy. "If many a person now offering his condolences with a properly funeral face, were to pass by the bier of the victims, the wounds would begin to bleed again."

There was still one other ordeal ahead of Storck. On July 3, a requiem mass for the murdered couple was held in the chapel of the Austro-Hungarian Legation. Several Serbian cabinet members attended it. Among them was Ljuba Jovanović, the Minister of Education who, like General Janković, had been present when Pašić had revealed his advance information about the plot. Jovanović's feelings, as he entered the chapel, were torn. On the one hand, he approved of Princip's deed. On the other, he agreed with Pašić's efforts to avoid trouble with Austria by acting in a wholly innocent manner. "Nevertheless," he wrote in what may have been the year's understatement, "both my action in going there and the short period during which we were in the church were unpleasant to me."

Three days earlier, before the Austrian government had even accused Serbia of any complicity in the crime, Jovanović had hastened to assure a visiting French diplomat that Belgrade had never aided the Bosnian revolutionaries in any fashion. We have treated Austria's Serbs, he said, "as though they had cholera."

Pašić, after returning to Belgrade, pursued the same line. On July 1, again before any formal Austrian charges had been made, he sent a circular instruction to all Serbian missions abroad. The deed, he wrote, had been generally deplored in Serbia. "It would be absurd to believe that at a time when Serbia is doing all it can to bring about better and more friendly relations with the neighboring monarchy, it would be capable of provoking such acts directly or indirectly."

A week later, the Prime Minister followed this up by a remarkable interview he gave to a correspondent of a Budapest newspaper. The double assassination, he said, had caused widespread and honest sympathy in Serbia. The criminals clearly were Austrian citizens, and not even citizens of voting age at that, but foolish children. His government had had no advance knowledge of the plot, nor had it been involved in it in any other way.

Having told one plain untruth—not only *had* he known about the plot beforehand, but he had failed to issue an adequate warning to the Austrians—he added a strange version of an incident that had taken place half a year earlier.

In the winter of 1913, the Belgrade police had sent a routine inquiry to the Austro-Hungarian Consulate, asking whether some personal data which Čabrinović had submitted to them agreed with what was known about him at the Consulate, or whether he had any criminal record in Bosnia. The Consulate sent an equally routine reply, saying that the information Čabrinović had given was correct; and that he did not in fact have any prison record.

If only the Austrian police had drawn our attention to Princip and Čabrinović when these two were in Belgrade, Pašić mournfully complained to the correspondent. (The Austrians, of course, did not realize that Princip was in Serbia, since he had gone there illegally. On the other hand, the Serbians did know about it, since he was taking the official high school examinations given by the Ministry of Education, and had met the Minister.) The Serbian Police, Pašić said, would have kept a sharp watch on them in that case. But it was not just that the Austrian police had been derelict about putting their Serbian colleagues on their guard. There had been something far worse. The Belgrade police, Pašić said, becoming suspicious of Čabrinović on the basis, presumably, of their own evidence, had intended to expel the young anarchist from the country. (Actually, the young anarchist was holding a job at the Serbian Government Printing Office that winter.) Upon hearing this, the Austrians had interceded in his behalf, and had used their efforts to save him from expulsion.

No Tears in Austria

In Vienna, rumors about an assassination first began to circulate in the early hours of the afternoon. It was terribly hot that Sunday, and the streets of the city were all but deserted. Most Viennese had either gone to the country and woods that surrounded Vienna, or had chosen to stay in the cool darkness of their homes. Even so, small crowds began to assemble, discussing the rumors. At 3:00 P.M., one-page extra editions reporting the news from Sarajevo reached the streets. At the same hour, the Imperial Chamberlain's office ordered the Burgtheater to cancel the evening's performance, and later in the afternoon, all other theaters staying open for the summer announced that they, too, would remain dark that evening.

Indignation against Belgrade ran high. It was taken for granted that the murder was Serbian inspired, and for several days, the police had their hands full in keeping the mobs away from the Serbian Legation. During one such scuffle, some ingenious rioters almost scored a brief victory when they threw live frogs at the line of mounted policemen barring their way, hoping to upset the horses. But despite the dark theaters and despite the riots, true sorrow for Franz Ferdinand was rare.

Some few people realized that the Archduke, had he lived to become Emperor, might have effected those painful reforms which Austria-Hungary needed to survive. Many more, however, seemed to share the feelings of a respected liberal politician who on June 28 wrote in his diary: "Perhaps [some day] one will be able to say: 'God meant to be kind to Austria by saving it from this Emperor.'"

Popular sympathy was reserved for Sophie and the orphaned children, but above all for the old Emperor.

Franz Joseph, in Ischl for his annual summer vacation, learned about the murder of his nephew through a telegram from Potiorek, which arrived within about an hour of the event. General Count Paar, his chief aide, took the telegram to the Emperor. Baron Margutti, another of Franz

Joseph's aides on duty in Ischl, has given an account in his memoirs of what he says Paar told him that evening about the Emperor's reaction. Franz Joseph, Margutti quotes Paar as telling him, seemed very much affected at first. He almost looked as though he had suffered a stroke. For several minutes, he closed his eyes, completely lost in his private thoughts, and not uttering a word. When he finally spoke, it was as though he was talking to himself rather than to Paar: "Terrible! The Almighty cannot be provoked!" And after a pause: "A higher force has restored that order which unfortunately I was not able to maintain."

Whether the Emperor's reaction to his nephew's violent death really did take the form of this almost blasphemous allusion to Franz Ferdinand's and Sophie's morganatic marriage is dubious at best. The quotation is a third-hand one— what Margutti, some years after the event, claimed Count Paar told him about what the Emperor, in turn, had told Paar, and Margutti's memoirs are full of entertaining but unsubstantiated gossip. Nor was the Emperor—as simple a man in his speech as he was in his other tastes—in the habit of speaking in such pretentious or blasphemous phrases. Unfortunately, however, Margutti's is the only account we have that was written by anyone present in Ischl at the time.

CHAPTER XIII

A Strange Funeral

"There Is No Need For Reproach, Your Majesty"

Having heard the news of Sarajevo, Franz Joseph gave immediate orders to prepare for the return to Schönbrunn, his residence near Vienna. Leaving Ischl at 6:00 A.M. on Monday, Franz Joseph and his retinue arrived at Schönbrunn five hours later. At the station, the Emperor was welcomed by Archduke Carl Franz Joseph, Franz Ferdinand's nephew. Owing to Franz Ferdinand's oath of renunciation—the price he had had to pay for his morganatic marriage in 1900—his children were excluded from the succession and Carl, the son of his younger brother Otto, had become the new Successor to the Throne. In 1916, in the midst of a hopeless war, Carl was to be crowned Austria-Hungary's last Emperor.

Together, Franz Joseph and his grandnephew walked out of the station—the Emperor had taken the young Archduke's arm—and drove to Schönbrunn castle. Many spectaators were lining the streets along their way. Some stood quietly to show their sympathy; others cheered the Emperor and Carl. In the courtyard, no words were spoken in welcome. The courtiers assembled there to greet the Emperor did so by bowing silently.

The Emperor either did not feel his nephew's loss very deeply, or else he was suppressing his emotions. Three days after his return to Schönbrunn, Colonel Bardolff came to give an eyewitness report of the assassination. Having listened to him in silence, Franz Joseph, in a low voice, asked only one question: "And how did the Archduke bear himself?"

"Like a soldier, Your Majesty," said Bardolff.

"That was to be expected from His Imperial Highness."

There was a brief pause. It was broken by the Emperor.

"And how were the maneuvers?" he asked, speaking in his normal tone of voice again, and changing the subject.

A few days later, he saw Baron Conrad, the Chief of the General Staff. Conrad originally had been one of Franz Ferdinand's favorites, but in recent years there had been many a bitter quarrel between them.

Franz Joseph's conversation with the Chief of Staff first touched upon the recent death of a general whom both had known.

"All are dying, only I can't die," said the Emperor.

"The Lord be thanked," said Conrad. "We're glad you're alive."

"Yes, yes, but one is *so* alone then."

The conversation moved on to the subject of the Bosnian maneuvers. He had feared a new conflict with Franz Ferdinand, Conrad admitted, but the Archduke had been kind and charming.

"Yes," broke in the Emperor. "He has changed recently, and for the better. Did he have any premonitions? I reproach myself. He was asking me whether he should not forget about the trip."

"But there is no need for reproaches, Your Majesty."

"He said he could not bear the great heat," said the Emperor, ready to abandon the subject again.

Potiorek To Resign?

Franz Joseph, noted Conrad, while reproaching himself, had no word of blame for Potiorek.

Here, in fact, is one of the strangest aspects of the murders. There was, it seemed, no intention to call Potiorek and Gerde to account for their negligence.

There was much public criticism of both men in Austria, and even harsher things were being said about them privately. The leading Socialist paper, the *Arbeiter Zeitung*, bitterly attacked Potiorek for his share of the responsibility. The widely respected Liberal paper, the *Neue Freie Presse*, asked editorially:

> Is it really so difficult to know who the fanatics are among the propagandized youth; would it really be impossible to keep these political birds of passage under observation? We do not think so, and it is precisely this which the police in the dangerous vicinity of the Balkans have to do if they are to fulfill their most basic duties.

In the same issue, the paper carried an outspoken dispatch from Vienna saying that "the insufficiency of the police in Sarajevo is a topic of general conversation."

Many people, reported the Conservative *Reichspost* from Sarajevo, "are reproaching General Potiorek and Police Commissioner Gerde for the poor security service."

The streets, these critics were arguing, should have been much better guarded, particularly after Čabrinović's attempt. "The heads of the Sarajevo police are generally held to be very much responsible, and it is likely that there will be some retirements." A week later, on July 7, the *Reichspost* reported a rumor according to which General Potiorek had been asked to submit his resignation.

"The most indescribable state of affairs must exist among the police," angrily exclaimed the Hungarian Prime Minister at a secret cabinet meeting about a week after the crime, "if on the day of the assassination six or seven individuals who were known to the police could take up their positions, armed with bombs and guns, along the route of the late Successor to the Throne, without the police observing or arresting a single one of them."

"If an archduke should be stung by a fly in some railroad station," the German Ambassador to Vienna privately told an Austrian friend, "the station master might well lose his job. But no one is as much as bothered for his share in this slaughter in the streets of Sarajevo."

Everyone, it seemed, was blaming Gerde and Potiorek—except for the Emperor. Not only did Franz Joseph abstain from uttering a single reproach against Potiorek, but in a conversation with Bilinski on June 29 he took pains, as the Minister reported to Potiorek, "to say some highly appreciative words of Your Excellency's person."

What accounted for the Emperor's attitude? Was it simply the resignation of a very old man? Franz Joseph had suffered so many personal losses during his long reign that the death of his nephew may have seemed no more than another inevitable blow of fate, to be borne in dignity and silence. Was it his dislike of Franz Ferdinand? The two certainly had never got on well with each other. Yet one wonders, for Franz Joseph was too much of a gentleman to have welcomed his nephew's death, and too much of a respecter of the law to close his eyes to the possibility of criminal negligence.

Was it friendship for Potiorek? The Bosnian Governor had the reputation of being one of the most capable generals of the Empire, and Franz Joseph had known and liked him for years. Gossip had it that in 1906, when the post of Chief of the General Staff fell vacant, Franz Joseph would have preferred to see Potiorek rather than Conrad appointed to it, and withdrew Potiorek's name only because Franz Ferdinand was totally unyielding in supporting Conrad's candidacy. But personal favoritism makes an unconvincing explanation too; for Franz Joseph was too honest a man and too good a ruler to let personal considerations influence his official decisions to this extent.

Whatever the motives, the facts remain that the Emperor, to all appearances, was absolving the Governor and the local authorities under him of any part of the responsibility; that Potiorek neither offered his resignation nor was asked for it; and that there was no investigation of the obviously insufficient security measures taken in Sarajevo. Perhaps parliament would have demanded such an investigation, but parliament was not in session. When it was, the country was at war—clearly not the proper time for an investigation which could uncover facts showing that there were Austrian officials who might have prevented the Sarajevo crime.

But if excuses exist why Potiorek and Gerde should have escaped the consequences of their negligence, none do for the manner in which the funeral of Franz Ferdinand and Sophie was arranged.

The Trip Home

At first, there seemed to be nothing out of the ordinary about the funeral arrangements. Resting in metal coffins, the bodies of Franz Ferdinand and Sophie, which military surgeons had embalmed during the night, were placed in the drawing room of the Konak on the day following the murders. The room, lined in black, soon filled with flowers and with mourners from the city. At six in the afternoon, Brother Mihačević, the Franciscan Provincial, and Archbishop Stadler, who was accompanied by the entire cathedral chapter, blessed the two bodies. Soldiers slowly carried the coffins to the waiting hearses, and a long cortège began its procession toward the station. A detachment of cavalry and several infantry battalions led the way, among them a battalion in which Bosnian Serbs predominated—the soldiers had volunteered for this duty in order to demonstrate their loyalty to the crown. Behind the troops walked Stadler, Mihačević, and the remainder of the clergy. They were followed by a car bearing the many wreaths sent to the Konak, by the two hearses, and by a group of mourners that included Baron Rumerskirsch, Colonel Bardolff, Countess Lanjus, Governor Potiorek, and every ranking officer and official of Sarajevo.

At the station, a special railroad car received the coffins. Stadler and Mihačević pronounced a final blessing, the car was sealed under the supervision of Baron Rumerskirch, and at a few minutes past seven, amid a twenty-four gun salute fired from the fortress cannon, the funeral train left the city in which Dimitrijević's men had murdered Franz Ferdinand and Sophie.

The coffins were returning by the same route by which Franz Ferdinand had arrived four days earlier—by rail and river to the coast, across the Adriatic on board the *Viribus Unitis,* and from Trieste to Vienna by train once more. Again, as on the Archduke's trip to Bosnia, large crowds, dressed in mourning this time, turned up all along the way between Sarajevo and the coast, and as the *Viribus Unitis* slowly crossed the calm Adriatic—the flag-draped coffins guarded by detachments of the ship's officers and men— boats of nearly every size and description came up to the battleship in a last and silent gesture of condolence.

Only when the *Viribus Unitis* anchored in Trieste two days later, on the afternoon of July 1, were there any indications that something was amiss. Instructions had been received from Vienna ordering a delay—the special train bearing the coffins was not to arrive in Vienna until ten o'clock the next evening, and thus well after dark. The author of this order was the Emperor's Lord Chamberlain, Prince Alfred Montenuovo.

Relations between Montenuovo and Franz Ferdinand had been badly strained during the latter's lifetime. No one could quite say why. Some gossip had it that the Prince, a distant relative of Sophie Chotek, felt slighted by her coolness toward him after her marriage, while according to other purveyors of scandal he was resentful over several alleged discourtesies on Franz Ferdinand's part. What made some of the people at court relish the hostility between the two men was a special bit of historic irony: Montenuovo, upholder of court etiquette and resolute opponent, so it was said, of Franz Ferdinand's morganatic marriage, was himself the descendant of a morganatic union. After Napoleon's exile to Elba, the Austrian Court had detailed a dashing general, Count Neipperg, to look after the Empress, Marie Louise, from whom Napoleon had been forced to part. The general fulfilled his duties so expertly that eventually, he and Marie Louise were married; and one of the grandsons of their morganatic union was none other than Prince Montenuovo.

As Lord Chamberlain, Montenuovo found himself in charge of all formal ceremonies surrounding the funeral. His first plan, it was said, was to enforce court etiquette with total cold-bloodedness. Franz Ferdinand was to be entombed in the Capuchin Crypt, the traditional burial place of the Habsburgs, but Sophie, who had no claim to such Imperial honors, was to receive a separate burial in the crypt which Franz Ferdinand had ordered built at Artstetten castle. The plan had to be revised when someone pointed out that Franz Ferdinand presumably in anticipation of the court's attitude, had included a passage in his will which specifically requested that he and Sophie be buried side by side in Artstetten.

Montenuovo had little choice except to give in, but he could raise a new objection. It would unfortunately be impossible, it appeared, to hold any memorial services in Vienna for the late Duchess without violating that holy of holies, court etiquette. Sophie, the Chamberlain's office reportedly ruled, having been born a mere Countess Chotek, could not possibly be allowed to lie in state next to her Habsburg husband in the Hofburg chapel.

At this point, the indignant new Heir to the Throne, Archduke Carl Franz Joseph, apparently went to see the Emperor. As a result of their talk, an Imperial command went out ordering joint requiem services. Montenuovo, unable to oppose the command directly, took refuge in what might be called a strategy of massive, administrative pettiness—there was to be no full ceremonial and no military parade; the coffins were to be brought from the station to the Hofburg chapel after dark, with only a minimum of soldiers lining the streets; the chapel was to be open to the public for four hours only, from eight in the morning to noon on July 3, and the position and decoration of the coffins was to make Sophie's morganatic position painfully obvious.

An Absence of Royalty

Neither Franz Ferdinand nor Sophie had ever been widely beloved, but thanks to the Lord Chamberlain's attitude they suddenly had more sympathizers than they had had in their lifetime. One open indication of this occurred as the train bearing their mortal remains arrived at the Vienna *Südbahnhof* on July 2. Among those awaiting the train could be seen Archduke Carl and all the officers of the Vienna garrison not on duty that evening, even though there was no provision for the presence of either the Heir to the Throne or of the officers in the elaborately worked out ceremonial. They accompanied the cortège from the station to the Hofburg chapel, making a spectacular procession even more memorable by their uninvited presence. For while Montenuovo had denied Franz Ferdinand the full honors due to an Heir to the Throne and Inspector General of the Armed Forces, it must be said that even a lesser Habsburg cortège offered some spectacular pageantry. Two grooms carrying lanterns opened the procession, followed by a squadron of the Seventh Lancers, courtiers in coaches and courtiers on horseback, the Lord Chamberlain and the Archduke's First Chamberlain, more grooms in braided court uniforms carrying lanterns, the two hearses, flanked by twelve royal guards to the right, carrying halberds, and twelve to the left, holding swords drawn. Franz Ferdinand, when alive, had never been so well guarded. Behind the hearses came more grooms, a court coach bearing Franz Ferdinand's retinue and another bearing Sophie's, and, finally, another squadron of Lancers.

When the public was admitted to the Hofburg chapel the next morning to view the bodies lying in state, the setting at first seemed solemn enough, too. The church was draped almost entirely in black; even the *prie-dieus* had been covered with black cloth. Masses were being read at every altar, and at ten o'clock, the court choir entered to chant the *Miserere*. Royal guards were keeping the death watch, and the two catafalques on which the bodies rested were gleaming in the light of enormous wax candles in silver candelabras.

As the visitor stepped closer to the silver and gold coffins, however, he was confronted with the final insult committed in the name of protocol. The two coffins had been placed side by side, but that of the Duchess—her former status as a lady in waiting apparently unforgiven even in death—was at a level lower than that of her hubsand's. Nor was this all. For while on top of the Heir to the Throne's coffin rested his medals, the crown of an Imperial Prince, a general's cap and sabre, and an Archduke's hat, all that could be seen on Sophie's coffin, in addition to her medals, were a pair of white gloves and a fan. In front of the catafalques lay a wreath of white roses sent by the orphaned children, bearing the simple inscription "Sophie, Max, Ernst," but none, the Archduke's friends noted, from the Emperor.

Sharply at noon, as the bells of the church started to toll, the attendants closed the doors of the church, admitting no more visitors, even though this meant turning away a good many Viennese who were still waiting outside to pay their last respects to the dead. The church was being cleared for the funeral requiem service that afternoon.

Four hours later, the brief requiem service began. The Cardinal Prince Archbishop of Vienna officiated, and the audience included the Emperor, all archdukes and archduchesses, ministers and generals, and the diplomatic corps. But brilliant though this assembly might be, there were some almost equally conspicuous absences. No foreign royalty had come to Vienna.

Kaiser Wilhelm of Germany, it seems, had almost immediately sent word that he was ready to attend the funeral services, and so had King Victor Emmanuel of Italy. King George of England was going to be represented by the Duke of Connought, Tsar Nicholas by Grand Duke Nicholas Nicolaievich. As late as June 30, the Austrian press still reported the impending arrival of both the German Emperor and the King of the Belgians as facts. Actually, however, the Austrian Foreign Ministry had let it be known the day after the murders that it would prefer to have no foreign monarchs or missions at the requiem services. The official explanation was that in view of the Emperor's advanced age, he should be spared the exertions of a long ceremony. But while the thought of avoiding, for Franz Joseph's sake, the tiring formal functions involved in the reception of foreign royalty may have been genuine enough, there must have been other, unspoken motives as well.

If any monarch was to be invited, all would have to be— including King Peter of Serbia. Yet it required no major feat of the imagination to picture the embarrassment which his presence would have caused to everyone concerned. Beside, the same guardians of protocol who had seen to it that the decorations on Sophie's coffin showed how far beneath her Habsburg husband she stood may have vetoed the presence of royal guests from abroad at even the requiem services for a former lady in waiting. Finally, the one monarch who out of his personal friendship for Franz Ferdinand might have made the journey despite court objections, Kaiser Wilhelm, was dissuaded from coming by an urgent telegram sent by the German Consul General in Sarajevo. An "absolutely reliable" informant, wired the consul, had told him that he feared an attempt might be made against Wilhelm's life in Vienna by either Russian or Serbian fanatics. The German Chancellor, apparently taking the warning seriously, strongly counseled against the trip, and Wilhelm gave in. A slight cold and a touch of lumbago, read a subsequent press release, had forced the Emperor—to his great regret—to cancel his Austrian travel plans.

From time to time, history staggers us with its might-have-beens—and this is one such instance. The absence of foreign royalty at the Hofburg chapel meant that the best possible opportunity for political conversations between Europe's heads of state was lost. Had the monarchs of the major powers met in Vienna at that time, and plainly discussed the political repercussions of Princip's crime, it is easy enough to imagine the totally different and happier course which events might have taken.

At a quarter past four, the requiem mass had ended. The Emperor was the first to rise and leave, without, as one of Franz Ferdinand's aides later wrote with ill-concealed bitterness, "casting as much as a glance at the two coffins." Franz Joseph, thought the aide angrily, had displayed no trace of emotion or sadness during the service either; instead, he had been looking around the assembly "with complete indifference and the same unmoved facial expression which he displayed toward his subjects during other occasions too. One had the involuntary feeling that Franz

Joseph was breathing more freely again, as though with a sense of liberation, and doubtlessly most of his old courtiers shared this feeling."

The Uninvited Mourners

When the last of the guests had left, the doors of the church were closed again, to remain shut until the removal of the bodies to the *Westbanhof* at ten o'clock that night, where the special train to Artstetten was waiting. During the move, there took place one more incident, at once bolder and more spectacular than Archduke Carl's earlier opposition to Montenuovo's protocol.

Since both coffins were to travel in the same cortège, the Lord Chamberlain had denied Franz Ferdinand the military honors which would have been due to him as Inspector General of the Armed Forces. Montenuovo had offered a compromise, however. The soldiers of the Vienna garrison, his office ruled, while not required to line the streets leading to the station were permitted to do so if they or their officers wished. Many of them had so wished, and the dark streets were full of bright uniforms now.

Almost as if foreseeing the results of his concession, Montenuovo had put pressure on the holders of high court honors—on the privy councilors, chamberlains, and knights of the Golden Fleece—not to accompany the cortège to the station. But here, Montenuovo had gone too far. Few among the aristocracy had any pleasant memories of Franz Ferdinand; not a few had had good reason to fear him. Still, most of them found the Chamberlain's attitude appalling. As one disgusted Hungarian nobleman put it, "Every ass was kicking the dead lion now." They would, they decided,

give a clear demonstration of how they felt about the way
the dead lion had been treated.

As the hearses, drawn by six black horses each, left the
Hofburg and headed for Vienna's main thoroughfare, the
Ring, there broke into the cortège over a hundred members
of the most ancient nobility of the realm. Some of them
bore the names of families that had fought the Saracens
during the Crusades, or the Turks outside Vienna, or the
Prussians of Frederick the Great in Silesia: Starhemberg,
Lobkowitz, and Pallavicini; Széchényi, Fürstenberg, Ho-
henlohe, Zichy, Thurn und Taxis, Hoyos, and Sapieha;
Kinsky, Esterházy, Schwarzenberg, Fugger, Thun-Salm, and
Liechtenstein. Many of them wearing their heavily braided
gala uniforms, they followed behind the cortège in a body,
walking all the way from the Ring to the station, where
they took up positions on either side of the two coffins.

As a priest pronounced his blessing over the bodies, his
audience was infinitely more illustrious than Montenuovo
had planned. Not only did the princes, counts, and barons
remain until the train's departure, but there had come to
the station—by a less conspicuous route but in equal dis-
regard of the Lord Chamberlain's original arrangements—
all the archdukes of the House of Habsburg, led by the
new Heir to the Throne, Archduke Carl Franz Joseph.

The numerous spectators who had turned up to watch
the passing of the procession showed, as one paper tactfully
put it, their "profound appreciation" of the appearance
of these unbidden guests; the more so since for many days,
the shabbiness of the funeral arrangements had been bitterly and publicly criticized. "Vienna," thought a French
writer not otherwise noted for his pro-Austrian sympathies,
"did not love Franz Ferdinand, but the people of Vienna
were lacking neither in tact, nor in dignity, nor in kind-

ness"—all qualities notable for their absence in the services arranged by Montenuovo. Surely court ceremonial was not that inflexible, commented the staunchly conservative *Reichspost*. When nine officers and enlisted men of the fledgling air force had been killed in a recent accident, the paper pointed out in a reasonable parallel, they had received a common military burial, at which the ceremonies for all had been those due to the highest ranking officer among them, a Captain.

When the dear departed [wrote the paper] was still on his bier it was important not to introduce any discordant note into a solemn hour. [Actually, there had been no such reticence.] But now our patriotic duty and the mood not only of Vienna and Austria but of the entire monarchy compel us to discuss the question why, according to the original arrangements, the funeral was to be so startlingly simple, and so insulting to the feelings of a grieving people. . . .

To quote the words of one of the highest generals of our army [the editorial concluded less reasonably], the funeral was . . . no different than one that would have been arranged for a six year old child.

Criticism might have become even sharper had there not been made public, on July 7, the following remarkable letter from the Emperor to the Lord Chamberlain:

Dear Prince Montenuovo:
For a number of years now, you have headed my court administration in the full possession of my confidence, and you have always exercised your office—one rich in responsibility—in accordance with my intentions and with complete success.

In recent days, the passing away of my beloved nephew, Archduke Franz Ferdinand—with whom relations of confidence and trust have always connected you—has made very extraordinary demands on you, my dear Prince, and has given you one more opportunity to prove your great and unselfish devotion to my person and my house.

I am glad to have this occasion to assure you of my most cordial gratitude and of my full appreciation of your excellent and faithful service.

Vienna, July 6, 1914

FRANZ JOSEPH

The letter contains some obvious ambiguities—were the funeral arrangements as much "in accordance with my intentions" as the Prince's earlier services?—and it is difficult if not impossible to say to what extent it implied Franz Joseph's approval of these much criticized arrangements. The two pieces of evidence we possess are contradictory. One of the few courtiers who later wrote about the affair, the wonderfully gossipy but often unreliable Baron Margutti, has definitely stated that the Emperor had little sympathy with Montenuovo's attitude, and that it was the Emperor who personally vetoed the Lord Chamberlain's original plan for holding separate requiem services. Franz Ferdinand and Sophie, he reports the old Emperor as having said, had died together as victims of the same conspiracy; they must therefore be allowed to receive their last rites together. On the other hand, the detailed ceremonial for the funeral services issued by the Lord Chamberlain's office are preceded by the very plain phrase "On the Emperor's orders."

But no matter which version is true, the Emperor's

22. The trip home. The funeral cortège passes through Trieste, July 2, 1914.

[...]he public learns the news. A special [...]n, printed in the early afternoon on [...] 28, and distributed free: "Heir to [...] Throne and Wife Murdered . . . [...] Sarajevo, horrifying, inconceivable [...] s being reported . . ."

24. The formal confirmation. The Official Gazette of June 29: "Official Part. His Royal and Imperial Highness, the Most Serene Archduke Franz Ferdinand, suffered a severe bullet wound on the morning of Sunday, June 28 inst., at Sarajevo, and died a short time later."

25. The trial. The defendants in the court room at Sarajevo.

[Handwritten manuscript in Serbian Cyrillic, signed and dated:]

12, мај 1916

Гаврило Принцип

26. A Princip manuscript, written in prison at the request of a visiting Austrian d
"On one occasion, we were discussing in company the question Kropotkin raised in his
versal Wealth:' 'What will the anarchists do in the event of the outbreak of a social
lution?' We all thought that what was involved was a phrase used by an old an
rather than any real and serious belief of his that such a revolution was possible a
time. Still, when we discussed this 'social revolution,' we almost all of us agreed i
was possible; but in our opinion it would first be necessary to create relations betwee
nations which would ameliorate the differences between the nations. But although w
read socialist and anarchist writings, we were nationalists, and did not concern ou
much with this question, for we thought that everyone of us had a different duty,
tional duty. May 12, 1916, Gavrilo Princip"

prestige was still so vast and unquestioned that his intervention on behalf of Montenuovo stilled any further public criticism.

Artstetten

As one follows the winding Danube westward from Vienna toward Linz, one reaches, after seventy miles or so, the lovely and romantic region of Pöchlarn. There is the town of Pöchlarn itself, the legendary Bechelaren of Margrave Rüdiger of the Nibelungen Epic. There are the many ruins of both ancient Roman fortresses and of medieval robber barons' castles, each built to overlook the river. There is the Benedictine Abbey of Melk, founded in the eleventh century, but rebuilt entirely in the eighteenth in the gold and marble splendor of the Austrian baroque; there is the ancient Habsburg Castle of Persenbeug, birthplace of the last Emperor of the Dual Monarchy; there is, set back not quite two miles into the woods and hills, its four red onion towers visible from afar, Franz Ferdinand's castle of Artstetten.

At Artstetten, Franz Ferdinand had spent some of the happiest days of his childhood. Having inherited the castle as a young man upon his father's death, he had undertaken some extensive restoration work, and shortly after his marriage had ordered a crypt built underneath the castle church. The builders soon ran into trouble; the excavations for the new structure, they discovered, were threatening the foundations of the old church. But the Archduke urged them on. It seemed, his Private Secretary has written, as though he was possessed "by an intimation of his impending fate, . . . and could hardly await its [*i.e.*, the crypt's] completion."

It was here that Franz Ferdinand had wished to be buried, and it was here that the final funeral ceremonies took place—free of the excesses of Spanish etiquette, but not free, unfortunately, of further bungling and confusion.

At 2:00 A.M., in the deepest dark of the night, the funeral train arrived at Pöchlarn, the station closest to Artstetten. Montenuovo had rejected all responsibility for the funeral arrangements beyond Vienna. "I shall get the bodies to the station"; was the gist of what he told Franz Ferdinand's staff, "I shall have them put aboard a train and see that they leave, but from then on, you must do with them what you want." Accordingly, the services of the Municipal Undertaking Establishment of the City of Vienna were engaged for the journey from the capital to Artstetten and for the local services—probably the first and only case in which this establishment, normally used to more bourgeois clients, had been asked to bury an Heir to the Habsburg Throne. The costs, however, were borne by the court after all. The Emperor, on hearing that the Archduke's children were hard put to pay for the funeral expenses, ordered Montenuovo to settle all of the Municipal Undertakers' bills.

Outside Pöchlarn station, large delegations of the region's social and civic organizations, ranging from the veterans' association to the local volunteer fire brigade, had taken their positions, for arrangements had been made to hold brief services in the station square. But just as the train was entering Pöchlarn, a violent thunderstorm broke. So much water suddenly came pouring down that it was difficult to see anything more than a foot away, much less to imagine how the clergy, in their ecclesiastical robes, would be able to proceed with the ceremony out in the open.

Still the bareheaded delegates, many of them war veterans well advanced in years, continued to stand stiffly at attention until Franz Ferdinand's Chamberlain, the sensible Baron Rumers Kirch, took pity on them. Would they, he sent word, please come and take refuge under the station roof.

Half an hour later, with no indication that the weather was likely to clear, the decision was reached to hold the ceremonies in the railroad waiting-room and not in the square outside. The coffins were placed on their biers, someone found a pair of candelabras, someone else brought in a few wreaths from the train. A guard of honor, consisting of six officers of dragoons and an equal number of uhlans, surrounded the coffins, and the mourners once more crowded into the small room after them. There was, it now turned out, no room for a single member of the local delegations. Why not, why someone in authority did not think of posting part of the guard of honor outside the door rather than by the coffins to allow at least a few of the local mourners to be admitted, is as incomprehensible as the choice of the hour of two o'clock at night for the arrival of the funeral train in Pöchlarn.

Since the railroad buffet was open, the foreseeable result was that many of the good veterans and firemen repaired there for some suitable refreshments, or, as Franz Ferdinand's Private Secretary put it tactfully: "that these people, who had walked for hours to get there, and who had been standing in the rain for some time as well, tried to warm up at the railroad buffet is possible or even probable." Later, all this gave rise to the most picturesque rumors about wild beer and sausage bacchanalia that were said to have been held by the bodies in Artstetten station, with the coffins doing service as buffet tables.

When the clergy had pronounced their blessings, the mourners entered some old and ramshackle taxicabs that had been hired for the trip to Artstetten, no court conveyances having been made available by Montenuovo. The roads were rough and rain-soaked, and wherever the climb up the hills became too steep, the disgruntled mourners had to leave their venerable vehicles and walk through the mud.

The hearses, each drawn by eight black horses which seemed to be shying at every thunderclap, were faring even worse. The storm was not letting up and some anxious moments passed before the horses, trembling with fear, could be brought aboard the Pöchlarn ferry by which the Danube had to be crossed.

The ferry had reached the middle of the river when the shaft-horses of one hearse, scared by a particularly loud crash of thunder, reared up. Only the fact that some quick-witted bystanders, realizing what was happening, rushed in to pull back the frightened animals, kept the hearse from slipping into the Danube. One wheel at least, noted an observer, was already hanging over the side of the ferry.

Later that morning, amid sunnier weather, more mourners arrived from Vienna. Among them were most of the aristocrats who had accompanied the cortège to the station. Their presence was another studied affront to Montenuovo, who was expecting them to attend an official requiem service at the Hofburg, which he had scheduled for precisely the same hour as the Artstetten funeral. Among them also were the Heir to the Throne, Archduke Carl Franz Joseph with his wife Zita, as well as one Herr Burg, who was seen to weep copiously. Herr Burg was none other than Franz Ferdinand's younger brother Ferdinand Carl, who had been stripped of his military rank, expelled from the territory of the monarchy, and deprived of his family name for marrying the daughter of a Vienna college professor some years before. The Emperor had lifted his exile for one day, so that he might come to Artstetten. He had not lifted the order forbidding any use of Ferdinand Carl's former titles. It did not matter, for faced with the ill and grief-stricken ex-Archduke nearly everyone took pains to address him as "Imperial Highness." There also were the murdered couple's childen—thirteen year old Sophie and her two brothers, Max, eleven, and Ernst, barely ten.

When all the guests had assembled in the flower-decked Artstetten church, the simple services began. The abbot of a nearby monastery consecrated the bodies. Lance corporals lifted the coffins, and with measured steps carried them into the crypt. At a sharp turn at the entrance to the vault, they apparently relaxed their attention for a moment, and knocked one coffin against the edge of the wall, breaking loose a small fragment of stone and mortar, but to the relief of the mourners there were no further incidents as the coffins were being set in their final resting place.

It is here at Artstetten, then, that the bodies of Apis' victims lie, and not in the customary burial place of the Habsburgs, the Capuchin Crypt in Vienna. It is oddly fitting that this should be so. In a historic sense, though not in a chronological one, the nineteenth century begins not in 1801, but in 1789, that is with the French Revolution, and ends not in 1900, but in 1914, with the First World War. It seems a strikingly symbolic coincidence, therefore, that the visitor to the Capuchin Crypt should miss, among the many royal dead, the sarcophagi of two Habsburgs— one that of Marie Antoinette, whose execution and burial in an unmarked Paris grave helped to usher in an age, the other that of Franz Ferdinand, whose murder helped to usher it out.

CHAPTER XIV

The Investigation

Sunday

In Sarajevo meanwhile, the law had very quickly gone into action. Even before Princip had fired his shots, the District Judge, Alois von Curinaldi, hurriedly ordered Judge Leo Pfeffer of Sarajevo to investigate Čabrinović's attempt against the Archduke's life. In no time at all, Pfeffer found that the simple task of interrogating a bomb-throwing young anarchist had become a vastly complex one, for as the second, more successful crime became known, and the police brought in Princip and dozens of others whom they suspected of complicity, Pfeffer saw himself appointed judge in charge of investigating the entire murder plot.

Pfeffer's first act was to have Princip brought before him. Princip was still suffering from the near-lynching the crowd had given him before the police managed to arrest him, and his head was swathed in white bandages. He was still sick, too, from the cyanide he had swallowed. The police doctor had assured the investigating judge, however, that the wounds were not serious, although he would not rule out the possibility of later complications.

From the very beginning, Princip managed to impress the hostile Austrian interrogator he was facing almost as much as he had impressed his partisans in Bosnia and Serbia. Pfeffer later described their meeting that Sunday. "The young assassin, exhausted by his beating, was unable to utter a word. He was undersized, emaciated, sallow, sharp-featured. It was difficult to imagine that so frail look-ing an individual could have committed so serious a crime. Even his clear blue eyes, burning and piercing but serene, had nothing cruel or criminal in their expression. They spoke of innate intelligence, of steady and harmonious energy. When I told him I was the investigating judge and asked him if he had the strength to speak, he answered my question with perfect clearness in a voice that grew steadily stronger and more assured."

The story which Princip now proceeded to tell Pfeffer was as plausible and simple as it was false. Years ago, he said, he had vowed on the grave of Žerajić to avenge that martyr to Serbdom. When, at Eastertime, he had heard that Franz Ferdinand was going to visit Sarejevo, he had chosen him as the fitting victim, since the Archduke seemed to embody all the forces of Austrian oppression. The decision to kill Franz Ferdinand had been entirely his own; and he had had no accomplices in executing his plan. The deed, in short, had been his and his alone.

But what about the fellow who had thrown the bomb, Pfeffer wanted to know.

I have nothing to do with him, said Princip. When I heard the explosion, I said to myself: here is someone else who feels as I do, but that was all.

With this, Princip had touched upon one of the weakest points in his story, for to accept this particular claim required a degree of belief in coincidence which no investigating judge could be expected to possess. Still, Princip persisted in denying any sort of acquaintance with Čabrinović for one more day. When he had heard the detonation of the bomb, he added the next morning, he had in fact been so startled that he had forgotten to shoot as the archducal party passed by him on the way to the City Hall. It was an ingenious explanation, and he might have stuck to it had not Čabrinović proved himself somewhat less skillful in the answers which he gave to Pfeffer.

On Sunday, Čabrinović's account still bore out Princip's. He had intended, the young typesetter admitted, to kill Franz Ferdinand with his bomb, but he had acted without any accomplices.

In that case, Pfeffer asked, where did the bomb come from?

From an anarchist in Belgrade, said Čabrinović.

What was the anarchist's name?

He could not tell his real name, said Čabrinović; he did not know.

What were his motives, then? Was he an anarchist too?

It was not quite that simple, said Čabrinović. Partly his motives were anarchistic, but partly they were nationalistic.

Monday and Tuesday

The next day Čabrinović, for no apparent reason, reversed himself on the issue of collusion. He had, he admitted, conspired to commit the crime with Princip in Belgrade. (All that Princip had been saying on this point was that he had spent three months in Serbia recently. It was a fact which the police were likely to discover anyway.) The weapons, Čabrinović added, had come not from an anarchist, but from former partisans with whom they had been associating.

Could Čabrinović name any of these men?

Yes, said Čabrinović—mentioning the least consequential of Apis' emissaries—there was one Ciganović.

Confronted with Čabrinović's admissions at noon, Princip quickly allowed that he had not told the whole truth in his previous interrogation. Yes, he said, he had acted in concert with Čabrinović. He had not wanted to implicate his friend before, he explained, but now that Čabrinović himself had talked, there was no need for him to keep silent about it any longer.

Thus far, even with Čabrinović's admission of complicity, the stories which the youths had offered Pfeffer amounted to a masterpiece of evasion. They had admitted the deed. They had provided a plausible motive—nationalism in Princip's case, nationalism plus anarchism in that of Čabrinović. They had satisfactorily explained the means —bombs and guns received from ex-partisans in Belgrade. Circumstantial and material evidence in the possession of the police bore them out. There was no shortage of witnesses to either crime. A police search had uncovered several revolutionary pamphlets at Čabrinović's Sarajevo residence and, as Potiorek put it in a report to Vienna, "a whole library" of pan-Serb literature in the house of Princip's brother. As for the arms, it was common knowledge that the Serbian partisans had secretly saved large stocks of just such weapons from the Balkan Wars. By and large, it was an account that made sense, and that would allow for the preparation of a strong indictment.

Between Sunday, June 28, and Tuesday, June 30, Pfeffer

knew neither that there had been five other assassins in the streets of Sarajevo nor that anyone other than Princip or Čabrinović had organized the crime.

He might never have found out. Pfeffer strikes one either as infinitely more solicitous over the rights of a suspect than one might normally expect someone in his position to be, or else as not a terribly competent investigator. He was reluctant, for example, to confront his witnesses with one another, or even to quote incriminating parts of one suspect's testimony to another. "Only independent, individual confessions could reveal the truth about the various facts to me," he later wrote. The one advantage such a system had, of not allowing any communication between the prisoners, was illusory from the first in this case, since Princip and Čabrinović as well as all those of their associates who were arrested afterward communicated between their cells by the simplest of secret systems, that of long and short knocks against the walls. They had learned about this method from a Russian novel.

At this point then, the assassination of Archduke Franz Ferdinand might still have remained a local murder, and not the cause of a world war. But the Sarajevo police, immediately after the shooting, had diligently if somewhat haphazardly begun to round up a large number of suspects. Some were known relatives and friends of Princip and Čabrinović, others were merely suspected of pro-Serbian sympathies. Among them were a great many innocents, such as Čabrinović's grandmother, or the proprietor of Sarajevo's best-known hotel, whose misfortune, under the circumstances, it was to have a former Serbian cabinet minister for a father-in-law. Among them also, however, was a school teacher and friend of Princip, Danilo Ilić.

Wednesday

Ilić's arrest was a matter of police routine. The authorities vaguely suspected him of being involved in subversive propaganda activities, and they knew that Princip had stayed at his house in Sarajevo recently. That was all they had—enough to justify detaining him briefly for questioning; not enough, on the other hand, to charge him with any specific crime. Had Ilić kept his head, and offered any sort of credible story to his questioners, the likelihood is that he would have been released again in a matter of days. But Ilić, not guessing how little evidence the police really possessed against him, was very badly scared.

As soon as he was taken before Pfeffer, Ilić proposed a bargain to the investigating judge. He would confess everything, he said, if Pfeffer would undertake to save him from the death penalty.

He could make no definite promises, Pfeffer answered, but it might interest Ilić to know that the law granted extenuating circumstances to any prisoner who turned state's evidence. What did Ilić have to tell him?

What Ilić had to tell him was short, to the point, and true. Princip and Čabrinović, said Ilić, had not been acting on their own. Instead, they were members of a conspiracy to kill Franz Ferdinand that comprised no less than seven members. Three of the assassins—Princip, Čabrinović, and Grabež—had come from Belgrade. Three more he, Ilić, had recruited locally.

Ilić's bland admission destroyed Princip's and Čabrinović's stories beyond any hope of repair. Pfeffer, interrupting the prisoner's confession, rushed to the telephone to issue urgent orders for the arrest of the accomplices named by Ilić. This time, arrests were not going to be made on the basis of general suspicions. Pfeffer now had a real case, although he must have suspected that Ilić was still with-holding certain essential facts.

First to be arrested was Grabež, whom the police brought in that same day. Ilić had volunteered the information about Grabež's probable whereabouts. It was likely, he said, that Grabež had gone to his home town of Pale, and would try to make his way to Serbia from there. It was an excellent guess.

After hearing Princip's shots on the morning of June 28, Grabež's first thoughts, as he said later, were to get rid of his arms and to escape. Trying to appear unconcerned, he walked from his post near the Kaiser Bridge to the house of an uncle of his in town. He hid the bomb in the toilet, and the gun under the coping of the roof, and strolled back to the scene of the crime. He then had lunch with another uncle of his in Sarajevo, a parliamentary deputy, spent the night at his house, and took the train home to Pale the next morning. His father was very much surprised to see him; he had expected him to be under arrest.

Deciding that his best protection lay in boldness, Grabež told everyone he met in Pale where he had just come from. No one, he reasoned, was likely to suspect him of being one of the assassins if he himself so obviously mentioned his having spent the day of the murder in Sarajevo.

On Tuesday, without telling his father what he was about to do, Grabež started out for Serbia and safety. On Wednes-day, the police arrested him in a small town some forty miles west of the Serbian border.

Taken back to Sarajevo, Grabež admitted his own role in the plot, and even added a precise description of where he had hidden the arms, but refused to implicate any of his friends. There was no need. The next day, the police found his gun and bomb where he had said they would, in his uncle's house, examined them, and discovered them to be of precisely the same make as those of Princip and Čabrinović —as tangible a bit of corroboration of Ilić's confession as Pfeffer might have wished for.

More Arrests

Grabež's arrest left three more assassins at liberty; Čubrilović and Popović, the high-school friends from Sarajevo, and Mehmedbašić, the Moslem carpenter and veteran of previous plots. On June 5, the Sunday after the murder, the police managed to arrest Čubrilović, and two days later, Popović joined him in prison.

Under interrogation, both of them, like Grabež before them, tried to protect their friends while admitting their own share of the guilt. Despite their good intentions, their admissions resulted in a wave of new arrests, for in their eagerness to be rid of their arms after Princip's shots, they had clumsily implicated a sizable number of people, many of whom in reality were innocent bystanders. On the morning of June 28, a pale and trembling Čubrilović had, by prearrangement, passed his gun and bomb to a young friend, Ivo Kranjčević, the son of a retired Austrian policeman. Kranjčević, rather than hiding the weapons himself, wrapped them up into a package and took them to the house of a couple he knew named Sadilo. He handed his lethal package to the Sadilos' five year old daughter, who happened to be at home alone, and told her to ask her parents to keep it for him for a while. A few days later, as he was going for a walk with his mother, he met Mrs. Sadilo in the street. What was in that package he had left, Mrs. Sadilo asked him.

Two old pistols, replied Kranjčević; my father is going to give them to the museum.

Please take them away again immediately, said Mrs. Sadilo. These are difficult times; I can't have any guns in my house. "Do you want to make us miserable?"

Mrs. Kranjčević, audibly angry with her son over this mysterious bit of mischief in which he seemed to have involved himself, picked up the package that same day. Opening it, either she or her son hid the bomb in the municipal park across from the main government building, and the gun in the Moslem cemetery, and there they still were when the police did their searching after young Kranjčević's arrest.

Popović, more daring than Čubrilović, had hidden his weapons himself, in the basement of a house on the Appel Quay close to his post. These, too, the police found, noting on examining them that it was not for lack of means that Popović had failed to act on the morning of June 28. The bomb was uncapped and ready to be thrown, and the revolver fully loaded.

Mehmedbašić

The only assassin who still eluded the police was Mehmedbašić. "It has not yet been possible to ascertain his whereabouts," wired Governor Potiorek to Vienna on July 3. Two days later, the police had managed to get on to the fugitive's trail, and Potiorek sent a more optimistic telegram. "His arrest," he wired, "is imminent."

It was not—at least not by the Austrian authorities. On July 13, Potiorek learned that Mehmedbašić had succeeded where all his accomplices had failed; he had safely crossed into neighboring Montenegro.

Officially, the small kingdom of Montenegro pursued a policy of neutrality between the powers, but popular sympathies were overwhelmingly pro-Serbian. Had Mehmedbašić curbed his tongue, he would probably have run into no trouble with the indulgent Montenegrin authorities. But once he had crossed the border, Mehmedbašić could not refrain from playing the hero, boasting loudly and publicly that he was one of those Sarajevo assassins everyone was talking about. On July 12, Montenegrin police took the self-confessed assassin into custody, and questioned him. Mehmedbašić not only admitted his boasts, but volunteered some additional information about a supposed meeting between the conspirators in Tours to arrange the details of the assassination. The latter was an invention that was to become the basis for one of the several myths about the origins of the conspiracy.

Montenegro's king and cabinet now found themselves in a fairly unenviable position. On the one hand, there existed a clear treaty of extradition with Austria, and hence no legal way of denying an Austrian demand for the surrender of one of Franz Ferdinand's admitted assassins. If, on the other hand, they should hand over Mehmedbašić to the Austrians for trial, an uncomfortably large part of the public—who tended to consider the conspirators heroes and not murderers—would be up in arms against them. It was a minor government functionary who found a way out of this dilemma. His solution had the simplicity of genius— Mehmedbašić's guards would allow him to escape.

On July 15, the Austrian Minister, acting on official instructions from Vienna, asked the Montenegrin Foreign Minister for the extradition of Mehmedbašić. Well, said the Foreign Minister, that is a very embarrassing affair. You are right; the police have arrested him, and he has made a full confession, but unfortunately, he managed to break out of prison just last night. The police are looking for him everywhere now; let us hope that they will be able to pick him up again very soon.

There the matter rested. Periodically, the Austrians repeated their inquiries about Mehmedbašić; just about as often as they did so, the Montenegrins apologized for the negligence of the police, and asserted that every effort was being made to recapture the fugitive. The well-informed French Minister summed up the whole little comedy neatly if cynically in a dispatch to the Quai d'Orsay. The Montenegrin Foreign Ministry, he reported, was swearing holy oaths that it had nothing to do with the escape, but "I do not think that the guilty official will have his future advancement retarded by the initiative he has taken in this affair." Nor, it so happened, did the Montenegrin police ever have any luck in picking up Mehmedbašić's trail again.

Mehmedbašić, during all this time, was still in the country of course, although he seems to have co-operated with his reluctant pursuers to the extent of behaving with somewhat greater circumspection than before. He remained until November, when he crossed into Serbia, where he enlisted in the partisans of Princip's old mentor, Major Tankosić.

The Circle Widens

From the point of view of the Sarajevo investigation, Mehmedbašić's escape made next to no difference. With Ilić's confession, and the arrests that followed it, the fictitious accounts which Princip and Čabrinović had offered Pfeffer could no longer be maintained in any case. The thread of the conspiracy had begun to unravel.

On July 4, the unfortunate Ilić introduced Miško Jovanović's name. It was from Jovanović in Tuzla, he told Pfeffer, that he had picked up the arms smuggled in from Serbia by Princip and Grabež. Arrested that day, and brought to Sarajevo, Jovanović at first attempted to deny any knowledge of the plot, but before long had to admit his meeting with the youths as well as his share in storing and transporting their weapons. His admission inevitably brought in the name of his relative, Veljko Čubrilović, the school teacher and Priboj, agent on the underground route. Čubrilović's arrest, in turn, made it impossible to protect any of the others who had sheltered or guided Princip and Grabež on their underground journey from the Serbian border to Sarajevo.

Earlier, Princip had confirmed Ilić's list of his Sarajevo recruits, explaining that he did not want any innocent persons to suffer. After Jovanović's admission and Čubrilović's arrest, both Princip and Grabež no longer withheld the details of their trip, although they pretended to be ignorant of the names of their helpers. This reticence offered no protection to those they had implicated; the police had enough leads now. Between mid-July and mid-August, the Sarajevo prison began to fill with the men who had aided them along the way. Jakov Milović, the smuggler who had taken them across the border from Isaković Island; his friend Mićo Mičić, who had brought him to Isaković; Obren Milošević, in whose cottage they had spent the first night on Bosnian soil; Nedjo Kerović and his unsuspecting neighbor, who had driven them from Priboj to Tuzla in his cart; Nedjo's two brothers and his old father, who had sheltered the boys and provided the cloth for wrapping the bombs and guns.

To deny the existence of a conspiracy had become wholly

futile. What Pfeffer did not yet know, however, and what the assassins could still try to hide from him, was the degree to which the conspiracy extended into Serbia.

Protecting Belgrade

Three men in Belgrade, it will be recalled, had been the principal actors in staging the assassination—Colonel Dimitrijević, called Apis, Chief of Serbian Army Intelligence, leading spirit of the Black Hand, and author of the crime; Major Tankosić, his Black Hand aide; and Milan Ciganović, Bosnian refugee and go-between. On July 2, Čabrinović volunteered Ciganović's name to Pfeffer.

It was Ciganović, he said, who had provided them with their guns and bombs. Ciganović, a humble employee of the Serbian State Railways, had not acted on his own, however, but on instructions received from none other than the Secretary General of the *Narodna Odbrana*, Milan Pribičević. Princip, he added, had introduced him to the Secretary General a few days after they had told Ciganović about their plan to assassinate Franz Ferdinand. Questioned the same day, Princip and Grabež confirmed the gist of Čabrinović's story. Princip disagreed on one detail only; he had not, he said, known Pribičević. Both Princip and Grabež were ready to admit, however, that their arms came from Ciganović. As far as they knew, they added, Ciganović was a member of the *Narodna Odbrana*.

It was a masterly story to tell the Austrian police. It was enough to explain the aid which they had plainly received in Belgrade, but not enough to enable the Austrians to find the real culprits. The part about Ciganović was true, of course, but Ciganović was the least consequential member of the conspiracy. Moreover, he was in Serbia, safely out of reach of the Sarajevo police. As for Pribičević and his organization, the *Narodna Odbrana* had become an all but harmless and open group ever since the formation of the Black Hand, and its Secretary General was a man who was firmly convinced of the superiority of moral suasion over murder and violence. As Apis must have known, however, the Austrians were not aware of these facts, assuming instead, in their vast ignorance of the Black Hand, that the *Narodna Odbrana* still aimed at detaching Bosnia and Herzegovina from the Empire by terror and subversion. Whether Apis had rehearsed Čabrinović, Princip, and Grabež in their story beforehand is a point on which we possess no direct evidence, but it is difficult to imagine how else they could have agreed on it so neatly and conveniently otherwise.

Quite possibly, Pfeffer would have been entirely satisfied with it, had not the hapless Ilić contradicted it three days later. The trio, said Ilić, indeed knew Ciganović in Belgrade, but the man to whom Ciganović had introduced them was a Major Tankosić. It was Tankosić, said Ilić, who had supplied the arms, given them their shooting lessons, and told them not to let themselves be taken alive.

Confronted with Ilić's statement, the three youths followed a strategy that led, by way of splendid confusion, from initial denial to reluctant—and incomplete—admission. Yes, there had been some shooting practice, said Grabež, but his and Princip's instructor had been Ciganović, and Čabrinović's had been a partisan named Milan Majić. A few days later, Princip was ready to grant Tankosić's existence, but denied that he had ever seen him. The only one among them, he said, who had any dealings with Tankosić in Belgrade was Grabež. Having said this, he abruptly changed the subject, and suddenly offered Pfeffer a great many details about the trip from Belgrade to Sarajevo.

No, said Grabež, Princip is wrong, I did not see Tankosić. If anyone did, it was Princip himself. In a way, said Čabrinović, both Tankosić and Pribičević were involved. We first intended to approach Pribičević about the weapons, but he was out of town. We thereupon turned to Ciganović, who told us on the eve of our departure from Belgrade that Major Tankosić had had to sign an IOU to pay for the arms.

Only a good two weeks after Ilić's admission did Grabež, Princip, and Čabrinović, following one of Pfeffer's rare confrontations, finally agree on Tankosić's involvement. As for their earlier contradictions about which one of them had talked to Tankosić, they now stated it was Grabež and not Princip who had done so. The Major, they explained, had told Ciganović that before handing over the arms, he wished to meet one of the would-be assassins to convince himself of their reliability, and since Princip felt that he was too weak physically to make the proper impression, Grabež had gone.

In all, it was another admirable performance. They had admitted the existence of Tankosić, but they had successfully devoted their considerable talents to holding back the one name that really mattered, that of Apis. Pfeffer's investigation had established the fact that there was a Sarajevo conspiracy, and that that conspiracy had had two rather shadowy helpers in Belgrade who had provided weapons and shooting lessons. What it had not brought out—for here even Ilić managed to keep silent—was that the origins of the conspiracy lay in Belgrade, that it involved an organization called the Black Hand, and that the crime's instigator was the Chief of Serbian Army Intelligence.

"Of A Black Hand I Know Nothing . . ."

Only once during the investigation was the Black Hand so much as mentioned. Early in July, the police picked up a bakery worker, named Trifko Krstanović, who had been overheard to say, shortly after the assassination, that such an act might have been expected. He explained to his interrogators that all he had meant by his remark was that in view of all the anti-Austrian propaganda that emanated from Serbia, he had not been surprised to see Franz Ferdinand killed. The police believed him, and decided to prefer no charges against him, but since he seemed to possess some information about the *Narodna Odbrana,* they interrogated him again as a witness on July 19.

The baker said he had illegally crossed over into Serbia some years before, and had met Tankosić at the Green Garland café in Belgrade. Subsequently, he had become a student at the Major's partisan academy. Later, he had broken with the *Narodna Odbrana,* and returned to Bosnia. At the end of his statement, he casually brought in the Black Hand, saying: "Of a Black Hand I know nothing definite, except for what I read of this Hand in the Serbian newspapers. I don't remember any more today what there was in the papers about this Black Hand."

That the police did not cross-question him on this is excusable; it was hardly a very specific reference and besides, they rightly considered him innocent of any participation in Princip's plot. What is less understandable is the general manner in which Pfeffer conducted his investigation.

Criticism that derives in part from the advantages of hindsight tends to sound petty and unfair; still, it should be said that some of Pfeffer's mistakes and omissions seem startling. There were serious indiscretions to the press on what the suspects had been telling the police; and the first such article to appear was based on an interview given by Pfeffer himself. There was the leisurely pace of the investigation; even if a suspect was found out in some patent untruth, days might pass before he would be interrogated again, giving him ample time to think up some more believable version. There was the absence of sharp and searching cross-examination, no matter how contradictory or rehearsed the suspects' stories might sound. Perhaps the resources of the Sarajevo police simply were not adequate to the investigation, but if so, why was not the help of the Vienna police requested?

As it was, Pfeffer did a great deal of listening, but very little probing. Possibly the most amazing but by no means atypical example of this took place near the end of the investigation, in an incident whose meaning is still obscure.

On August 15, Čabrinović, out of a clear sky, said that he regretted his deed, but that he had one consolation: the idea of killing Franz Ferdinand had not been his. If Princip should permit him to do so, he said, he would name the instigators of the crime.

Confronted with his friend, Princip said, and these were his precise words: "If someone made you do it, say so," whereupon Čabrinović would speak no more.

When interrogated again the next day, Čabrinović said that his lips were sealed; Princip had forbidden him to talk. What happened next was—nothing. Pfeffer simply left it at that. He pressed neither Princip nor Čabrinović about the episode, nor did he insist on obtaining some solution to the puzzle of why Princip's statement should have been the signal for Čabrinović's lapse into silence.

CHAPTER XV

War

The Wiesner Investigation

In Vienna, the piecemeal reports which Potiorek was sending on the progress of the investigation—at least one or two such telegrams from Sarajevo would usually arrive each day—were causing some understandable confusion. In the wake of Franz Ferdinand's assassination, the Austrian government was considering the presentation of an unequivocal ultimatum to Serbia, demanding an end to all Serbian-inspired subversive activities against Austria. To lend emphasis to such a demand, it was imperative to know to what extent—if at all—the Serbian government was incriminated in the murder plot. Had it been Pribičević who supplied the assassins with arms? Were there any provable connections between the *Narodna Odbrana* and the assassins? What links, if any, existed between that organization and the Belgrade government? All these were points on which Potiorek's daily summaries of Pfeffer's investigation seemed to provide no clear answer. In consequence, it was decided, on July 9, to appoint someone who was to go over all the available facts, and to put together a dossier that would provide an intelligible picture of the whole conspiracy. The man entrusted with this task was Sektionsrat Friedrich von Wiesner, a career official of the Foreign Ministry.

Earlier that month Wiesner had been looking over both the Foreign Ministry's and the Ministry of Finance's files on Serbian activities without finding any very significant material at either place. On July 10, he left for Sarajevo, where he arrived on the morning of the eleventh. During the next two days, he kept frantically busy. There were conferences with Potiorek and with the Governor's principal administrative assistant; with Pfeffer and with Pfeffer's superior, the Chief of the Bosnian Administration's Justice Department; with Gerde, the Sarajevo Commissioner of Police; with the Head of Army Intelligence; and with the general in charge of the frontier guards. In between, he read all the major Administration files dealing with subversive activities, and the latest summaries of Pfeffer's interrogations. He did not, however, attend or conduct any interrogations of Princip, Čabrinović, or any of the other suspects.

The first night, he stayed up until 4:00 A.M., working his way through the files in his hotel room, nor did he get to bed much earlier the second night. On July 13, after perhaps four hours' sleep, and some final morning conferences, Wiesner drafted the dispatch for which Vienna was waiting.

The suspects' admissions, he wired, proved the following facts to be true beyond a reasonable doubt: the decision to assassinate Franz Ferdinand had been made in Belgrade. The assassins had undertaken their Belgrade preparations with the aid of the employee of the Serbian State Railways,

Ciganović, and of the Serbian Army Major Tankosić. The latter had provided the bombs, guns, ammunition, and poison. The bombs had come from the Serbian Army arsenal of Kragujevac. Princip, Grabež, and Čabrinović had crossed the border with the aid of certain Serbian officials, most notably that of the border captains at Šabac and Loznica.

What had not been proven, however, was this. Pribičević's complicity could not be accepted as a fact. The bombs' origin was indisputable, but there was no way of telling whether Tankosić had withdrawn them for the purposes of the assassination, or whether they were left over from the supplies issued to the partisans during the Balkan Wars. As for anti-Austrian propaganda activities in Bosnia and Herzegovina, there was no doubt either of their existence or of the support they received from private Serbian organizations, yet "the material dating from the period prior to the assassination offers no evidence that [this] propaganda has been sponsored by the Serbian Government."

But the really crucial passage of Wiesner's report consisted of two short and fateful sentences. He was to rue them for the rest of his life, part of which he was to spend in writing articles that intended to prove that on the one hand, no other conclusion had been tenable at the time, and on the other, that his words did not really mean what they said:

> There is nothing to indicate [wrote *Sektionsrat* von Wiesner from Sarajevo on the morning of July 13, 1914], or even to give rise to the suspicion, that the Serbian Government knew about the plot, its preparation, or the procurement of arms. On the contrary, there are indications that this is impossible.

It was the triumph of Apis' planning.

Austria's Ultimatum

On July 23, nine days after Wiesner's return from Sarajevo, the Austrians presented Serbia with an ultimatum based on his findings, to which they demanded an answer by July 25. Vienna had decided to seek a showdown with the Serbians. Either Serbia was to agree to the demands of the Austrian ultimatum unconditionally—"acceptance *pure et simple*," as the Austrian Foreign Minister put it— or Austria was prepared to go to war against Serbia. There was no longer any other way, the Austrians felt, of stopping the dissolution of their Empire.

The presentation of the ultimatum in Belgrade took place amid some curious byplay. Pašić, the Prime Minister, was in the country making election speeches, and the Austrian envoy, Baron von Giesl, had had to make his appointment with the Minister of Finance, Paču, who was acting as Pašić's deputy. He would like to draw the Minister's attention to the fact, said Giesl when he had been shown into Paču's office at six o'clock in the evening, that there was a definite time limit to the note he had with him. Should there be no Serbian answer within forty-eight hours, or should that answer be unsatisfactory, he and the Legation staff were under strict instructions to leave Belgrade.

Paču, by way of reply, desperately tried to temporize. He could not really accept the note, he suggested. This was election time, he explained, and several ministers were absent from the capital. It might be physically impossible to call a full cabinet meeting at such short notice for a discussion of the Austrian demands.

This is the age of railroads, of the telephone and the telegraph, replied Giesl curtly. Surely the return of the ministers could take a few hours at the most. Beside, he reminded Paču, he had hinted earlier in the day that it might become necessary to get in touch with the Prime Minister. All this however, he concluded, was an internal Serbian affair and no concern of his.

Paču continued to hesitate. He still did not see how he could accept the note, he said.

If you will not take it from my hands, declared Giesl, abruptly ending the conversation, I shall leave it on the table and you can then do as you wish with it, and having said this, took his leave from Paču.

As soon as Giesl was gone, two of Paču's colleagues who had quietly been waiting in an adjoining room, entered, and together went over the note. Their reaction, as they did so, must have been a mixed one—worry, on the one hand, over the stiffness of the Austrian conditions; relief, on the other, over the false premises on which these conditions were based.

The principal Austrian demands, they read, ran as follows: The Belgrade government was to put an immediate stop to all Serbian-sponsored subversive activities on the territory of the Austro-Hugarian monarchy, and to all anti-Austrian propaganda in Serbia. The *Narodna Odbrana* was to be dissolved. Judicial proceedings were to be instigated against anyone in Serbia who was an accessory to the Sarajevo crime with "agencies delegated by the Imperial and Royal [Austrian] Government" taking part in any investigation that might be undertaken in Serbia in this connection. Tankosić and Ciganović were to be arrested "forthwith." The Serbian government was to co-operate in putting an end to the illegal arms traffic across the border, and the frontier officers in Šabac and Loznica were to be punished for their share in helping Princip and Grabež cross secretly into Bosnia. Vienna, finally, was to be informed without delay of all measures taken by the Serbian authorities to satisfy the foregoing demands.

Appended to the ultimatum was a summary of the findings of Pfeffer's investigation. Nowhere, either in the summary or in the note itself, was there a single mention of Colonel Dimitrijević or of the Black Hand.

"Secret Society: The Black Hand in Serbia"

It was an omission that immeasurably weakened the Austrian case. "One did know vaguely," wrote Wiesner in one of his many later attempts to justify the blunder, "that there was a 'Black Hand,' and that this secret military faction was exercising a sinister influence. But that the 'Black Hand' was engaged in irredentist and foreign as well as in domestic activities one did not know, at least not in Austria." Yet why should not one have known?

The Austrian diplomatic reports for the period were not without some occasional hints about the Black Hand and its involvement in the murder, but these reports were filed and disregarded. If the material in the hands of the Austrian Intelligence Services was any better, the people responsible for drafting the ultimatum to Serbia certainly never heard about it. The most valuable information on Apis and his organization available to the Foreign Ministry apparently was contained in a folder bearing the label "Secret Society: The Black Hand in Serbia." It consisted of random press clippings covering the period from September, 1911, to May, 1912, as well as the month of October, 1913—with no material at all on the time between June, 1912, and September, 1913, or on the eight months prior to Sarajevo. Some of the material contained in these clippings was surprisingly correct—there was a list of prominent Black Hand members, for example, that included Apis' name—some of it was wildly misleading—one story quoted an early membership figure of no less than 2,500. No one, it appears, ever made any effort to evaluate the material. Worse, even the raw file seems to have been unavailable when the ultimatum to Serbia was being prepared.

"Among the documents . . . I went through," wrote Wiesner after the war, "there was not a single one concerning the Black Hand. . . . The only explanation . . . which I can offer is that they must have been indexed in such a manner that the archivists could not find them."

"Absolutism mitigated by sloppiness," had been the famous definition of Austria's system of government in an earlier epoch. By 1914, absolutism had become archaic; sloppiness had not.

In fairness, it should be said that a close study of the diplomatic documents from the archives of Britain, France, and Germany shows these powers to have been similarly ill-informed about the Black Hand. But to these nations, Serbian activities were not a matter of life and death, as they were to Austria. Nor did their police hold a number of confessed assassins, who knew some very essential facts about the Black Hand, and who, under more skillful questioning, might have been made to tell what they knew.

To realize how strong the Austrian position might have been, and what the failure of the investigation meant, one ought to picture an imaginary American parallel. Let us assume that there existed a treaty of mutual assistance, in case of attack, between Mexico and a number of South American states. Let us assume further that for years, there has been an active movement—headed by the Chief of Mexican Army Intelligence and condoned, if not aided, by the Mexican government—to unite Texas, Arizona, and

Southern California with Mexico, and that these regions have been flooded with propaganda, arms, and underground agents sent from Mexico City. Let us assume finally that in 1914, on the anniversary of the battle of San Jacinto, the Vice-President of the United States, visiting Texas in the course of his official duties, is assassinated in the streets of Houston by a group of young Mexican-Americans, trained and equipped with bombs and revolvers in Mexico City, and acting under the orders of the Mexican Chief of Intelligence.

What assistance would Mexico receive from its allies if the United States, possessing proof of the crime's Mexican origins, decided to seek a radical end to all such activities in the future; and on whose side would international opinion be if it came to war between the United States and Mexico over the issue?

Had the Austrian ultimatum of July 23, 1914, begun with the words: "The responsibility for the murder of Archduke Franz Ferdinand has been traced to a secret Serbian society called the Black Hand and its leading member, Colonel Dimitrijević, whose immediate arrest we demand," it is more than doubtful that Serbia would have received the aid which the Allies extended it in the days that followed. For faced with such a charge, Pašić would have been caught in a dilemma which even he could not have escaped. He would have been forced either to reject the Austrian demand—the more likely course in view of the Black Hand's power in Serbia—thus putting himself in the wrong before world opinion, or to accede to it, thus running the risk of exposing the extent to which high Serbian government officials were involved in pan-Serb activities.

But as it was, the Austrian case lacked conviction and

Pašić knew it. Hence, he was able to engage in a magnificent bit of temporizing.

Serbia's Answer

On July 25, at 5:58 P.M.—precisely two minutes before Vienna's ultimatum was about to expire—the Austrian envoy to Belgrade received the Prime Minister's answer. Conciliatory and moderate in tone, the Serbian note fully accepted several of the Austrian demands, and indicated Serbia's readiness to compromise on most of the others. It failed to meet Vienna on two points only, one concerning the investigation, the other the arrest of Ciganović. On both of these, compliance might have meant disaster to the Serbians.

The Serbian government, read the note, was unable to agree to the participation of any Austro-Hungarian agencies in the investigations that might be held concerning the assassins' Serbian connections, since such participation "would be in violation of [Serbia's] Constitution and criminal law." As to the demand for Tankosić's and Ciganović's arrest, the police had taken Tankosić into custody on the very evening the Austrian note was received, but unfortunately, the note said, Ciganović had managed to evade his captors so far.

The details of how Ciganović was allowed to escape are not known to this day, and it is unlikely that they ever will be. What apparently happened, however, was that almost immediately after the Sarajevo assassination, Pašić ordered a police inquiry into its Belgrade origins. Its findings were never made public, but someone either in the police or the government soon suggested to Ciganović that he disappear from sight. Tankosić's arrest, Pašić may have reasoned, was one thing, for the Major was a Serbian citizen, and any number of obstacles could be placed in the way of his extradition to Austria; Ciganović, on the other hand, was an Austrian subject, whose extradition, should it be demanded, could hardly be refused. (It was absolutely essential, of course, to keep Ciganović from talking to the Austrians.) Ciganović, at any rate, took the hint. On July 1, a comfortable three weeks before the Austrians asked for his arrest, he requested a months' sick leave from his job at the Serbian State Railways, and under an assumed name left Belgrade for the provinces, where, oddly enough, all the resources of the Serbian police proved unable to locate him.

War

Faced with the evasions of Pašić's reply, the Austrian Minister and his Legation staff departed from Serbia on the morning of July 25. Three days later, exactly one month after Franz Ferdinand's death, Austria followed the break in relations with a declaration of war against Serbia. "If the monarchy must perish," said Franz Joseph sadly, "let it at least perish decently."

The further sequence of events is a familiar one. Russia, which had long and loudly claimed for itself the role of protector of all Slavs, mobilized its troops in support of Serbia—as the Russian military attaché in Belgrade had reportedly assured Apis that it would. Any other course, St. Petersburg felt, might lead to the most grievous loss of Russian prestige and influence in the whole Balkans. The Russian mobilization did not deter the Austrians, who knew that if the conflict over Serbia should spread, they would probably not have to fight alone. An Austro-German military alliance, first signed in 1879, and periodically renewed since, obliged either nation to assist the other in case of attack by Russia. The alliance had remained no secret, and expecting the Germans to join their Austrian ally now, Russia mobilized its army not only along its Austrian, but also along its German frontier. Germany, still hoping that the Austro-Serbian conflict might be localized, demanded an end to Russian mobilization, but receiving no answer, declared war against Russia on August 1.

Germany's action meant the war's westward as well as eastward extension, since the twenty-year old Dual Alliance between Russia and France provided for mutual assistance if either power should be attacked by Germany. Convinced that Russia would invoke the French alliance, and that the French would honor their treaty obligations, Germany decided not to wait, and declared war against France on August 3. Among the major European powers, this left Great Britain as the only neutral. Britain and France frequently pursued common policies in the early part of the twentieth century, but the so-called *Entente Cordiale* between them was something of a misnomer, since no binding Anglo-French alliance existed. What made Britain go to war, too, was a German blunder. In a single-minded attempt to win the war in the west before the Russians could break through German's eastern defenses, the German army invaded neutral Belgium in order to outflank the French. On August 4, Great Britain, very much concerned over the specter of German possession of the Channel coast and outraged over the violation of Belgian neutrality, declared war on Germany, joining France and Russia.

The Austro-Serbian war that had begun over Sarajevo thus had become a world war, with Serbia drawing in Russia, with Austria drawing in Germany, and with Russia and Germany drawing in France and Great Britain. Before it was over, there were few neutrals left in the world. The number of soldiers and civilians known to have been killed in its course has been given at ten million; the number of wounded, including the totally disabled, at twenty million. History has recorded few other single acts of violence with consequences as bloody as the crime organized by Dimitrijević and executed by Princip.

CHAPTER XVI

The Trial

The Indictment

On Monday, October 12, 1914, at eight o'clock in the morning—some two months after the beginning of the war—the trial against Princip and his associates opened in the district court of Sarajevo. There were twenty-five defendants in all; the assassins were being tried along with all those accused of helping them either before or after the crime. The charges against the six youths as well as against their principal helpers were murder and treason, since under Bosnian (as under American) law, an accessory to murder was considered guilty of the deed itself. The maximum penalty for either charge was death. However, the law provided that if an offender was under twenty at the time he committed his crime, a prison sentence of not more than twenty years was to replace the death penalty.

The list of court officers and defense counsel sounded like the multinational, multiracial Empire in microcosm. The three judges trying the case were Councilor Bogdan Nau-

mowicz, Dr. Mayer Hoffmann, and Judge Alois von Curinaldi, with Curinaldi presiding. The prosecutor was Franjo
Svara; the court reporter Nikola Rašić. Principal defense
counsel were Dr. Max Feldbauer (for Princip and several of
the lesser helpers), Dr. Konstantin Premušić (for Čabrinović, Miško Jovanović, and two of the farmers), Court Secretary Wenzl Malek (for Ilić), Dr. Felix Perišić (for some of
Ilić's local recruits), Franz Strupl (for Grabež) and Dr.
Rudolf Zistler (for Velijko and Vaso Čubrilović).

There was no jury, since under Bosnian law it was the
judges who would decide on the defendants' guilt or in-
nocence. Another manner in which Bosnian trial procedure
differed from that of an American court—but conformed to
that generally followed on the Continent—was that prosecution and defense counsel were to do next to no cross-ex-
amining. Instead, the questioning was to be done by the
judges—chiefly the presiding judge—who could base their
line of inquiry on the findings of the pretrial investigation
and on any other pertinent depositions and documents they
had studied before the opening of the trial.

The trial's scene was a small and bare courtroom of the
Philipović barracks in Sarajevo. The twenty-five defendants, guarded by eight soldiers carrying drawn bayonets, sat
on wooden benches in the middle of the room, facing the
court. The room at times was stiflingly hot, and most of the
defendants looked pale and tired.

The trial was not secret, but the bailiff admitted a handful of spectators only—the Mayor, a parliamentary deputy,
some police officials. The Austro-Hungarian press was adequately represented, and was to do a fair and accurate job
of reporting the trial. Reporters from Serbia, Russia, and
France, or any other enemy belligerent were necessarily
absent; what is less understandable is that no neutral cor-

respondents had apparently been invited. *The New York Times,* for example, was to carry a few fragmentary dispatches on the trial only, none of them written by its own correspondents. What follows here, in fact, is the first complete summary of the proceedings ever given in English.

In some ways, it was an unsensational and at times even a dull trial. There were no brilliant cross-examinations and little impassioned oratory. In other ways, the record of the Sarajevo proceedings is full of suspense, for the trial represented the Austrians' final chance to discover and expose the true scope of the conspiracy.

The prosecutor, Franjo Svara, spent the better part of Monday morning reading his indictment. Calmly, he described the facts which Pfeffer's investigation had brought out: the Belgrade preparations, the assassins' trip, the deed itself. His opening speech foreshadowed the prosecution's entire case—only the actual assassins and their local helpers, it ran, were in the dock, but behind them, and beyond the reach of the court, stood the propagandists of the *Narodna Odbrana* in Belgrade.

"Only I Thought of the Assassination"

The first defendants to take the stand were Princip, Čabrinović, and Grabež. Čabrinović, subdued for once, quickly entered his plea before the presiding judge:

Judge Curinaldi: "Nedjelko Čabrinović, do you feel guilty?" ("Do you feel guilty," or "are you guilty" rather than the Anglo-Saxon "how do you plead" were the standard questions.)

Čabrinović: "Yes."

Curinaldi: "Guilty of what?"

Čabrinović: "I am guilty of the crime of Archduke Franz Ferdinand's assassination."

Grabež, too, admitted his guilt:

Curinaldi: "You are Trifko Grabež? Do you feel guilty?"

Grabež: "Yes."

Curinaldi: "Guilty of what?"

Grabež: "Of having attempted an assassination."

Princip alone was defiant.

Curinaldi: "Do you feel guilty?"

Princip: "I am not a criminal, for I have removed an evildoer. I meant to do a good deed."

Curinaldi: "And the Archduchess?"

Princip: "I did not mean to kill her; I killed her unintentionally."

Curinaldi: "You do not consider yourself guilty then?"

Princip: "No."

That day and the next, the three defendants proceeded to give their account of the origins of the plot. They were opposed to Austrian rule, they said, and when in Belgrade, had resolved to kill Franz Ferdinand together. They had done so, they added, after receiving an anonymous news clipping from Bosnia around Easter time, which reported the Archduke's impending trip. At one point, their eagerness to shift the whole blame onto themselves, and to divert the court's attention from their Serbian associates, resulted in this curious argument between Princip and Čabrinović over the honor of being the crime's instigator:

"Did you not say that the first idea of committing the assassination was yours," Curinaldi interrupted one of Princip's statements, turning to Čabrinović.

Čabrinović: "When I received the news clipping, I told Princip about it, and showed it to him."

Princip: "I did talk with him about the assassination at the 'Acorn Garland,' but I had decided all by myself to do it. It was I who spoke of it first, before Čabrinović received the clipping, [saying] that I would commit the assassination. I know positively that I spoke to him about it before he received the clipping."

Čabrinović: "I received anonymous information. However Gavro asserts. . . ."

Curinaldi, interrupting him: "He claims that he was already in agreement with you."

Čabrinović: "I don't remember."

Princip: "I know it positively."

Čabrinović: "Princip says that the idea of the assassination was his before I received the news clipping. . . ."

Curinaldi, interrupting once more: "He says that he decided on it before."

Čabrinović: "There was frequent talk about the assassination between us, but I don't recall when the definite decision was arrived at."

Princip: "The definite decision was made when we received the news clipping. Before that, only I thought of the assassination."

Curinaldi, instead of pursuing the point, changed the subject. "Do you know anything of Žerajić," he asked, turning to Princip.

Princip could have wished for no better cue. Indeed he did, he said. Žerajić, the would-be assassin of the Austrian Governor, and hero of Bosnia's pan-Serbs, had been his model, he told the court. It was on Žerajić's grave in Sarajevo, he said, that he had sworn to avenge the dead martyr. Nor did he leave any doubts about his admiration for Žerajić later in the trial. In the session of October 20, Gaćinović's

fiery pamphlet in praise of Žerajić, *The Death of A Hero,*
was read into the evidence.

"Are there any comments," Curinaldi asked both prosecution and defense when the reading of the pamphlet was
finished.

There was silence, and then a shout from Princip:

"Hurrah for Žerajić, that is all!"

The court rose for a brief recess. When Curinaldi returned to the bench, he warned that anyone interrupting
the trial again would find himself excluded from the courtroom.

Princip: "If it's forbidden, all right. But it is still the way
I feel."

Curinaldi: "One must not express it; that is a punishable
act."

"Don't Think of Turning Us In, Sir."

Princip's strategy, and that of his two friends who had
come from Belgrade with him, thus was apparent from the
very beginning. They would describe the crime as local in
origin, born of Bosnian resentment against Austrian rule
and against Franz Ferdinand, "the evil genius of the Slavs,"
as Grabež put it. They would avoid implicating or even
mentioning the Black Hand. They would accept full responsibility for the crime's execution themselves, and do
their best to parry any indiscretions that might be committed by any co-defendant or witness. It was a strategy that had
an excellent chance of success. Of the other assassins, only
Ilić and Mehmedbašić were fully aware of Belgrade's involvement. Mehmedbašić was safely across the border,
and Ilić, when put on the stand, recovered the composure
he had lost during the pretrial investigation, and kept ab-

solutely quiet about what he knew of Apis and the Black Hand.

Ilić's two Sarajevo recruits—Čubrilović and Popović—knew little or nothing of what had gone on in Belgrade, and hence were in no position to betray the Black Hand even if they had wanted to do so. The assassins' various helpers, similarly ignorant, were far too busy trying to exculpate themselves. In this, Princip and Grabež supported them as much as they dared.

Under Curinaldi's questioning, few details of the underground journey from Belgrade to Sarajevo remained hidden from the court. The youths' crossing with Mičić and Milović; their meeting with Veljko Čubrilović, the Priboj schoolteacher; their stopover at the farm of old Mitar Kerović and his three sons, where they had rested; the part which Miško Jovanović had played in hiding their arms at Tuzla—all became part of the trial record. To make up for these fatal admissions, Princip and Grabež volunteered that it was their fault if their helpers had failed to turn them in to the Bosnian police before or after the crime.

"It seems to me that Kerović saw the bombs," said Grabež, when the admission could no longer be avoided. "I can't say exactly whether he did see them, but I told him. . . ."

Curinaldi: "Whom?"

Grabež: Blagoje [Kerović, one of the three sons of old Mitar Kerović]. I threatened him not to tell anyone that we had come by his place. 'You should pay dearly for any imprudence; you will be punished by people who will come here who are stronger than any soldiers and policemen, and who will kill all the men in your family.' "

Curinaldi: "Someone suggested these words to you?"

Grabež: "It was my own idea to say them. There was

absolutely nothing behind these threats, but they scared the peasant, of course."

The peasants were understandably eager to confirm these accounts of having been threatened, as was Miško Jovanović, the Tuzla businessman and *Narodna Odbrana* agent. What could I have done, Jovanović asked in his defense. My wife was seven months pregnant, and here was Princip telling me: "Don't think of turning us in, Sir, for I would destroy you and your family." What choice did I have but to hold their weapons and hope that in the end, the youths would decide against using them?

Princip firmly upheld Jovanović. He could not very well deny having given Jovanović the arms to keep, but he insisted that Jovanović had had no more of an idea of what they planned to do with them than did Veljko Čubrilović or the peasants.

"Didn't he ask you for what purpose you were carrying these implements," asked Curinaldi increduously.

"He did not ask us and we did not say any more about it," answered Princip.

The skill and persistence with which the assassins obscured the parts played by their helpers in Bosnia and Serbia demand admiration. It is worth remembering, however, that their efforts exposed them to no major risk. Except for Ilić, who was twenty-three at the time of the murder, all the assassins were under twenty years of age, and thus safe from the death penalty. Čubrilović was nineteen, as was Grabež; Popović was eighteen, Vaso Čabrinović seventeen. Only about Princip's age did some questions exist, and the most critical part of his defense concerned not his participation in the plot, but the precise date of his birthday.

Princip, the prosecution contended, was born on June

26, 1894, and had therefore passed his twentieth birthday when he shot his two victims.

No, claimed Princip, his birthday came on July, not June, 26.

To settle the issue, two depositions were read into the trial record. One was by Princip's mother. The other was by the parish priest of his native village of Oblej.

The July 26 date was the correct one, Mrs. Princip had deposed.

Could she remember the birthdays of her other children? she was asked by the examining magistrate.

No, she could not.

The parish priest's testimony was somewhat more convincing.

According to the official church register, the priest had deposed, Princip was born on July 26, 1894. According to another equally official church record, on which the entries were not strictly chronological, but on which the vital statistics for all the members of one family were listed together, the date was June 26. He thought that he could explain the reason for the contradiction, said the priest. At the time, he had been assistant to the old parish priest, and it had been part of his duties to make most of the entries in the church records for him. The old priest did not write too well, and would simply jot down the date by pencil on any scrap of paper that was handy. Sometimes, these penciled notes would pile up for weeks before he could copy them into the church register, and this was what had happened in Princip's case.

Inviting no additional testimony, and without recalling Princip to the stand, the court took the matter under advisement, delaying a definite decision until the time of the verdict.

"Do You Think I Am An Animal?"

The court's reluctance to probe any further was indicative of the trial's tone and progress. In going over the trial record, one has the impression that on most major questions the court, even when it must have had strong doubts about the stories told by the defendants, made only feeble efforts to uncover the full facts. The court did, however, manage to illuminate some interesting side issues. One of these was the apparent disingenuousness of many of the plotters' associates.

"Are you a member of any organization?" Curinaldi asked young Dragan Kalember, a Sarajevo high-school student very much on the outer fringes of the conspiracy, who now found himself in court on the dual charge of having had prior knowledge of the plot, and of having withheld evidence.

Kalember: "No. I am a progressive, but I don't belong to any organization."

Curinaldi: "What does the word 'progressive' mean?"

Kalember: "To me it means 'always forward.' "

Curinaldi: "What is your opinion of the Yugoslavs? What should they do, according to you?"

Kalember: "I know nothing about that."

Curinaldi: "You did talk about it. No doubt you've forgotten?"

Kalember: "Perina [a classmate of his, on trial on the same charges as Kalember] once told me 'Be a nationalist,' and I replied 'all right.' But what it means, I don't know."

"Are you guilty?" Curinaldi asked Nedjo Kerović that same day.

"It is possible that I am a little guilty," pleaded Kerović, weeping. He continued to weep during much of his testimony that followed.

The assassins' other helpers took a line of defense similar to Kerović's, that of being "a little guilty." They had met Princip, Grabež, and Čabrinović on their trip to Bosnia or in Sarajevo, they admitted, but they had had no idea what these young men were planning to do. Now that they did, they bitterly regretted their unwitting share in the plot, they said.

He was sorry for both the murdered couple and for the deed's political consequences, said Veljko Čubrilović, the schoolteacher who had arranged transportation for Princip and Grabež and the arms they were carrying from Kerović's house to Tuzla. "I am an opponent of assassinations and revolutions," he explained, "for the traces they leave behind are too bloody. That is the case here. I believe in the evolution of the spirit, of ideas; I rely on progress, not on action."

With the exception of Ilić, the assassins themselves did not choose to curry the court's favor in this fashion. All they were willing to show remorse for was Sophie's death, which they swore had been unintentional—his second shot, Princip asserted, had been meant for Potiorek—and the fact that the crime had resulted in general war.

The deed itself, said Grabež under questioning by Judge Naumowicz, was "one of the greatest works of history."

Naumowicz: "Did you know what the consequences would be?"

Grabež: "I did not dream of them."

"I am happy to say that I have no regrets," Čabrinović bluntly told Curinaldi. "However, this act has had consequences which one could not possibly forsee or calculate, and if I would have known what was going to happen, I would have sat down on these bombs and let them tear me to pieces."

Only once did their braggadocio desert the assassins; only once did their attitude suggest that they considered their deed anything beside the impersonal removal of a villain who could not be allowed to live.

On the fifth day of the trial, Curinaldi read into the record a factual and moving affidavit by Count Harrach describing the events of June 28. Harrach, who had been standing on the running board of the archducal car that morning, had been a witness to most of the details of the crime and its aftermath, and it was he who heard and recorded the last words which Franz Ferdinand had gasped to his wife: "Sophie dear! Sophie dear! Don't die! Stay alive for our children!"

As the reading of the affidavit progressed, all the defendants lowered their heads. Princip closed his eyes. When it was over, Curinaldi, who had been very much moved by it, called a five minutes' recess. During the recess, one of the defense counsel walked up to Princip. Hadn't Harrach's account left some impression on him, he asked?

Thrusting up his hands in one violent motion, Princip answered with an anguished question: "Do you think I am an animal and have no feelings?"

Čabrinović's Fumble

But no matter what their private feelings, the defendants never allowed themselves the luxury of forgetting their main purpose, which was to clear Belgrade. The *Narodna Odbrana*, they asserted, was a purely "cultural organization," which had had nothing to do with the preparation of the crime. Ciganović and Tankosić they could not well deny knowing, since their names had come out in the pre-trial investigation. What they could and did do, however, was to confuse the court on the role these men had played.

"Tankosić," testified Grabež, "was a secondary figure. The chief culprit, if one wants to use the word culprit, was Ciganović."

"I don't know," said Čabrinović, "if Ciganović and Tankosić were members and leaders of the *Narodna Odbrana;* others who know Tankosić better than I claim that he is in opposition and even in conflict with the *Narodna Odbrana.*"

The defendants did not always manage to mix truth and untruth that smoothly, however. Čabrinović in particular would occasionally fumble. When this happened, Princip was usually there to help him, but on one occasion a slip made by Čabrinović came so close to revealing Dimitrijević's name that their whole house of cards was suddenly on the point of collapse.

"Nobody was in a position to know anything about the project," said Čabrinović heatedly during the session of October 18, in an effort to discredit a witness who had given testimony hostile to Belgrade, "except for Ciganović, Tankosić, and a friend of the latter, for if others had been informed the police would have found out."

"What is the name of this friend of Tankosić's of whom you just spoke?" asked Curinaldi quickly.

Čabrinović had caught his mistake: "A former officer whose name I forget."

Princip, realizing that the danger was not yet over, broke in. "Yes, an ex-officer. A theology graduate was also in the know."

Curinaldi allowed himself to be deflected. "Who was this theology graduate?" he asked.

Princip: "It was said that he was Djuro Šarac." (The name was no invention of Princip's. There did live a theology student and ex-partisan by that name in Belgrade. Moreover, Šarac may have known about the plot. According to one account, it was Šarac who was sent to Bosnia in the unsuccessful attempt to dissuade the youths from killing Franz Ferdinand after the Black Hand's vote against Apis early in June.)

All would have been well, had not Čabrinović needlessly mentioned "this friend of Tankosić's" again a minute later.

Now his defense counsel, Dr. Premužić, intervened.

"What does this friend of Tankosić's do?"

Čabrinović: "I don't know. He is a very mystical [*sic*] person."

Premužić: "Do you know his name?"

Čabrinović: "I don't know it."

Again, Princip thought it wise to interrupt. "He called himself Kazimirović," he offered, "and he studied theology in Russia."

Princip's defense counsel, Dr. Feldbauer, rose. "Princip, what are you saying about this Kazimirović?"

"I say that this is what he calls himself, and that he studied theology in Russia. Ciganović mentioned him to me. He did not want to become a priest, and I believe that he finished his studies at Kiev." (Here too, Princip was using some partially correct details. Dr. Radovan Kazimirović, a graduate of the Kiev Theological Seminary, was a high-school teacher in Belgrade at that time. To what extent, if any, he was involved in the plot is still a matter of conjecture, however.)

Masons and Mayerling

It was late in the afternoon, and the court was about to adjourn. Before it did, Princip engaged in another diverting maneuver.

Some days earlier, he had suggested that Ciganović was a Freemason. He now came back to this point, and hinted that Kazimirović might be a Mason too. "When Ciganović alluded to the Freemasons," he said, "he told me that he would speak to Voja Tankosić and to this man. . . . I told him that I would have no part in the assassination if others knew about it; he repeated that this man was safe, that he was a good friend, and that his name was Kazimirović."

That night, it seems, Princip and Čabrinović agreed, by the covert system of knocks which the prisoners used to communicate between their cells, to pursue the subject of the Masons. The next day, they volunteered more details about Kazimirović.

Kazimirović, implied Čabrinović, was the mysterious man behind the scenes. He could seldom be found in Belgrade, he said; one day he would be in Budapest, another in France, yet another in Russia. "When the other man returns," he quoted Ciganović as having said to him, the youths would get their arms. "Ciganović then told me," he went on, "that two years before, the Freemasons had condemned Franz Ferdinand to death, but that they could not find the men to execute the sentence. When he brought me the gun and the ammunition, he said: 'That man came back from Budapest last night.' I knew that his trip was concerned with the affair, that he had gone abroad, and that he had conferred with certain circles."

As Čabrinović's stories about Kazimirović grew wilder,

Curinaldi broke in. "Aren't these fables you are telling us?"

Čabrinović: "It is the pure truth and a hundred times more truthful than all your documents about the *Narodna Odbrana.*"

Cross-examination would shake neither his nor Princip's testimony. Since Čabrinović's statement of the previous afternoon, someone had hurriedly checked up on what was known about Kazimirović, and had found him to be a contributor to a Belgrade theological journal called *The Christian Messenger*, which published such non-Masonic articles as "Our Young Theologians," "The Religious Policy of Dubrovnik," and "Second Marriages of Ministers."

"How can one simultaneously be a Freemason and a contributor to *The Christian Messenger?*" asked Curinaldi, sensibly.

"The Freemasons," said Čabrinović simply, "get into all sorts of circles, and work everywhere for the realization of their aims."

Curinaldi remained incredulous. Owing to the defendants efforts, the court was to remain wholly in the dark about the Black Hand's involvement, but it would not accept their fabrications about the Freemasons. "In regard to this particular," the sentence was to read, "the court is of the opinion that the statements on Freemasonry are part of the attempt to hide the activity of the *Narodna Odbrana* and the complicity of Serbian official circles."

If the judges had substituted "Black Hand" for "*Narodna Odbrana,*" they would have described the full truth.

The court's findings, incidentally, did not keep a number of later writers from elaborating on Princip's and Čabrinović's inventions, and from insisting that the Masons had indeed killed Franz Ferdinand. The editor of the German version of the trial record, the Jesuit Father Puntigam, so mutilated the record that the Masons' involvement appeared possible. General Ludendorff, a brilliant German military planner during the war, and a man dedicated to somewhat less brilliant political causes afterwards, published several books and pamphlets intending to prove the Masons' guilt. The World War, he wrote, had been decided on years before its actual outbreak by what he called the "metanational forces," the Jews, the Freemasons, and the Jesuits. Among the reasons they had chosen to start it in 1914 was that $1 + 9 + 1 + 4$—the numbers making up 1914—added up to 15, a number sacred to these forces. It was followed, Ludendorff further explained, by the "second Yahve year 1915," containing the numerical values of $1 + 9 = 10$, and of 15. Beside, the Jewish year for 1914, when put into Hebrew letters, meant "War on Earth."

Dimitrijević, Tankosić, and Ciganović, the general went on, were all Freemasons. They had prepared their plot with the aid of a secret department in the British Foreign Office which specialized in political assassinations, and which had a budget of five million pounds sterling. "Čabrinović and Princip," Ludendorff wrote simply, "were Freemasons too, and Princip was a Jew. His first name was the promising name Gabriel."

Undaunted by the difficulty of explaining why the Jesuits should have co-operated with their sworn enemies, the Masons, the general advanced the following thought:

> The Jesuits let the Freemasons go ahead. They did not prevent the Archduke's trip to Sarajevo, even though Roman circles, too, looked toward Sarajevo with much suspense. With strange zeal, they then directed people's attention to the guilt of the Freemasons.

Much of this nonsense was repeated by other writers. Even as respectable a journal as the *Mercure de France* printed an article in which the Masons were accused of having sentenced Franz Ferdinand to death, and of having chosen Sarajevo as the place of execution. "Perhaps," the author of the article suggested ominously, "light will be thrown some day on these words uttered by a highly placed Swiss Freemason on the subject of the Austrian Heir Apparent: 'He is a good man; it is a pity that he has been condemned; he will die on the steps of the throne.' "

The Masonic myth was not the only one to be told about Sarajevo. Some writers blamed the Hungarians for the assassination, arguing that Budapest was eager to manufacture a pretext for war against Serbia. Others blamed the Austrians. Wickham Steed, a former editor of the London *Times,* and a man with nearly as many prejudices as General Ludendorff, published an account of the crime's origins in which he hinted strongly that its instigators should be sought in Vienna. "In any case," he wrote with a neat bit of innuendo, "the possibility of a 'removal' of the Heir Presumptive and his consort . . . was not thought entirely deplorable from the point of view of the Hapsburg family." Franz Ferdinand's death, said yet others—and their story was at least as credible as the rest—was his punishment for once having shot a white stag at Konopisht.

But the most picturesque myth of all is the one that made Sarajevo the result of Mayerling. Properly speaking, there are two versions of this story. According to one, Princip was none other than the illegitimate son of Archduchess Stefanie, the wife of Archduke Rudolf, the suicide of Mayerling. Holding Franz Ferdinand responsible for Rudolf's death, she had made young Princip kill the Heir to the Throne in Sarajevo. According to the other, which is set forth in a

French novel entitled *Taïa,* Rudolf definitely did not commit suicide at Mayerling, but was assassinated, together with his mistress Marie Vetsera, by his cousin Franz Ferdinand. Unbeknown to the world, however, Marie had given birth to an illegitimate daughter by Rudolf. This daughter, to avenge her mother, armed Princip and sent him to Sarajevo.

Taïa is prefaced by a statement declaring crisply: "This is not a work of fiction. This book, in essence, is a true history." It must be admitted that unlike the other stories— except that of the white stag—it offers the reader romance and the illusion of poetic justice, and not just sheer bigotry. Like the others, however, it lacks the least amount of truth.

CHAPTER XVII

The Penalty

"I Have No Words To Condemn This Crime"

On October 22, the tenth day of the trial, the last witness left the stand, and the prosecutor rose for his summing up. Svara began with the kind of heavy, old-fashioned oratory that countless lawyers, no matter in what part of the world, have found effective: ". . . a bomb explodes, a gun is fired, and the life of two noble hearts is brutally ended. I have no words to condemn this crime, and one cannot imagine that men could be found to commit such a deed. The grief of every patriot, of every citizen of the monarchy of Austria, becomes even more terrible, more profound, when one remembers how the two august guests arrived full of confidence, how the Archduke moved openly in the midst of his people, and how his noble spouse nourished for our youth a maternal love."

Growing more restrained, Svara proceeded to give a competent outline of the facts of the crime. His analysis came remarkably close to the truth, except that in place of Apis, he named Kazimirović as the crime's principal instigator in Belgrade, and that he made no allusion to the Black Hand, but put the blame on the *Narodna Odbrana*.

"Official circles" in Serbia, he insisted, wishing Franz Ferdinand's death for reasons of their own, had arranged the killing. He was contemptuous of the defendants' claims that the crime's idea had been their own, and that they had hated the Archduke because they thought him an enemy of the Slavs. To show how unlikely this explanation was, he did not hesitate to allude to the painful details of Franz Ferdinand's marriage:

> It [the accusation that Franz Ferdinand was anti-Slav] was nothing but a maneuver on the part of Serbia, of Serbian circles, to convince children to commit this horrible act. The august spouse of the Archduke was Czech, and thus of Slav origin, and due to this marriage the late Archduke has had difficulties [a wonderful piece of understatement]; he would never have decided on it if he had been an enemy of the Slavs.

No more than three among the twenty-five defendants in the dock, he concluded, should be acquitted of treason. They were Mr. and Mrs. Sadilo, and Mrs. Sadilo's father, Ivan Momčinović, in whose house Čubrilović's arms had briefly been hidden after the crime with the explanation that they were antiques about to be presented to the Sarajevo museum. These three, he said, were guilty only of being accessories after the fact. The remaining twenty-two defendants were guilty as charged, and should be convicted of treason. All of them were, "to the same degree, the direct authors of the assassination." Treason was punishable by death, and this was the penalty he was demanding wherever the law allowed it. Nine among the twenty-two, he explained, were clearly under twenty at the time of the murder, and should therefore be sentenced to prison and not to death. In the case of Princip, he admitted that the evidence concerning his birthdate was conflicting. He himself was convinced, however, that Princip had passed his twentieth birthday when he fired the fatal shots, and hence should suffer the death penalty.

Not As Black As Beards

When Svara had sat down, the first lawyer to rise for the defense was Dr. Feldbauer, counsel for Princip. Shrewdly agreeing with the prosecutor that the true responsibility for the crime lay beyond the border, he pleaded with the court to consider Princip no more than the tool of others, "the victim of the Greater Serbia movement." Insisting that July, and not June, was his client's birthdate, he ended his brief appeal by recommending Princip to the mercy of the court.

Feldbauer also was defending three of the assassins' helpers—Blagoje Kerović, the farmer's son, Jakov Milović, the smuggler, and one Nikola Forkapić, a Sarajevo student accused of having had prior knowledge of the conspiracy—and he could do more for them than he could for Princip. The case against Forkapić, he said, had simply not been borne out by the evidence. Blagoje Kerović had had no idea of what was going on when the youths stopped at his father's house; "his peasant's mind does not know the meaning of the words 'assassination plot.' " Milović finally, who had guided the youths across the border, might be "a common smuggler," not an offense with which he was charged, but he was no traitor, an offense with which he was. All three, Feldbauer demanded, should be acquitted.

He was followed by Dr. Premužić, counsel for Čabrinović, Miško Jovanović, and two of the lesser helpers—Mitar Kerović, and a seventeen year old student named Branko Zagorac, who was accused of having received advance information about the plot from Vaso Čubrilović. Old Mitar Kerović, the defense counsel said, was an illiterate peasant, with no understanding of the assassins' intent. Nor could Zagorac be expected to have lent any credence to the tales told him by Čubrilović, "a virtual child." Neither, therefore, was guilty as charged.

In Čabrinović's and Jovanović's cases, Premužić could hardly ask for an acquittal, of course, but he could and did plead extenuating circumstances. The court, he asked, should erase from its mind the character sketches the prosecution had drawn of his clients. "The prosecutor thinks that Miško [Jovanović]'s soul is as black as his beard." But this was untrue. Jovanović had had no idea that the arms he was keeping were to be used in an act that constituted treason. Admittedly, he had been the Tuzla representative of the *Narodna Odbrana,* but he had thought of that organization as a purely cultural one. He might have been an unwitting accessory to murder, but never to treason.

In Čabrinović's case, one should bear in mind his unhappy home life, as well as the fact that during the trial, he had shown more "sincerity" than any of the other defendants. "He has revealed," said Premužić with an irony that was totally unintentional, "the existence of Kazimirović [the alleged Mason] to us." If Čabrinović had been an anarchist, it had been because of the Christian elements in anarchism. Assuredly, he had not been the crime's true instigator. Like Princip, he had merely acted as the tool of others. He would recommend no specific penalty, concluded Premužić, but he again wished to ask the judges, in arriving at the proper sentence, to remember the crucial role played by Kazimirović.

The next two defense pleas offered no surprises. The third one did.

Dr. Perišić demanded acquittals for Momčinović and the two Sadilos, saying that they could not conceivably have known that the package left at their house contained arms used in the assassination of Franz Ferdinand, and were thus innocent of any offense. For Cvijan Stjepanović, one of Princip's and Grabež's lesser helpers along the route, he pleaded ignorance; "this simple peasant," he said, had had no inkling of the object of the trip. Coming to his most heavily incriminated client, Cvijetko Popović—one of the seven assassins—he begged the court to be lenient. At eighteen, Popović was terribly young still, he said, and what he had known about the meaning of violence had all come from books. He had grown up in an atmosphere poisoned by pan-Serbian propaganda, but "at the bottom of his soul, he is no revolutionary." He was not a member of the inner conspiracy, nor had he known about the true motives of the rest of the group. Above all, when presented with his opportunity to kill Franz Ferdinand that bloody Sunday four months ago, he had refrained from taking any action.

The following morning, October 24, Dr. Strupl demanded the acquittal of two of his clients—Mićo Mičić, accused of having helped to smuggle Princip and Grabež across the border, and Jovo Kerović, another of old Mitar Kerović's sons, at whose farm they had stayed afterwards. Neither had known that the youths were planning an assas-

sination, he argued, and hence the prosecution had failed
to establish any treasonable act. He pleaded extenuating
circumstances for his two other charges—Trifko Grabež,
the only one among the three Belgrade-trained plotters who
had failed to act on June 28, and Marko Perina, one more
Sarajevo high-school student accused of having known
about plans for the assassination. Perina, he said, had been
unaware of any of the plot's details; moreover, he had been
very much afraid of what might happen to him if he talked
to the police. As for Grabež, Strupl did not deny his part
in the conspiracy, but he pleaded that Grabež, rather than
acting on his own volition, had been drawn into it by others.
Beside, like Popović, he had refused to kill when face to
face with his intended victim.

A Parliamentary Oversight

All these had been highly competent, if unstartling,
pleas. But when Dr. Rudolf Zistler rose to address the three
judges, the atmosphere of the courtroom suddenly changed.
Zistler's clients were Vaso and Veljko Čubrilović, the Sarajevo assassin and his Priboj cousin; Ivo Kranjcević, the Sarajevo student who had helped to hide Vaso Čubrilović's arms
after the crime in the Sadilos' house; and Nedjo Kerović,
last of Mitar Kerović's sons, who had weepingly pleaded "It
is possible that I am a little guilty." What Zistler was attempting to prove now was nothing less than the total in-
nocence, under the law, of every one of his clients.

The judges, he said, must not allow themselves to be influenced by the passions of war; they "must judge this case
purely from a legal point of view." They must be perfectly
objective, and "not be guided by their hearts."

You, My Lords, you are the priests of the blindfolded God-dess, that blind divinity who in one hand holds the scales and in the other the sword, who seeks only the objective truth, who makes all men equal before the law, and judges each according to his merits.

Some of the defendants, said Zistler, might be accused of murder, but none of them was guilty of treason. Zistler's manner was long-winded and digressive; at one point Curinaldi had to stop him when he embarked on an explanation of some of the intricacies of Croatian law, at another point he had to call him to order when he tried to launch into a history of European nationalism from "the end of the middle ages onward." The gist of his case, however, was forceful and simple.

The defendants' actions, Zistler argued, "not only do not constitute, under our laws, the crime of treason, but are not even punishable acts." The reason was this: Under the Peace of San Stefano of 1878 and the subsequent Treaty of Berlin, Austria-Hungary had been allowed to occupy the provinces of Bosnia and Herzegovina, but not to annex them. Since the provinces were thus not an integral part of the monarchy, no one could be accused of treason for trying to detach them.

In 1880, Zistler went on, the Austrian parliament had passed a law concerning the occupation, which specifically provided that no change in the territorial status of Bosnia-Herzegovina could be affected without the consent of the legislative bodies of Austria and Hungary. There had, of course, been a recent change, he said, since on October 5, 1908, the Austro-Hungarian government had proclaimed the annexation of Bosnia-Herzegovina, and the Turkish government, formerly sovereign over the region, had renounced its local rights. The annexation, however, was not legally valid—for parliament had forgotten to ratify the annexation.

Bills legalizing the annexation had been submitted to parliament in Vienna and Budapest, but no action had been taken so far. "Consequently, the union of Bosnia and Herzegovina with the monarchy exists *de facto* but not *de jure;* in other words, the sovereign rights of our most gracious Emperor extend to Bosnia and Herzegovina not as integral parts of the Austro-Hungarian monarchy, but as political units distinct from, and located outside of, the monarchy."

The Prosecutor: "I object."

But if Svara acted shocked by Zistler's argument, Zistler was scornful about the prosecution's entire case. The treason charge, he said, had been introduced only because Austria and Serbia were at war. The prosecutor was a government official, and the government he was serving wished to do as much damage as possible to Serbia before world opinion. By accusing the defendants of both treason and murder, he implied, the prosecution had admitted the falseness of the treason charge. "The indictment is very foresighted: it figures that the court might find that there was no treason, and is ready to fall back on the murder charge."

Zistler was too good a lawyer to put everything on one card, however, and to end his speech on this note. Instead he went into the extenuating circumstances which he felt his clients could claim in the event that the court should uphold the treason charge.

Veljko Čubrilović, he said, was a man devoted to his family, a man of kindness and intelligence. His only part in the crime had been to aid Princip and Grabež on their trip to Sarajevo; and here the court must consider how terribly frightened he had been by the two young men's threats. If found guilty, he did not deserve death, for he had only been an accessory to the crime, and not its instigator.

Vaso Čubrilović, one of Ilić's recruits, was only seventeen —a difficult age in anyone's life. He had been a victim of pan-Serb propaganda, whose answers in court had shown how profound his political naïveté was. He might have been an accessory to planning the murder, but when Franz Ferdinand actually passed him, he had made no use of his bomb or gun. "Saul became Paul; the criminal became a just man." The court should set him free: "I feel that Vaso Čubrilović would benefit from an acquittal."

Kranjčević had helped Vaso Čubrilović to hide his arms only because he had taken pity on "a repentant criminal." His loyalty to the monarchy was beyond doubt, and he had had just about as much to do with the plot "as Pontius Pilate with the Apostles' Creed." Nedjo Kerović, finally, was "a big child," a peasant wholly ignorant of politics. When told to transport some students and their baggage by Veljko Čubrilović, a learned schoolteacher, how could this simple soul refuse? "That is the extent of Nedjo Kerović's participation. Where is the intention of detaching Bosnia and Herzegovina from the monarchy?"

Reverting to his dramatic mood once more, Zistler ended his plea with this appeal to the court:

> I am profoundly convinced that if you were to address yourselves to those who have perhaps suffered the most, really, from the death of the Heir to the Throne, because they have lost their family, if you were to address those who every night before falling asleep bathe their pillows in tears— if you were to address the children of the deceased princely couple, asking them if they demanded the heads of the defendants, they would spare their lives.

We must not lose sight of the fact that this is a historical trial; that the eyes of the whole world look on this illustrious court today; and that the world waits curiously for the sentence that will be pronounced in this hall of judgment.

Future generations and historians will speak of this trial. For this reason, the sentences must not be brutal; they must be just and endure as a bright page in the annals of criminal jurisprudence, before the tribunal of civilization, and of posterity.

My Lords, if you will imbue your minds with this idea, I am convinced that in considering the defendants in general and my clients in particular, you will give proof of leniency and generosity.

"We Have Loved the People"

After this direct attack on the whole basis of the trial, one might have expected any plea that followed to sound anticlimactic. In a sense it did, for the last counsel to rise for the defense, Court Secretary Wenzl Malek, decided to take an approach that was infinitely less aggressive than Zistler's. At the same time, he was really saying very much the same things Zistler had in defense of his individual clients, except that it was doing it in a manner designed to win the sympathy of the court.

Zistler had begun by casting doubts on the judges' objectivity. Malek began by making clear his personal distaste for defending the people who were his clients. "If I hear," he quoted Cicero, "that someone has undertaken to defend a man guilty of treason against his country, I consider him an accomplice to the crime." In the much-maligned Austro-Hungarian monarchy, the Court Secretary went on, matters were different, and the country's magistrates themselves might be charged with defending men accused of treason. "That is my duty, too, much as I would prefer sitting among you, My Lords, to standing before this bar."

Having said this, Malek launched into a skillful and lucid defense of his four clients—Ilić, Djukić, Kalember, and Milošević. Ilić, he said, had committed no overt act of treason. His part in transporting the arms from Tuzla to Sarajevo might make him an accomplice to Princip's crime, but not its instigator. Beside, in deciding whether or not he had committed treason, it was essential to weigh his motives. Whatever Ilić's role in the assassination, there was no evidence that he had been driven by any desire to see Bosnia and Herzegovina detached from the monarchy, as charged by the prosecution. The true reason for his involvement was the dominating influence exerted over him by Princip.

Regarding the murder charge, Ilić's only involvement again consisted in transporting the arms, an act of "indirect participation" at most. The real crime, argued Malek, did not begin until the conspirators assembled on the Appel Quay on June 28. By that time, Ilić had abandoned the whole murder plan, and was trying to dissuade the others from going through with it.

In considering Ilić's penalty for the lesser charge of complicity, the court should hold in his favor the fact that he had acted under Princip's orders, and it should remember his genuine regrets after the crime, regrets that had led him to make a full confession to the investigating judge.

Malek's pleas for his remaining three charges were short. Djukić, accused of having recruited Vaso Čubrilović for the assassination, had never really taken the plot seriously, and thus been without any treasonable intent. Nor had Kalember, accused of having heard about the crime from Čubrilović and of having withheld evidence, harbored any such intent. Čubrilović was known as a fellow addicted to wild talk, and there was no reason why Kalember should have believed his "Wild West novel" tales about an assassination. Milošević, finally, who had sheltered Princip and Grabež after they had crossed into Bosnia, and who had carried their arms for them, had known neither who his visitors were, nor what was in their bags. All the defendants, said Malek, had agreed on the stand that Milošević had not been told one word about the plot.

In Djukić's case, he begged the court to take into account his youth and his good record; as for Kalember and Milošević, he was demanding an acquittal.

With this, the defense rested its case. Under Bosnian trial procedure, the prosecution now was allowed a last brief summing up, after which the defendants themselves would be given an opportunity to make any final statement they wished.

Svara, the prosecutor, concentrated on Zistler's charges in his closing words. Zistler, he said, might be right when he claimed that parliament had failed to act on the annexation. The issue was immaterial, however, since the trial was being held under Bosnian, not Austrian law, and "the law in force among us" made the crime one of treason. "I reiterate," were the final words Svara uttered in the trial, "the entire indictment."

Judge Curinaldi turned to the defendants. Was there anything they wished to add?

Three of them made use of their right on this last day of the trial, Friday, October 23—Veljko Čubrilović, Nedjelko Čabrinović, and Gavrilo Princip.

Čubrilović spoke for a minute only, and the school teacher's sole point was to stress again that his part in the crime had been of no real consequence.

Čabrinović's statement was of a very different sort. He would like to explain, said the young man who had thrown the bomb at Franz Ferdinand, "in clear terms the circumstances that influenced us before the assassination."

"We did not hate Austria," he said, but the Austrians had done nothing, since the occupation, to solve the problems that faced Bosnia and Herzegovina. In particular, they had failed to relieve the economic misery of the Bosnian farmer. "Nine-tenths of our people are farmers who suffer, who live in misery, who have no schools, who are deprived of any culture. We sympathized with them in their distress." The court should understand this, and "not consider us criminals. We loved our people."

The assassination, Čabrinović went on—his voice betraying his deep emotion—had arisen from an atmosphere in which there was daily talk of violence, and in which assassins were celebrated as heroes. "We thought that only people of noble character were capable of committing [political] assassinations." There had been no personal hatred for Franz Ferdinand, but "we heard it said that he was an enemy of the Slavs. Nobody directly told us 'kill him'; but in this environment, we arrived at the idea ourselves."

Čabrinović ended by voicing a sentiment he had steadfastly suppressed during the trial so far:

I would like to add something else [he said, as tears showed in his eyes]. Although Princip is playing the hero, and although we all wanted to appear as heroes, we still have profound regrets. In the first place, we did not know that the late Franz Ferdinand was a father. We were greatly touched by the words he addressed to his wife: 'Sophie, stay alive for our children.' We are anything you want, except criminals. In my name and in the name of my comrades, I ask the children of the late successor to the throne to forgive us. As for you, punish us according to your understanding. We are not criminals. We are honest people, animated by noble sentiments; we are idealists; we wanted to do good; we have loved our people; and we shall die for our ideals.

Weeping, he sat down. Both the audience and one of the judges, noted a local reporter, had been moved to tears by his words.

The last defendant to face the bar was Princip. As he rose, he looked pale and calm; "his voice," wrote the same reporter, "does not show the least trace of emotion." What he had to say he put into four terse sentences:

In trying to insinuate that someone else has instigated the assassination, one strays from the truth. The idea arose in our own minds, and we ourselves executed it. We have loved the people. I have nothing to say in my defense.

Curinaldi: "The trial is ended. Sentence will be pronounced here on Thursday, the 29th, at 8:30 A.M."

The Sentence

Six days later, as Curinaldi had announced, the court reconvened to hear the decision of the judges.

Five of the six assassins—Princip, Čabrinović, Grabež, Popović, and Vaso Čubrilović—were found guilty of treason and murder. Since all but Princip were indisputably under twenty years of age at the time they had broken the law, they were not subject to the death penalty, however, and even in Princip's case, the judges ruled that the conflicting evidence about his birthdate must be interpreted in his favor, and the defendant be considered underage. Princip,

Grabež, and Čabrinović accordingly received the maximum term of twenty years in prison; while the less actively involved Vaso Čubrilović was sentenced to sixteen years, and Popović to thirteen. Except for Popović, the judges added, the prisoners were to suffer one fast day each month, and every June 28, they were to spend twenty-four hours in solitary confinement, "in a darkened cell, and on hard boards."

Danilo Ilić, the last of the assassins, and four of the plotters' principal helpers—Veljko Čubrilović, the Priboj schoolteacher, Miško Jovanović, the Tuzla businessman, Nedjo Kerović, who had driven Princip and Grabež to Tuzla, and Lazar Djukić, who had recruited Vaso Čubrilović for the assassination—were found guilty of treason and of being accessories to murder. Djukić got off with a prison term of ten years, but the four others were sentenced to death by hanging.

Found guilty of the treason charge, but innocent of murder, were Mitar Kerović, head of the Kerović clan, and Jakov Milović, Princip's and Grabež's guide across the border. The sentence against Milović was death, that against Kerović prison for life. Guilty of being accessories to either treason or murder, for having failed to inform the police of the plot, were four of the killers' associates: Kranjčević, Stjepanović, Zagorac, and Perina. Their sentences were prison terms of between three and ten years.

Nine of the defendants—Mr. and Mrs. Sadilo and Mrs. Sadilo's father, accused of having hidden Čubrilović's arms; Jovo and Blagoje Kerović, accused of having aided Princip and Grabež on their trip to Sarajevo; Forkapić and Kalember, accused of having withheld evidence; and Mičić and Milošević, accused of having accompanied Princip and Grabež during and after their border crossing—were acquitted on all charges.

The five death sentences cannot but strike one as harsh, yet it should be borne in mind that under Anglo-Saxon law, too, death is the ultimate penalty for treason, and that anyone conspiring to commit an act of murder is fully as guilty of that murder as the person striking the fatal blow. In all, it had been a fair and objective trial, held at a time, moreover, when the war—the direct result of the crime—was endangering the very existence of the monarchy which the accused had betrayed. They had had all the latitude which the law permitted to defend themselves and their action; their judges, throughout, had indeed shown themselves to be "priests of the blindfolded Goddess." The court's observance of the rules of evidence had been so scrupulous that the conflicting testimony about Princip's birthdate had been resolved in the defendant's favor, and that two of the assassins' principal helpers—Mičić and Milošević—found themselves acquitted. To realize just how fair the trial had been, one only needs to recall some of the circumstances of the trial of Lincoln's assassins, in which defense counsel was treated with contempt and abuse by the court, in which the government offered perjured testimony, in which people on the mere fringes of the plot, like Mrs. Surratt, whose guilt is in doubt to this day, were sentenced to death, and in which, finally, the condemned prisoners' pleas for clemency were suppressed and never reached the President.

The Sarajevo sentences, subsequently, were appealed to a higher court. The higher court upheld all of them, except for the death sentences against Jakov Milović and Nedjo Kerović. It changed Milović's sentence to imprisonment for life, and Kerović's to twenty years.

Those sentenced to prison were then taken to various

places of confinement; where, we do not always know. Some apparently stayed in Sarajevo; others, like Princip and Čabrinović, began to serve out their terms at the fortress prison of Theresienstadt in Bohemia. With the end of the trial, they fell back into the obscurity from which they had come. Many people must have seen them or talked to them in prison, but there are next to no descriptions of any such meetings, or of the circumstances of their confinement. The terrors of the war, it seems, made the fate of its instigators a matter of very minor interest.

The execution of the three men whose death sentences had been confirmed took place, some three months after the trial, in the courtyard of the Sarajevo prison. There is no known record of it other than the barest newspaper accounts, and the official telegram sent by the Bosnian Administration to the Joint Ministry of Finance in Vienna on February 3, 1915. The telegram reads as follows:

Trial sentence against Veljko Čubrilović, Miško Jovanović, and Danilo Ilić executed today between 9 and 10 A.M. without incident.

CHIEF, ADMINISTRATION [NO.] 1439.

"On this Historic Spot"

The Salonica Murders

Few of the remaining plotters, either in Austria or in Serbia, survived the war. Major Tankosić, arrested in Belgrade after the receipt of the Austrian ultimatum, but released again after the declaration of war, was killed in action during the retreat of the Serbian army before the Central Powers in 1915. Ciganović, Apis' go-between, joined Tankosić's company after the Serbian mobilization, but he was more fortunate than the major. In 1917, Prime Minister Pašić furnished him with some money and with a false passport, and sent him to the United States, where he waited out the war. In 1919, he returned to Serbia, received a small grant of land from the government, married, and settled down. He died in 1927, the only one among the principal plotters to die from natural causes outside prison. The price Ciganović had to pay for his survival, however, was the open betrayal of Dimitrijević.

The betrayal was needed in the judicial murder of Apis

and his friends by the Serbian government. Toward the end of 1916, Prime Minister Pašić decided to break up the Black Hand once and for all, and to destroy its leaders. What his reasons were is not clear. The Serbian army had suffered a series of disastrous defeats, and the government had been forced to take refuge on Greek soil. One possibility is that Pašić thought of negotiating a separate peace with the Austrians at this time, and that he as well as the Prince Regent were mortally afraid of what Apis might do to them if he should hear of this. Another is that Apis was actively intriguing against Pašić's regime. Yet another is that Pašić was very much concerned lest Apis, on some occasion, reveal the truth about Sarajevo, and thus expose the guilty knowledge of the Serbian government.

Whatever the motives, between December 1916 and March 1917 the Serbian police arrested Apis and a great many of his associates, including Mehmedbašić, the Moslem carpenter who, alone among the Sarajevo assassins, had succeeded in escaping to Serbia. In May 1917 these men were tried before a military tribunal in the city of Salonica. There were two charges against them. One was treason. They had, the prosecution claimed, planned to overthrow the legal Serbian government, and to conclude peace with the country's enemies. The other was attempted murder. In August 1916 according to the indictment, they had made an unsuccessful attempt against the life of the Prince Regent, Alexander. One charge was as baseless as the other.

The trial, in which Ciganović appeared as one of the government's star witnesses, was a travesty of justice. The judges chosen were personal enemies of the defendants. The prosecution produced eighty witnesses, but none had anything concrete to say about the treason charge, and only one claimed to have been present at the scene of the supposed attack on Alexander. That witness had to be brought in from prison, where he was serving a sentence for murder. The most important part of the evidence, that against the Black Hand, was incomplete, since the government was intent on keeping out of the record anything bearing on either the Black Hand's general activities abroad, or on its share in the Sarajevo assassination. Apis, patriotically, agreed before the trial's start to introduce no such evidence himself. Thus, there is something of the quality of Koestler's *Darkness at Noon* about the proceedings. Apis, one realizes as one reads between the lines of the Salonica trial record, must have known that one of the reasons the government was so anxious to see him dead was his participation in the Sarajevo plot. Yet there was no way in which he could defend himself against this unspoken charge—if only to explain his motives—except by revealing facts which would harm the case of Serbia. This Apis could not bring himself to do.

Only once did a possible allusion to Sarajevo get into the record. It happened when Djuro Šarac, one of Apis' Black Hand associates who had either known about or aided in Franz Ferdinand's murder, testified for the government that he had once heard Ciganović say something that implied that Tankosić had once murdered or tortured some people outside Belgrade. (This bit of third-hand, hearsay evidence was fairly characteristic of the testimony heard during the trial as a whole.)

Dimitrijević interrupted the witness: "That is a lie."

"No!" shot back Šarac. "That is no lie! It hurts my soul when I consider what you made of us, and what you still intended to make of us. One can't mention everything here in court. You know that very well. But the time for that will come. I knew no evil before I fell into your hands. Horror seizes me when I think what you made of us!"

The legal farce had a tragic ending. On May 23, 1917, Apis and six of his fellow officers were sentenced to death; the remaining defendants received long prison terms. Mehmedbašić was sentenced to fifteen years in prison for his alleged part in the alleged assassination plot against the Prince Regent. On appeal to a higher court, four of the death sentences were commuted to long prison terms, but those against the three others—Apis among them—were upheld. The Prince Regent, for his part, rejected a final appeal for clemency.

A Necessity of State

Before informing the defendants of the decision of the higher court, one of the judges paid a visit to each of the prisoners in their cells. Would they, the judge asked, give him a full and secret statement describing their involvement in the Sarajevo plot.

Apis, for one, complied, writing a confession which was a curious blend of truth and untruth. He admitted his own share in Franz Ferdinand's murder, and gave a largely correct account of the crime's genesis, but took pains to mention a co-defendant of his named Malobabić, rather than Tankosić, as his link with the assassins.

A few days later, having been told that the court of appeal had upheld his death sentence, Apis wrote his last will and testament. Into it, he inserted a number of references to Sarajevo, which he must have hoped later readers would understand—as indeed they can. The text reads as follows:

My Last Will and Testament

Although sentenced to death by two competent courts, and deprived of the mercy of the Crown, I die innocently, and in the conviction that my death is necessary to Serbia for higher reasons.

This conviction gives me the peace of soul with which I await my last hour.

Provided that Serbia be happy, and that our holy oath—the union of all South Slavs and all that is South Slav—be fulfilled, I shall be happy even after death.

The pain that I feel over dying by Serbian guns shall be sweet and dear to me, since I am convinced that the guns are aimed at my chest for the good of Serbia and the Serbian people, a cause to which I have dedicated my entire life.

I may, without wishing to, have committed errors in my work as a patriot. I may even, unknowingly, have hurt Serbian interests. But in taking any action one almost always runs the risk of being sometimes wrong. I am certain, however, of having committed no intentional errors, and of always having wished to serve no other cause than that of Serbia.

May these mistakes be forgiven me, at least by the Serbs, and I shall pray to God to show me His inexhaustible mercy.

What property remains to me I distribute as follows:

1. I request that my money be sent to my nephew Milan Živanović, refugee in France, a student at the *Grand Lycée Neuf* in Nice.

2. I request that my horse "Blücher" be offered first to the state, and that the money from the sale be sent to my nephew.

3. As for my horse "Zvesdana," I leave it to those best able to judge the matter whether this horse is still capable of

rendering some service. If he is, I donate him to the state; if not, I ask that he be killed.

4. All my other possessions should be distributed among poor refugees, with the canned goods, food, and tobacco going to the soldiers and policemen who have guarded me in prison, as a gift toward the repose of my soul.

5. I request that my watch, a souvenir from my brother-in-law, Živan Živanović, be sent to my nephew Milan Živanović as a souvenir.

This is my last will and testament.

I request, finally, that after the execution of my bequests, this testament be sent to my nephew Milan Živanović in Nice.

June 11 [Old Style] 24 [New Style], at Salonica.

DRAGUTIN DIMITRIJEVIĆ—APIS, m[anu] p[ropria]

"No One Was Hit in the Head"

Less than forty-eight hours later, during the night of June 25, the executioners came to fetch the condemned men from their cells. Apis, who in his single-minded pursuit of the Greater Serbian idea had not hesitated to sacrifice either individuals or nations, showed them no weakness and no self-pity. Whether Apis' life deserves admiration or blame will always be a matter of argument, but there can be no question that his death was that of a hero. Here is the account of his last hours, written immediately after the event by an official witness to the execution, Lieutenant Colonel Ljubomir Dabić, of the Judge Advocate's Division of the Royal Serbian Army:

"After having made their confessions to arch-priest Zdravko Paunković, the condemned men Dimitrijević and

Vulović gave him letters for their families; the arch-priest will pass them on today to the commanding officer. The condemned Malobabić gave him keys and combinations in order to withdraw money from a bank, which is to go to the state.

"Dimitrijević, Vulović, and Malobabić were taken to the place of execution in a closed car at 1:00 A.M. [of June 26].

". . . We arrived at the place of execution at 1:30. All along the narrow path that led to it from the car Vulović talked animatedly with Lieutenant Joseph Protić [apparently a guard officer in command of the policemen who were charged with the execution]. Dimitrijević said three times: 'This is a special military service we are made to perform,' talking all the while with Captain Milan Stojković [apparently another officer of the guards] in a low voice. Malobabić said nothing.

"At the precise spot of the execution, we had to wait for twenty minutes, the time necessary to make the preparations. It was then that Dimitrijević and Vulović asked repeatedly not to be executed before dawn, and to tell the policemen to aim well, so that they would not be massacred in the dark. This was granted. When he saw me, Dimitrijević asked if I had come on behalf of the court, and when I replied that I had, and that I was obliged to read the sentence to him, he said in a bantering tone: 'Understand what has happened to me; I assure you that I am innocent.'

"I replied that as a man and a comrade I felt sorry to see him die in his best years, when he still could have rendered so many services to his country, but that according to the law he was guilty, and that he might find consolation in the certain knowledge that his death was necessary for the country and for public order. He seemed to be pleased to hear these words, for he said: 'I beg you, tell my friends that I do not regret dying under Serbian bullets, since it is for the welfare of Greater Serbia, which I hope with all my heart will soon come about. Yes, according to the law I am guilty, and what will happen had to happen. Relations [with Pašić's government?] had become too strained through my fault, and that is why it is necessary that I go.'

"Then he continued jestingly: 'But why could not one have chosen a better place for the execution, preferably on a hill, from which one could have gazed at the sea. You know, what this country lacks is a bit of solemnity.' His attitude was one of firmness; he was, however, quite changed, his face was pale and his voice trembled slightly. From time to time he consoled Rade Malobabić. When the latter reproached him by saying that it was due to him that he found himself in this spot, he replied: 'It's fate, Rade. If you had not been with me, it would not have happened to me either. If you had stayed at Kurchumlia, you and I would have remained alive.' [Malobabić, an Austrian citizen, had been Apis' top espionage agent in Austria-Hungary. After the outbreak of the war, he had been arrested and maltreated by the Serbian police. When Dimitrijević heard about this, he effected Malobabić's release. Kurchumlia was the place to which he took the "more dead than alive" ex-spy to recover from the effects of his prison experiences. As the enemy advance into Serbia continued, Malobabić begged Apis not to let him fall into Austrian hands, and Apis agreed that he should leave Kurchumlia, and accompany him on the Serbian retreat into Greece.]

"Vulović bore himself best of all. He did not lose his sense of humor for a moment. He admitted having been guilty, but not of the crime of which he was accused. When I asked for some water while reading the sentence, and when I had drunk, he addressed me with the words: 'Give me some water too, please, namesake.' Taking the jug, he added: 'Let's hope you don't have syphilis,' to which I replied that it was too late now for such worries; he laughed in an entirely natural manner.

"Malobabić was the most discouraged and beaten; he reproached himself all the time for finishing his life in this manner instead of being able to offer it freely in the cause of Serbia.

"After the sentences of both courts and the orders from headquarters concerning the executions had been read, which took from 2:00 to 4:30 [A.M.], Dimitrijević and Vulović took leave from all the officers present, bidding them adieu. Dimitrijević turned to the priest and kissed his hand, and in a low voice spoke some words to Colonel Dunić [another officer detailed to attend the execution]. The three condemned men embraced, and Dimitrijević turned toward us, saying, as he put his hand on Malobabić's shoulder: 'I affirm again that this man was a good patriot and that he was always acted for the welfare of Serbia.'

"Then the three condemned men stepped down into the ditches that had been dug for the purpose, and placed themselves in front of the stakes, Dimitrijević on the right, Vulović in the middle, and Malobabić on the left. When stepping down, Dimitrijević said: 'It seems that the ditch is not quite deep enough for me.' When it came to blindfolding Malobabić, and the latter asked that one dispense with it, Dimitrijević said: 'Let them do it, Rade, the law requires it.' After being blindfolded, Dimitrijević and Vulović cried: 'Long live Greater Serbia!' and Dimitrijević added: 'Long live Yugoslavia!' At the last moment, Vulović said: 'Adieu, Dragutin' to Dimitrijević once again, and

Dimitrijević passed on this farewell to Malobabić, adding: 'Adieu, Rade,' to which the latter made no reply.

"Although it had taken more than two hours and a half to read the sentence, dawn had not broken yet, and the three condemned men waited calmly, talking to each other from time to time in low voices. At one point, Malobabić turned almost entirely away from us, and there was talk that he was thinking of escaping and was looking for a way to do so. However, he did no such thing. All he did was to give some more instructions concerning his property which he was leaving to his family.

"The condemned Vulović threw his cane over his head from the ditch, asking that it be given to Major Alexander Savić, who should take it to his wife, and asked that his wallet be taken from his pocket.

"Malobabić succumbed after the first five shots, while the two others suffered longer, twenty shots having to be fired at each of them. No one was hit in the head.

"The doctor made the usual examination, and the condemned men were buried.

"The execution was over on June 13/26, 1917, at 4:47 in the morning."

There remains one postscript to record about the trial and execution of Apis. Thirty-six years later, in 1953, the Supreme Court of the Federal People's Republic of Yugoslavia (Princip's dream has taken on a very different shape today) retried the case of Dimitrijević and associates, and found them innocent of the charges on which they had been convicted at Salonica. The posthumous acquittal led to a public debate in Yugoslavia whether Dimitrijević and the Black Hand might not, perhaps, be considered early "progressives." The debate was ended when a government spokesman declared that while the reversal of the Salonica sentence was fully justified, the Black Hand's ideals bore no resemblance to those of modern, Communist Yugoslavia. Hence no monument, no tablet, and no street name proclaims the fame of the author of the Sarajevo murders to this day.

Prison and Death

What happened to the others? Not everyone involved in Franz Ferdinand's murder ended as violently as Dimitrijević, or the three men executed at Sarajevo. Yet for the survivors, life never was the same after the First World War and the peace that, ending it, decreed the dissolution of Austria-Hungary and the establishment of a number of successor states which included the new kingdom of Yugoslavia.

Curinaldi, the Presiding Judge at Princip's trial, quietly lived out the last years of his life at a Jesuit retreat in Sarajevo. Pfeffer, the Investigating Judge, was appointed District Attorney a year after the trial. At the end of the war, he asked for his retirement, and subsequently published some reminiscences of Sarajevo in which he absolved the Serbian government of any responsibility for the crime, and implied that certain people in Austria—whom he would not name—might have been behind the assassination.

Zistler, the most temperamental among the defense counsel, also opted for Yugoslavia, and in the late nineteen-thirties went on a lecture tour to raise funds toward the construction of a memorial to Princip. Grbić, the Serbian border guard who had helped Princip and Grabež cross into Bosnia, was wounded and taken prisoner-of-war by the Austrians in August, 1914, but was never brought to trial.

Governor Potiorek and Minister of Finance Bilinski, whose Ministry in Vienna held the ultimate authority over the affairs of Bosnia and Herzegovina, engaged in a bitter and protracted argument in which they accused each other of not having done enough to prevent Franz Ferdinand's murder. Potiorek, who had long thought war with Serbia inevitable, and who immediately after the crime urged Vienna to use force against Belgrade, was put in supreme command of the Southeastern front when war came. He won some brilliant initial victories, which brought his troops deep into Serbia, but in December, 1914, he was forced to retreat in disastrous haste, and was relieved of his command. His greatest failing, apparently, had been his ignorance of actual conditions in the field. He directed all operations from his office at headquarters, communicating even with his chief of staff by means of written notes only. For all his considerable talents, Potiorek had always been an unsociable and lonely man, but an added reason why he would never leave his office for an inspection of the front, Vienna gossip had it, was that ever since Princip had almost shot him instead of Sophie on June 28, he lived in perpetual fear of his personal safety. He died in the Austrian province of Carinthia in 1933, at the age of eighty. "When," read one obituary, "he walked through the streets of Klagenfurt in simple civilian clothes, rucksack on his shoulders to do his shopping, as he did until the last years of his life, no one could have seen that this man had once been so powerful, proud, and unapproachable."

Bilinski, when peace came, for a while served in the government of the newly created Republic of Poland as Minister of Finance, but as an acquaintance noted, "he soon returned to Austria, chagrined, and lived mostly in Vienna, or during the summer in Ischl, amidst his memories of the Empire that was no more." Emperor Franz Joseph, at the age of 86, collapsed while going over some state papers on a cold November morning in 1916. He had been trying to observe his usual work schedule despite his age, and despite the fact that he was suffering from a severe case of pneumonia. He died during the evening of November 21, surrounded by his daughters, by the Heir to the Throne, and by a number of old servants.

Konopisht castle, from which Franz Ferdinand had started on his fateful journey, was seized by the government of the new Czechoslovak republic after the First World War. In 1938, after the Nazi occupation of Austria, the Gestapo arrested both of Franz Ferdinand's sons, Duke Maximilian and Duke Ernst, and sent them to Dachau concentration camp. One of their Austrian fellow-inmates remembers having met them, "unbowed, and encouraging everyone by their example. Even in their dirty, torn prison clothing they remained gentlemen, true noblemen. In what little free time we had, they sat in the dusty road with us, sharing the few pieces of sugar one had somehow got hold of. There was not a person in the whole camp who did not speak of the 'Hohenbergs' with the greatest respect." After the end of the Second World War, Duke Maximilian von Hohenberg for several years served as mayor of Artstetten, and in 1956, his son Franz Ferdinand—namesake and grandson of the murdered Archduke—married Princess Elizabeth of Luxembourg in Luxembourg's Cathedral of Notre Dame.

Pašić, the Serbian Prime Minister, played a leading role in Yugoslav politics until his death in 1926. In the final years of his life, he was rumored to be working on a manuscript which would tell his side of the Sarajevo story, but no such book ever appeared.

Of the assassins and their helpers, only a handful lived long enough to witness the defeat of Austria, and the creation of the Yugoslav state for which they had hoped and killed. Old Mitar Kerović, the farmer, died in prison, as did young Marko Perina, Čabrinović's friend, who had been among those initiated into the plot. Nedjelko Čabrinović, the bomb-thrower and ex-anarchist, died in Theresienstadt prison at the end of January, 1916, of the tuberculosis he had contracted before his arrest. At the end of the previous year, Franz Werfel, the playwright and novelist, who was serving with the Austrian army at the time, happened to see him briefly, and came away profoundly impressed by the meeting. Čabrinović, he wrote later, was pitifully weak, and looked like "a ghost who is about to dissolve." Yet the expression of his face looked to Werfel "turned deeply and nobly inward," and a power born of his obvious convictions seemed to radiate from him—"I do not believe that anyone dealing with this shadow [of a man] could escape this force." A month after Čabrinović's death followed that of Grabež. In his case, too, the cause was tuberculosis.

Princip, deeply grieved by the loss of his friends, and suffering, as they had, from tuberculosis in its most cruel form, died during the last year of the war, on the evening of April 28, 1918, in the hospital of Theresienstadt prison. His illness seems to have made his last years a period of physical torture. Not enough is known of the conditions of Princip's and his friends' imprisonment to pass any judgment on their jailers, or to say what might have been done to ease their final sufferings, but the evidence of three deaths in two years alone reflects little credit on the Austro-Hungarian authorities.

Not one among the youths ever revealed what he really

knew about Sarajevo. Even when visited by a psychiatrist in 1916, Princip, while speaking freely about his dreams and feelings, took care to emphasize that the idea of the murder had been his and his alone.

Only three of the assassins survived the war—Popović, Čubrilović, and Mehmedbašić. Young Cvijetko Popović, sentenced to thirteen years in prison at the Sarajevo trial, was released after the collapse of Austria, as was the other young local high-school student, Vaso Čubrilović. Čubrilović, after teaching high school in Sarajevo for a number of years, went on to become a university professor. After the Second World War, he joined Tito's government as minister of forests, and at present is a professor of history at the University of Belgrade, where he is offering a course in nineteenth-century Serbia. Popović also chose an educator's career. He advanced to high-school supervisor and at present is Curator of the Ethnographic Department of the Sarajevo Museum. Muhamed Mehmedbašić, pardoned in 1919, along with the other survivors of the Salonica trial, went back to Sarajevo, where he made a modest living as a gardener and occasionally as a carpenter, his old trade. There he died during the Second World War.

In 1920, the mortal remains of Princip, Čabrinović, and Grabež were solemnly transferred from Theresienstadt—now in Czechoslovakia—to Yugoslavia, and reburied in the Sarajevo cemetery, in a simple and impressive grave, whose only ornament consists of three large stone slabs. Princip rests in the middle, under a raised slab; to his left lie Čabrinović and Grabež, and their mentor Žerajić; to his right lie the men who were executed after the Sarajevo trial, or who died in prison.

A memorial which the Austrians had erected in honor of Franz Ferdinand and Sophie near the place of the assassination was razed soon after the war. The Lateiner Bridge, where Princip fired his fatal shots, now bears the name of Princip Bridge; the street in which Ilić's house stands, and where Princip stayed with his friend after returning from Belgrade, has been renamed Ilić Street. On the pavement in front of Schiller's store, Princip's footprints have been scooped out, to show exactly where he stood when he shot his two victims, and after the Second World War, a Princip Museum was founded in Sarajevo. Some years before this, a black marble tablet was unveiled over the door of Schiller's store, in the presence of Ilić's aged mother, and of other relatives of the assassins. The inscription, in gold letters, reads: "On this historic spot, Gavrilo Princip initiated freedom on Saint Vitus' Day, June 15/28, 1914."

dispensable works on their general subject, contain a great deal of original material on Franz Ferdinand and Sarajevo. A short biographical essay that is interesting primarily because of its author is Winston Churchill, "The Victim of Sarajevo," *The Saturday Review*, CLII (London, 1931), pp. 388–389.

Personal recollections which mention Franz Ferdinand and his family in passing are *Im Weltkriege* (Berlin, 1919), by Count Ottokar Czernin, who became Austro-Hungarian Foreign Minister at the end of the World War; and *Ein Leben für Ungarn* (Bonn, 1953), by Admiral Nicholas von Horthy, a former aide to Franz Joseph, and Regent of Hungary in the postwar period. (An English translation of Horthy's book entitled *Memoirs*, appeared in London in 1956.) Franz Ferdinand's own description of his world tour, *Tagebuch meiner Reise um die Erde* (2 vols., Vienna, 1895–96) is too carefully edited to be very revealing.

One of the best accounts of Mayerling is that by Egon Caesar Conte Corti, *Elisabeth* (Salzburg, 1934), pp. 412–428, (translated as *Elizabeth, Empress of Austria* [New Haven, 1936], pp. 388–403.) and a summary of most of the rumors extant about the tragedy will be found in Ernest Cormons (the pseudonmym for an Austro-Hungarian official named Emanuel Urbas), *Schicksale und Schatten* (Salzburg, 1951), pp. 34–45. For a strange premonition which Rudolf seems to have had that not he but his cousin Franz Ferdinand would inherit the throne, see Count Hoyos' contemporary memorandum on Mayerling in Jean de Bourgoing, ed., *Briefe Kaiser Franz Josephs an Frau Katharina Schratt* (Vienna, 1949), p. 137.

On Franz Ferdinand's illness and character, two authors should be consulted in addition to the biographies and recollections cited above. One, whose approach is friendly, is his military aide—Carl Freiherr von Bardolff, *Soldat im alten Österreich* (Jena, 1938), and "Franz Ferdinand," *Die Kriegsschuldfrage* (hereafter cited as *KSF.*), V (1927), pp. 599–608. (Published from 1923 to 1944, *KSF.*—its subtitle varies, and its main title was changed to *Berliner Monatshefte* in 1929—is a journal that will be cited frequently here. Aided by a covert subsidy from the German Foreign Ministry, *KSF.* set itself the admitted task of disproving the Versailles allegation of Germany's war guilt. But despite its obvious bias, *KSF.* yields much valuable and original material on Sarajevo, particularly in its translations of Serbo-Croatian articles not easily accessible otherwise.) The other, which is much more critical, is Albert Freiherr von Margutti, *Vom alten Kaiser* (Leipzig and Vienna, 1921). Margutti was for many years aide to Emperor Franz Joseph. His memoirs, while always entertaining and gossipy, must be read with some caution, since some of the stories he tells fall short of being wholly reliable. Perhaps the most revealing single document is a character sketch written by a military associate of Franz Ferdinand's, Colonel Brosch, in 1913 (it was so frank an evaluation that Brosch thought of burning it), which is printed in Chlumecky, pp. 354–362. For the Archduke's marriage, see the notes on the following chapter.

CHAPTER II: Emperor and Nephew

To see the story of both Franz Ferdinand's marriage and of his relationship with his uncle, the Emperor, in perspective, one must examine the literature on Franz Joseph as well as that on Franz Ferdinand. Oddly enough, there is no really satisfactory biography of the Emperor. Of the three existing full-length biographies, two—Eugene Bagger, *Francis Joseph* (New York, 1928) and Karl Tschuppik, *Franz Joseph I* (Hellerau, 1928)—are too superficial and unreliable to be of any real value. The third—Joseph Redlich, *Emperor Francis Joseph* (New York, 1929)—while very much superior to the other two, is perhaps the least successful work of an otherwise distinguished scholar. A more recent book, Ottokar Janatschek, *The Emperor Franz Joseph* (London, 1953) is almost pure fiction. The best account is a brief and sensitive sketch by Heinrich Ritter von Srbik, "Franz Joseph I," which appeared in the *Historische Zeitschrift* (hereafter cited as *H.Z.*) for 1931 (CXLIV, pp. 509–526).

Important memoirs and documents bearing on the conflict between Emperor and Archduke, and on the latter's marriage, are Czernin; Friedrich Funder, *Vom Gestern ins Heute* (Vienna, 1952); Nikitsch, Margutti, and Rudolf Sieghart, *Die letzten Jahrzehnte einer Grossmacht* (Berlin, 1932), which contains the texts of some of Franz Ferdinand's desperate appeals for help to the Austrian Prime Minister during the height of the marriage crisis. Franz Joseph's letters to his friend Frau Katharina Schratt, edited by Bourgoing, yield disappointingly little.

From an American point of view, Theodore Roosevelt's impressions during his visit to Vienna in 1910 are particularly entertaining and illuminating. He met Franz Joseph, with whom he spoke in French, and he obviously loved Viennese society, although he noted that its world was "as remote from mine as if it had been in France before the Revolution"; Elting E. Morison, ed., *The Letters of Theodore Roosevelt*, VII (Cambridge, 1954), pp. 369–370. For some of the motives behind the German Emperor's friendly attitude toward Franz Ferdinand, see Bernhard Fürst von Bülow, *Denkwürdigkeiten*, I (Berlin, 1930), pp. 400–401 and 624–626. More official material can be found in Robert A. Kann, "Emperor William II and Archduke Franz Ferdinand in Their Correspondence," *The American Historical Review*, LVII (January 1952), pp. 323–351.

The newly married Archduke's letters about Sophie are cited from Sosnosky, pp. 34–43, where on pp. 34–35 there will also be found the text of his oath of renunciation. The story of his break with his younger brother Ferdinand Carl over the latter's marriage to a professor's daughter is told in Nikitsch, pp. 17–21. The evidence on whether Franz Ferdinand intended to observe the oath of renunciation is inconclusive. Nikitsch, p. 31, and Funder, pp. 495–496, think that he was just as happy to see his sons grow up as country gentlemen; on the other hand, Margutti, p. 141, and Albertini, II, pp. 2–3, make it clear how widely Sophie was suspected of intending to have the oath annulled after Franz Joseph's death.

Judgments on Old Austria differ widely, of course. At one end of the scale, there is the concept of the Empire as a *"Völkerkerker,"* a veritable "dungeon of nations"—or, in the words of Mazzini, "a land of slavery, of inertia, of death; an anomaly in the nineteenth century; a mystery of immobility in the universal movement of Europe." At the other end, there is Sir Winston Churchill's anger, in *The Gathering Storm* (Boston, 1948), at the peacemakers of Paris for destroying a country that "had afforded a common life, with advantages in trade and security, to a large number of peoples. . . . There is not one of the peoples or provinces that constituted the Empire of the Habsburgs to whom gaining their independence has not brought the tortures which ancient poets and theologians had reserved for the damned." His comment seems to echo Prince Otto von Bismarck's startling prophecy, made when the Chancellor successfully opposed those who favored the destruction of the Austrian Empire after the Austro-Prussian War of 1866. ". . . I could imagine," Bismarck recorded in his memoirs, "no future for the nations forming the Austrian monarchy that was acceptable to us, if the latter were destroyed by Hungarian and Slavic revolts, or if its independence was to be destroyed forever. What system was to take over in that part of Europe which up until now had been filled by the Austrian state from the Tyrol to the Bukovina? New formations in this region could only be of a permanently revolutionary nature."

This is not the place for an exhaustive bibliography on Austria-Hungary. Among more recent books in English, A. J. P. Taylor, *The Habsburg Monarchy 1809–1918*, (New Edition, London, 1948), and the early sections of Gordon Shepherd, *The Austrian Odyssey* (London, 1957) make perhaps the best starting point; the reader will easily find his way from there. Taylor has an excellent selected bibliography, which is brought up to date by Shepherd's listing of books on the subject published since the end of the Second World War. One other title worth mentioning—it seems to be listed in no bibliography—is a great novelist's charming and nostalgic panegyric to Royal and Imperial Austria: Robert Musil, *Der Mann ohne Eigenschaften*, I (Berlin, 1921), chapter 8, which has at long last been translated into English (by Eithne Wilkins and Ernst Kaiser), *The Man Without Qualities* (London, 1953).

On Franz Ferdinand's political plans, the following are essential: Fay, II, pp. 6–27; Bardolff, pp. 136–179; Kiszling, pp. 87–260 (this is revealing also for Franz Ferdinand's anti-Magyar and other prejudices); Funder, pp. 505–507; Albertini, II, pp. 7–18 (the broken pot quotation will be found on p. 16); Chlumecky, "Franz Ferdinands Aussenpolitik," *Berliner Monatshefte* (hereafter cited as *B.M.*), XII (1934), pp. 455–466; and the pro-Serbian R. W. Seton-Watson, *Sarajevo* (London, n.d.), pp. 80–91.

CHAPTER III: The Trip to Sarajevo

The precise date of Potiorek's first invitation is in some doubt, as are his motives for extending it. The fullest account of the trip's genesis, based on voluminous notes taken at the time, will be found in the memoirs of the Chief of the Austro-Hungarian General Staff and close associate of Franz Ferdinand, Count Franz Conrad von Hötzendorf, *Aus meiner Dienstzeit*, III (Vienna, 1923), pp. 445–447, 622, 700, and 702. The chagrin which the manner of Franz Ferdinand's acceptance caused at court is recorded in Margutti, pp. 145–147.

The definitive account of the annexation crisis and its origins is Bernadotte E. Schmitt, *The Annexation of Bosnia 1908–1909* (Cambridge, 1937). For a shorter summary, there is the excellent *History of the Modern World* by R. R. Palmer (New York, 1954). Doré Ogrizek, *La Yougoslavie* (Paris, 1955) has a handsomely illustrated description of the region involved, while the detailed maps in that classic among travel guides, Karl Baedeker, *Austria-Hungary* (Leipzig, 1911) are unsurpassed. Franz Ferdinand's worried comment about the annexation is from Chlumecky, pp. 99–100. For similar thoughts expressed by other Austrians see Conrad, I, p. 174; Margutti, p. 27; and Nikitsch, pp. 119–120. A good account of Bosnia-Herzegovina's postannexation constitution, of the quality of Austrian administration, and of conditions in general is that by Josef Brauner, "Bosnien und Herzegovina. Politik, Verwaltung und leitende Personen vor Kriegsausbruch," *B. M.*, VII (1929), pp. 313–344, which should be compared with the revelant passages in Jozo Tomasevich, *Peasants, Politics, and Economic Change in Yugoslavia* (Stanford, 1955). The connection between the region's economic ills and the Sarajevo plot is stressed in Wladyslaw

Gluck, *Sarajewo, Historja Zamachu Sarajewskiego* (Cracow, 1935).

A sympathetic description of the Greater Serbia movement and of the 1903 Revolution is that of Seton-Watson. A more balanced work, based on many Serbo-Croat sources generally inaccessible to the Western reader, is Wayne S. Vucinich, *Serbia Between East and West, The Events of 1903–1908* (Stanford, 1954). The best summaries in English of the Bosnian revolutionary movement and of Gaćinović's life and writings are in Fay and Seton-Watson, where suggestions for further reading will also be found.

Several writers have claimed that Vienna received some more or less concrete warnings against the trip, but with the evidence so far available the truth of these claims is impossible to establish. The following sources should be consulted on this subject, which is well summed up in Bernadotte E. Schmitt, "July 1914: Thirty Years After," *The Journal of Modern History* (hereafter cited as *J.M.H.*), XVI (1944), p. 173; Bardolff, p. 181; "Dr. Bilinski über das Attentat von Sarajevo," *Neue Freie Presse*, No. 21479, Vienna, June 28, 1924; August Urbański von Ostrymiecz, "Mein Beitrag zur Kriegsschuldfrage," *B.M.*, IV (1926), pp. 84–85, and the same author's "Conrad von Hötzendorf und die Reise des Thronfolgers nach Sarajevo," *ibid.*, VII (1929), p. 466; Funder, pp. 480–485; Maurice Muret, "L'Attentat de Sarajevo," *La Revue de Paris*, LX (1932), p. 102; Anton Rémy-Berzencovich, "Die Wahrheit über Sarajevo," *Neues Wiener Tagblatt* (hereafter cited as *N.W.T.*), October 3, 1925; Emil Seeliger, "Aus den Geheimakten des Sarajevoer Attentats," *ibid.*, June 29, 1924; and I. A. Žibert, *Der Mord von Sarajevo und Tiszas Schuld an dem Weltkriege* (Ljubljana, 1919). Rémy-Berzencovich and Seeliger are dubious sources, and Žibert is a totally unreliable one. On the responsibility for the security arrangements see, in addition to the above, the letter from Bilinski to Potiorek of July 3, 1914, in the collection of Austrian diplomatic documents edited by Ludwig Bittner and others, *Österreich-Ungarns Aussenpolitik von der Bosnischen Krise 1908 bis zum Kriegsausbruch 1914* (hereafter cited as

Ö.-U.), VIII (Vienna, 1930), pp. 289–291; Albertini, II, pp. 111–115; Fay, II, pp. 48–49; and Seton-Watson, p. 107.

On the subject of the Archduke's forebodings, real or alleged, see Czernin, p. 57; Funder, p. 498; Conrad, III, p. 700; Prince Ludwig Windischgraetz, *Vom roten zum schwarzen Prinzen* (Berlin, 1920), pp. 49–50 (this is another very dubious source); and also Joseph M. Baernreither, *Fragments of a Political Diary* (London, 1930), p. 158. The incident of Bardolff's call is told in Nikitsch, pp. 210–211. For the rumors as well as the facts about the Konopisht meeting with Emperor Wilhelm, see the summary in Fay, II, pp. 32–43; the personal recollections of Andreas Freiherr von Morsey, "Konopisht und Sarajevo; *B.M.*, XII (1934); the fanciful allegations by Henry Wickham Steed, *Through Thirty Year,* I (New York, 1924), p. 396–399 and by Jules Chopin (the pseudonym of Jules E. Pichon), *Le Complot de Sarajevo* (Paris, 1918); and Minister von Trautler's version of the actual events in Karl Kautsky, ed., *Die Deutschen Dokumente zum Kriegausbruch 1914,* I (New Edition, Berlin, 1927), pp. 5–8.

The principal unpublished documents from the Austrian Archives (the *Österreichisches Staatsarchiv* at Vienna) bearing on Franz Ferdinand's and Sophie's trip to Bosnia are the travel program issued by the Archduke's Military Chancellery, of which 400 copies were printed for official distribution, and the report written after the event by the captain of the *Viribus Unitis*: "Programm für die Reise Seiner k. u. k. Hoheit des durchlauchtigsten Herrn Generalinspektors der gesamten bewaffneten Macht Erzherzogs Franz Ferdinand nach Bosnien und der Herzegovina vom 23. bis 30. Juni 1914;" and "Bericht S. M. S. 'Viribus unitis' vom 1. Juli 1914 über Vorfallenheiten in der Zeit vom 23. Juni bis 1. Juli 1914; Res. Nr. 382." A microfilm of these documents and of all other material from the Austrian Archives here cited—most of which comes from the *Kriegsarchiv*—has been deposited in the Hoover Institution on War, Revolution, and Peace at Stanford.

The principal published sources on the trip and its incidents are: Nikitsch, pp. 209–213; Morsey, *B.M.*, XII, pp. 490–491; Paul Höger, "Erinnerungen an die Todesfahrt," *Österreichische*

Wehrzeitung, No. 26, June 27, 1924; "Der Reiseweg des Erzherzogs Franz Ferdinand nach Bosnien und die Wege der Attentäter von Belgrad nach Sarajevo," *KSF.*, V (1927), pp. 226–230 (which has a good map, as does Fay, II, p. 47); Conrad, IV, p. 13; and Kiszling, pp. 291–292. Of considerable value for details and local color are contemporary press reports, particularly those of the *Sarajevoer Tagblatt* (the speech of the Mayor of Mostar has been translated from the issue of June 26, 1914).

CHAPTER IV: The Conspirators

Fay, II, pp. 76–85 has an excellent summary of the *Narodna Odbrana's* activities. One of his most useful sources is a book which, while written to plead the Serbian case, inadvertently revealed far more than the author intended: Stanoje Stanojević, *Ubistvo Austriskog Prestolonaslednika Ferdinanda* (Belgrade, 1923); German translation by Hermann Wendel, *Die Ermordung des Erzherzogs Franz Ferdinand* (Frankfurt, 1923).

The indispensable primary source on the Black Hand is the transcript of the trial of Dimitrijević and associates at Salonica in 1917, which is described in chapter XIX: *Tajna Prevratna Organizatsija* (Salonica, 1918). This is as strange a document as any. It is a garbled and censored record: most of the proceedings are paraphrased rather than quoted in full, and the evidence bearing on the Black Hand's foreign activities has been deleted. Published by the Serbian Government in an effort to destroy Dimitrijević's reputation, it was withdrawn when it became apparent how much incriminating material the record still contained and today is a bibliographical rarity. A German translation was published in 1933 (*Der Saloniki Prozess*, edited by Professor Hans Uebersberger); but no English translation has ever appeared. When supplemented by a number of postwar revelations, it is possible to reconstruct many of those Black Hand secrets which the faithful member was supposed to take into the grave with him.

The most important of these sources—whose reliability is often less than certain, and whose facts need constant checking—are the following books and articles by Miloš Bogićević: *Le Procès de Salonique Juin 1917* (Paris, 1927); *Le Colonel*

Dragutin Dimitrijević (Paris, 1928); "Die serbische Gesellschaft 'Vereinigung oder Tod,' genannt die 'Schwarze Hand,' " *KSF.*, IV (1926), pp. 664–676; and "Mord und Justizmord," *Süddeutsche Monatshefte*, XXVI (1929), pp. 331–369, a summary of *Le Procès* and *Le Colonel.* (Bogićević, a Serbian diplomat before 1914, chose to become an émigré after the war, publishing a great deal of pro-Dimitrijević and anti-Pašić literature, in which the facts are not always easy to separate from liberal amounts of rumor and conjecture. The spelling of his name differs in various publications). Further sources are: Stanojević; [Čedomir A. Popović], "Das Sarajevoer Attentat und die Organization 'Vereinigung oder Tod;' " *B.M.*, X (1932), pp. 1097–1121 (an attempted exoneration of the Black Hand, this is a translation of the major portion of an article which originally appeared in the Zagreb *Nova Evropa*); Henry Pozzi, *Black Hand Over Europe* (London, 1935); the reader had best be very skeptical here, for Pozzi's reliability is next to impossible to assess); and Dobrovoi R. Lazarević, *Die Schwarze Hand* (Lausanne, 1917); wildly prejudiced against Pašić and the Black Hand, Lazarević makes perhaps the most questionable of all the witnesses listed here).

There are English translations of some key documents in Edith M. Durham, *The Sarajevo Crime* (London, 1925). This is a book whose value is marred by its extreme anti-Serbian bias. An outstanding recent account, based on all the available sources and on interviews with Black Hand survivors, will be found in Albertini, II, pp. 25–35, which has the additional attraction to the reader unfamiliar with Italian of offering some extensive quotations from Luciano Magrini, *Il Dramma di Saraiewo* (Milan, 1929).

Most of the titles cited above should also be consulted for the facts of Apis' career and for the genesis of the plot. In addition, Vucinich, pp. 47–51, has an excellent description of Apis' role in 1903, which has been followed here. The same author is planning a review article on recent Serbo-Croat publications on Dimitrijević, which is to appear in the *Journal of Modern History*. The difficulties of arriving at the truth about the origins of the assassination are compounded by the fact that the few surviving plotters who could be persuaded to talk about the subject usually did so only years afterwards, and that the youths who were arrested and tried by the Austrians in 1914 deliberately and quite legitimately lied in order to obscure the role played by their associates in Belgrade.

For Apis' confession, see Stoyan Gavrilović, "New Evidence on the Sarajevo Assassination," and Bernadotte E. Schmitt, "Comment," *J.M.H.*, XXVII (1955), pp. 410–414. The story of Ilić's trip has been told by Colonel Popović to Albertini (II, p. 79). On the Toulouse meeting, and on Mehmedbašić's fiasco, see *ibid.*, pp. 78–79; as well as Miloš Bogićević, "Nouvelles dépositions concernant l'attentat de Sarajevo," *KSF.*, IV (1926), pp. 21–28. The Italian friend to whom Pašić revealed his fears about Franz Ferdinand was Count Carlo Sforza, Italy's Foreign Minister after both the First and Second World Wars. It is recorded in his *Makers of Modern Europe* (Indianapolis, n. d.), p. 50. For Apis' contacts with the Russian military attaché, see *J.M.H.*, XXVII, pp. 410–414; Albertini, II. 81–86; Miloš Bogićević, "Weitere Einzelheiten über das Attentat von Sarajevo," *B. M.*, III (1925), pp. 15–21 and 437–444; and Victor M. Artamonov, "Erinnerungen an meine Militärattachézeit in Belgrade," *ibid.*, XVI (1938), pp. 583–602. Perhaps the most intriguing of recent theories about Apis' motives as that set forth by A. J. P. Taylor in "Murder at Sarajevo," *The Observer*, November 16, 1958. Apis, the distinguished British historian maintains, was guided entirely by domestic considerations, and Sarajevo was to be nothing but a tactical move in his power struggle with Pašić. In the absence of any supporting evidence, and in the face of some definite misstatements (such as the claim that no precautionary arrests at all were made in Sarajevo in June, 1914, or that the news of Franz Ferdinand's visit had not yet appeared in the press when Princip said it had, and that he therefore must have received the information from Dimitrijević) Taylor's theory, while novel, remains pure conjecture.

CHAPTER V: The Preparations

By far the major source here is the transcript of the trial of Franz Ferdinand's murderers held at Sarajevo. There are three versions of the trial record. The first to appear was a German edition, *Der Prozess gegen die Attentäter von Sarajevo, Nach dem amtlichen Stenogramm der Gerichtsverhandlung akten-mässig dargestellt* (Berlin, 1918), edited by "Professor Pharos," a pseudonym for the Jesuit Father Puntigam. This is a disgraceful piece of work. There are frequent deletions in the text, with no editorial indication that such deletions have been made; elsewhere, different statements have been made; elsewhere, different statements have been combined into one or paraphrased, again without any open acknowledgment that the original text has been tampered with. A vastly better edition is the French one: Albert Mousset, ed., *Un Drame historique, L'attentat de Sarajevo, documents inédits et texte intégral des sténogrammes du procès* (Éditions Payot, Paris, 1930). Here, too, one can not be sure that the text always reproduces precisely what was said in court, although Mousset claims to be offering a straight translation of the daily shorthand reports of the trial sent from Sarajevo to Vienna. It is a far more reliable source than Pharos, however. More recently there appeared a Croatian version of the record which is also superior to Pharos: Vojislav Bogićević, *Sarajevski Atentat, Izvorne Stenografske Bilješke Sa Glavne Rasprave Protiv Gavrila Principa i Drugova, Održane u Sarajevu 1914 G* (Sarajevo, 1954), which claims to be more accurate than either Pharos or Mousset. That the claim is true in the case of Pharos is evident; whether it is so in that of Mousset is open to doubt. An English translation of Bogićević is being planned; it is to be hoped that it will appear before too long. All quotations here are from Mousset.

Next in importance to the trial record are the interrogation reports of which sometimes several a day were sent from Sarajevo to Vienna during the police investigation of the crime. Practically all of these are printed in the Austrian diplomatic documents, *Ö.–U.*, VIII; only one or two others will be found in the Austrian Archives. Needless to say, what was said at the trial must be read skeptically. (Many writers, for example, have followed the story told by Princip and Čabrinović that they resolved to kill Franz Ferdinand only after receiving a mysterious press clipping from Bosnia, an explanation which does not ring true, and which therefore has not been emphasized here.) If evaluated critically, however, the court record will yield a very great deal of information.

On the biographies of the major participants, on the Belgrade preparations, and on the assassins' trip, the trial transcript and interrogation reports are again indispensable, and only a few additional details can be obtained from the following (in addition to Albertini, Fay, and Seton-Watson): For the Belgrade atmosphere, and for the actual preparations: Borivoje Jevtić, *Sarajevski Atentat, Sećanja i Utisci* (Sarajevo, 1924), this has been partly translated into German, but not into English, under the title "Weitere Ausschnitte zum Attentat von Sarajevo," *KSF.,* III, pp. 657–686); Stanojević; and Ljuba Jovanović, *The Murder of Sarajevo* (London, 1925). On the biography of Tankosić: Stanojević. On that of Princip, three books of doubtful reliability: José Almira and Giv. Stoyan, *Le déclic de Sarajevo* (Paris, 1927; this is a strongly anti-Austrian account—"Its [Bosnia's] schools were closed, after the occupation, to become prisons or barracks"—which tries to compensate for its lack of facts by a false lyricism— [Princip arrived in Sarajevo] "with a heart that was entirely open and pure and a soul that was as white and chaste as the snow of his mountains;" Géza Herczeg, *Von Sarajevo bis Lodz* (Munich, 1916); the report of a Hungarian journalist who went to Belgrade a few days after the crime to retrace Princip's steps; his accuracy is questionable, but the book is worth looking at: *Gavrilo Princips Bekenntnisse* (Vienna, 1926; prison conversations with one Dr. Pappenheim; vague and unrevealing); and the document reproduced in Miloš Bogićević, *Die Auswärtige Politik Serbiens 1903–1914,* II (Berlin, 1929), pp. 525–526. On the question of whether Ciganović was Pašić's agent: Fay, II, p. 90, and Vaso Trivanović, "The Responsibility for the Sarajevo Assassination," *Current History,* XXIX (1929), pp. 987–992. For a picture of the bombs, and a description of the manner in which they worked: K. u. k. AZD., Sarajevo, to Ministry of War, July 13, 1914, in the Austrian Archives.

CHAPTER VI: PAŠIĆ

Since Serbia, alone among the powers, has never opened its diplomatic archives, many of the details about the warning to Austria must remain conjectural. The disclosure that Pašić possessed advance information about the plot, and made a futile attempt to stop the assassination, was first made in 1924, in an article written by Ljuba Jovanović, who in 1914 had been Minister of Education in Pašić's Cabinet. (Jovanović, *Sarajevo*, p. 3.) The Yugoslav press, realizing the disastrous implications of Jovanović's admissions, violently attacked his article, and it is possible that his indiscretion cost him the premiership that year. In 1926, after a good deal of impatient prompting by those of his partisans who had been maintaining official Serbia's total ignorance of Sarajevo, Pašić publicly denied Jovanović's charges, and assailed his former cabinet colleague for his "unpardonable conduct."

Jovanović, expelled from his party, and his political career ended, refused to withdraw his story. All he would grant was that Pašić had made his statement not in a cabinet meeting, but in the course of a private conversation. If the Prime Minister and the Foreign Minister, he added, would take the responsibility for his doing so, he would submit documentary proof of his original assertion. Both refused. (See Albertini, II, pp. 93–94; and Seton-Watson, pp. 153–59.) Even so, to reiterate the point, the evidence on the whole subject of the Serbian warning is far from conclusive. The most that can be claimed for the version of it given in this chapter is that having considered all the fragmentary evidence that is available, it seemed plausible to the present author. What cannot be claimed for it is that it is based on incontrovertible fact.

Of the Serbian envoy's luckless interview with Bilinski, only one version has been told. It is that of Jovanović; Bilinski, in his memoirs, made no mention of the episode. Jovan Jovanović, "Meine Warnung an den Erzherzog Franz Ferdinand," *N.W.T.*, June 28, 1924, pp. 3–4. For additional evidence, and for the whole bitter argument on the question of Pašić's foreknowledge and of Jovanović's warning, which for all its violent allegations and counterallegations in the end produced little or nothing that was not contained in Jovan and Ljuba Jovanović's original disclosures, see the following:

The opposing testimony given by Roderich Gooss and Hermann Wendel before the Reichstag committee investigating the causes of the war in *Die Vorgeschichte des Weltkrieges*, X (Berlin, 1930); Alfred von Wegerer, "Neue Ausschnitte zum Attentat von Sarajevo," *KSF.*, IV (1926), pp. 400–414, "Die serbische Warnung," *ibid.*, VIII (1930), pp. 539–546, "Die Erinnerungen des Dr. Velizar Janković," *ibid.*, IX (1931), pp. 851–869, and "Der ehemalige serbische Kriegsminister über den Ausbruch des Weltkrieges," *ibid.*, IX, pp. 990–998; as well as these notes and articles in the same journal: I, pp. 82–83, II, p. 282, III, pp. 213–220, 270, and 286, VIII, pp. 324–329; Albertini, II, pp. 89–109; Fay, II, pp. 61–74 and 152–166; Seton-Watson, pp. 152–159; Bilinski, Friedrich von Wiesner, "Der Sarajevoer Mord und die Kriegsschuldfrage," *Das Neue Reich*, VI (1924), pp. 969–976; Pierre Renouvin, *The Immediate Origins of the War* (New Haven, 1928); pp. 28–29; Harold Temperley, "The Coming of the War," *Foreign Affairs*, IX (1931), pp. 330–331; *Documents diplomatiques français* (hereafter cited as *D.D.F.*), Third Series, X (Paris, 1936), No. 466 (this is a key document, since it records a statement made by the Serbian Minister in Paris, in July, 1914, to the effect that the Austrians had been warned by Serbia about the Sarajevo plot. If true, Pašić obviously must have had that foreknowledge which he later denied); *Ö.-U.*, VIII, pp. 219–220 and 220n.; Leopold Mandl, "Zur Warnung Serbians an Österreich," *KSF.*, II (1924), pp. 108–111; [Flandrak], "Die falsche Deutung der Bilinskischen Warnung durch Senator de Jouvenel," *ibid.*, VI (1928), pp. 1152–1154; Miloš Bogićević, "Die Warnung vor dem Attentate in Sarajevo," *ibid.*, II (1924), pp. 231–238; and "Weitere;" and [Edmund von Glaise-Horstenau], "Der Thronfolgermord im Lichte der heutigen Geschichtskenntnis," *N.W.T.*, June 29, 1924, pp. 2–3.

For a brief biography of Pašić, see Heinz Sasse, "Staatsmänner und Diplomaten der Vorkriegszeit, Nicola Pašić," *B.M.*, XVI

(1936), pp. 23–42. Count Carlo Sforza, *Fifty Years of War and Diplomacy in the Balkans, Pashich and the Union of the Yugoslavs* (New York, 1940), is a disappointing book.

For the meeting of the Black Hand's Central Committee, and for Apis' unkept promise, see Stanojević, p. 56; Alfred von Wegerer, *Der Ausbruch des Weltkrieges 1914*, I (Hamburg, 1939), pp. 96–97; and "R.D.I. 5 Nr. 9," *B.M.*, XII (1934), p. 507; and Popović, pp. 114–115.

CHAPTER VII: Crossing the Drina

This chapter is based almost entirely on the transcript of the Sarajevo trial (Mousset and Bogićević). On the topography of the region, and on the number of Austrian frontier guards, compare Ludwig Schnagl, "War der Grenzübertritt? . . .," *B.M.*, XIII (1934), 957–965, with the translation of Vogislav Bogićević's *Nova Evropa* article, *ibid.*, pp. 990–991. The letter from Captain Prvanović which opens the chapter was captured by Hungarian troops which occupied Mali Zvornik in August, 1914. It is printed in Wiesner, "Die Schuld der serbischen Regierung am Mord von Sarajevo," *KSF.*, VI (1928), pp. 334–335.

All quotations from the trial follow the transcript, of course. Conversations that took place during the assassins' trip are placed in quotation marks only if this is the way they appear in the transcript or in the account of some other reliable witness; conversations that are paraphrased in the sources also are paraphrased in this narrative. In other words: the temptation to make people say what they *might* have said, but did not—as far as we know—in fact say, has been resisted; neither here nor in any other part of this book are there any imaginary conversations. Admittedly, even the literal quotations of the sources are subject to some doubt, of course, since no unseen companion took any shorthand notes of what Princip said to Grbić on Isaković Island for example, and the exchanges quoted in court are plainly reconstructions made some four months after the event. To quote as Princip's words what he himself so quoted seemed justifiable, however, quite aside from the monotony that would have been produced by a dramatic narrative in which none of the protagonists is ever allowed to speak for himself.

CHAPTER VIII: Waiting

Here, too, the principal source is the trial transcript and, to a lesser extent, the interrogation reports in *Ö.-U.*, VIII. The story of the correspondence between the conspiracy's one Moslem member and Gacinovic was told by Mehemedbašić himself to Albertini (II, pp. 78–79). For an illustrated description of Ilic's house and of the room in which Princip stayed, see René Pelletier, "Les Souvenirs du drame chez la mère du régicide," *L'Illustration*, CLXXXVIII (1934), pp. 434–437. The best account of the waiting period—aside, again, from the facts uncovered at the trial—is that of Jevtić, from which Princip's "matchbox" quotation has been taken.

CHAPTER IX: Maneuvers

The story of the archducal couple's surprise visit to Sarajevo has largely been reconstructed from contemporary press accounts. The date of the visit is definitely June 25, not June 26, as assumed by some writers. (See Fay, II, p. 51; *Ö.-U.*, VIII, p. 216; and *KSF.*, V, pp. 226–227). The chance encounter between Princip and Franz Ferdinand on that occasion, and Čabrinović's trip to Ilidže that same day, have been described by Jevtić. Also worth looking up in this connection are [Albert] T'serstevens, "Étapes Yougoslaves, II, De Raguse à Sarajevo," *Revue des Deux Mondes*, XLIII (1938), pp. 127–148, which is a questionable source; and Albert Mousset, "L'Attentat de Sarajevo," *Revue d'Histoire Diplomatique*, XXXIX (1925), pp. 44–68, which is more solidly based on ascertainable fact.

Estimates on the number of troops taking part in the maneuvers differ wildly, with one Serbian writer setting it as high as 250,000 (see *B.M.*, IX, p. 854; for a wrong Austrian estimate, see Urbański, "Conrad," p. 469). The sources mainly relied on here are the printed instructions issued by Potiorek's office in the Austrian Archives, "K. u. k. Armeeinspektor in Sarajevo, Nr. 3000 von 1914, Detailbestimmungen für die grösseren

Manöver in Bosnien-Herzegovina 1914 und Anordnungen der Manöverleitung"; and the following books and articles: Conrad, VI; Ludwig Schnagl, "Die Manöver in Bosnien im Jahre 1914," *KSF.*, IV (1928), pp. 873–881; "Reiseweg"; and Höger. The story about the peddler comes from the Vienna *Reichspost* (which had sent its own special correspondent to Bosnia), No. 296, June 28, 1914; that about the court photographer from Schnagl, p. 879. Franz Ferdinand's directive to the troops is printed in Bardolff, pp. 181–182; the passage from the telegram to the Emperor of June 27 is taken from the copy in the Austrian Archives (No. 170/168).

For Sophie's trips into Sarajevo, and for the details of the farewell dinner at Ildže, see T'Serstevens, "Étapes;" and Morsey, "Konopischt." Funder, p. 484, has a report of the conversation between Sophie and Sunarić.

Morsey, p. 491; Bardolff, p. 182; and Nikitsch, pp. 214–215 agree on how close the June 28 visit came to being cancelled. The program for the day is that from the Austrian Archives which was mentioned in the notes on chapter IV.

On the matter of Ilić's alleged trip to Belgrade, see the depositions by Bastaić and Golubić in Bogićević, "Nouvelles dépositions," pp. 27–28. The other preparations have been reconstructed from the trial record, and from the story Mehmedbašić told to Albertini (II, 49). Jevtić (pp. 34–35) is the witness for Princip's last party; a later description of Semiz' wine shop is that of T'Serstevens, "Étapes."

CHAPTER X: Čabrinović

The sources for the events surrounding the departure from Ilidže and the arrival in Sarajevo—aside from the program in the Austrian Archives, from contemporary press accounts, and from the trial record—are: Höger; Nikitsch; Morsey, "Konopischt," and "Der Schicksalstag von Sarajevo, Nach eigenen Tagebuchaufzeichnungen," *Reichspost*, No. 177, June 28, 1924, pp. 1–3; Chlumecky; and Conrad, IV. Of lesser value are two tendentious accounts, one pro-Austrian, the other pro-Serb: *Sérajevo, La Conspiration Serbe contre la monarchie Austro-*

Hongroise (Berne, 1917); and Raymond Recouly, *Les Heures tragiques d'avant guerre* (Paris, n.d.).

Auffenberg-Komarów, *Aus Österreichs Höhe und Niedergang* (Munich, 1921), pp. 133–134; Baron Carl Collas, "Auf den bosnischen Spuren der Kriegsschuldigen," *KSF.*, V (1927), p. 22; Funder, pp. 445–446; and Rémy-Berzencovich, pp. 2–3, describe the security measures taken in 1910. An idea of how General Potiorek had himself guarded during major public appearances can be gleaned from Nikola Stojanović, *Le Serbie d'hier et de demain* (Paris, 1917), p. 108. The most significant unpublished document on the number of troops in Sarajevo on June 28, 1914, is the report which General von Appel sent to the War Ministry in Vienna on July 17, 1914, which is at variance with the General's undated letter printed in Chlumecky, p. 363. ("K. u. k. 15. Korpskommando an das k. u. k. Kriegsministerium, Präs. Nr. 2535" in the Austrian Archives.) For published material on the 1914 security arrangements, see, in addition to the 1910 sources, Sosnosky, p. 207; Conrad, IV, pp. 65–66; Schnagl, *B.M.*, XII, p. 964; Seton-Watson, pp. 112–114; Mousset, *Drame*, pp. 491–493; Pokrowski, ed., *Die internationalen Beziehungen im Zeitalter des Imperialismus* (the official collection of Russian diplomatic documents, hereafter cited as *I.B.*), Series I, vol. IV (Berlin, 1932), p. 123; and Albertini, II, pp. 111–115.

The account of Čabrinović's crime and arrest, and of the actions—or, more accurately, the inaction—of his associates on Franz Ferdinand's way to the City Hall has been reconstructed almost entirely from the trial record. Additional sources are the interrogation reports in *Ö.–U.*, VIII; the testimony given by Mehmedbašić and Čubrilović to Albertini, II, pp. 46–49; the affidavits from Bernstein, Morsey, and Harrach in Sosnosky, pp. 215–221; Colonel Bardolff's report in Conrad, IV, pp. 19–20; the description by General Appel in Chlumecky, pp. 363–364; Wiesner, "War Nedjéljko Čabrinović [sic] ein österreichischer Konfident?" *KSF.*, V (1927), p. 884; Seton-Watson, p. 114; Morsey, "Konopischt," pp. 492–494 and "Schicksalstag," p. 2; Recouly, p. 183; and various newspaper dispatches, particularly in *The Times* of London, and the

Neue Freie Presse (hereafter cited as *N.F.P.*) and *Reichspost* of Vienna, all of which had their own special correspondents in Sarajevo.

CHAPTER XI: Princip

This chapter, too, is based mainly on the trial transcript. Additional details come from newspaper accounts, and from the reminiscences of the various participants that were mentioned before, especially Morsey, Höger, Nikitsch, Sosnosky, and Bardolff.

Of considerable interest for the City Hall reception is the report which the Vice-Mayor of Sarajevo wired to the *N.F.P.* on the day of the murder, and which appeared in its issue of June 29: Vancas, "Die Letzten Worte des Erzherzogs Franz Ferdinand." The text of the Mayor's speech and of Franz Ferdinand's reply has been translated from the *Reichspost* of the same day (No. 298). For the City Hall discussion on the new route to be followed, Conrad, IV, pp. 20–21 should be consulted in addition to the trial record. A supposed collection of eye-witnesses' statements which appeared ten years after the event, Leonhard [...], "Der Mord von Sarajevo," *Berliner Tageblatt*, June 28, [...], is of questionable accuracy. Sophie's decision to stay with her husband is described in Morsey, "Konopischt"; her "No, Franz, I am staying with you," is from the story in the *N.F.P.* of June 29, 1914.

On the crime itself, from Princip's choice of Schiller's to the death of his victims, only one major statement will not be found in the trial transcript. It is Princip's "I aimed at the Archduke . . ."; which is recalled in L[eo] Pfeffer, *Istraga u Sarajevskom Atentatu* (Zagreb, 1938), and translated in Albertini, II, p. 43. On the precise nature of Franz Ferdinand's and Sophie's wounds, Bogićević, pp. 427 and 437, contains some medical evidence omitted in Mousset, but otherwise, the key documents are the same in both versions of the transcript. The Jesuit Father Puntigam, who came to perform the last rites at the Konak, and "Professor Pharos," editor of the mutilated German edition of the trial record, are one and the same person.

CHAPTER XII: Riots and Sympathy

The most revealing unpublished document on the riots, and on the attitude of the Sarajevo authorities toward them, is General von Appel's long letter to the Vienna War Ministry of July 17, 1914 ("K. u. k. 15. Korpskommando an das k. u. k. Kriegsministerium, Präs. Nr. 2535," in the Austrian Archives). To round it out, the following published material should also be consulted: Bilinski's reports to Vienna in *Ö.-U.*, VIII; Appel's letter to Brosch in Chlumecky, pp. 364–365; the diplomatic dispatches in G. P. Gooch and Harold Temperley, ed., *British Documents on the Origins of the War, 1898–1914* (hereafter cited as *B.D.*), XI (London, 1926), p. 15, and *I.B.*, IV, 234, pp. 236–237; and the reports in the *Arbeiter-Zeitung*, *N.F.P.*, and *Reichspost* of Vienna, and *The Times* of London. The proclamation announcing martial law is printed in the official *Wiener Zeitung (Abendpost)*, June 30, 1914. The correspondence between Bilinski and Potiorek will be found in *Ö.-U.*, VIII, pp. 227–231, 288–290; and in Conrad, IV, pp. 64–66. On the funds collected for a monument, see *Reichspost*, No. 304, July 2, 1914; and *Sarajevoer Tagblatt*, particularly the issues of July 4 and 7.

The source for Emperor Wilhelm's condolences is Kiszling, p. 303; for President Wilson's, *Papers Relating to the Foreign Relations of the United States, 1914* (Washington, 1922), p. 25. International reaction to the news of the assassination can be judged most dispassionately from the diplomatic correspondence of time: Bogićević, *A.P.S.*, I, pp. 424–425; *B.D.*, XI, pp. 19–20, 28, 55–56, *D.D.F.*, X, pp. 659–660, 662, 668, 673–679, 684; *I.B.*, IV, pp. 152–153; Kautsky, I, p. 16; *Ö.-U.*, VIII, pp. 209–212, 218–219, 270–271, 292–293, 296–297, 321, 325–326, 361, 376–380, 699–700.

The Mussolini comment is cited from Sosnosky, p. 224. Other editorial opinion is summarized in Albertini, II, 270–271. Janković's experiences have been recounted by himself (*B.M.*, IX, pp. 851–869) as were Jovanović's (*Murder*, p. 8). Additional sources worth consulting, particularly for the repercussions in

Austria, are newspapers and the following memoirs: Bilinski, *N.F.P.,* pp. 9–10; Cormons, pp. 156–158; Funder, p. 485; Nikitsch, pp. 216–217; Redlich, *Tagebuch,* I, p. 235 (which contains the "God meant to be kind to Austria" quotation); Sieghart, pp. 242–243; Stanojević, pp. 43–44; Windischgraetz, p. 50. Franz Joseph's alleged "A higher force" comment is recorded in Margutti, pp. 147–148. Its accuracy is questioned in Kiszling, p. 344, n. 18, and Sosnosky, p. 233 n. For a very different account of the Emperor's supposed first words ("Horrible, horrible! No sorrow is spared me") see the story in *The New York Times* of June 29, 1914.

For the reception of the news in Hungary, where perhaps even fewer tears were shed than in Vienna, see the dispatch of the British Consul General in Budapest reporting "an especially large attendance at the races" on June 29 (*B.D.,* XI, pp. 55–56) and the alleged comment of the Hungarian Prime Minister: "God has wanted it this way, and we must be grateful to God for *everything*" (Stanojević, pp. 43–44).

CHAPTER XIII: A Strange Funeral

There is a moving account of Franz Joseph's return to Schönbrunn in Margutti, p. 153, which is borne out to be the *N.F.P.* report of June 29, 1914, and by Conrad, IV, p. 32. Bardolff, p. 183, and Conrad, IV, p. 37, quote the author's conversations with the Emperor.

The date of the *N.F.P.* editorial criticizing the Sarajevo authorities is June 30, 1914. Tisza's blunt comment was made during a meeting of the Council of Ministers in Vienna on July 7 (*Ö.–U.,* VIII, p. 347); Franz Joseph's kind words for Potiorek were recorded by Bilinski (*ibid.,* p. 227).

Unpublished documents in the Austrian Archives on the return of the bodies to Vienna, and on the whole, sad funeral farce, are General Paar's telegram to the War Ministry in Vienna of June 28, 1914; the "Bericht S. M. S. *Viribus Unitis,*" Res. Nr. 382, of July 1; the War Ministry's telegram to the 2. and 3. Korpskommando of July 2, 9:30 A.M.; the dispatch, Res. Nr. 848 M.A., sent by the Seebezirkskommando, Trieste, to the

War Ministry on July 3; and, as the key document, Montenuovo's "Zeremoniell der Einholung, Exponierung, Einsegnung
und Überführung der Leichen weiland Seiner kaiserlichen und
königlichen Hoheit des durchlauchtigsten Erzherzogs Franz
Ferdinand von Österreich-Este und Ihrer Hoheit Sophie
Herzogin von Hohenberg," which was printed for official distribution only, and which has been relied on heavily here.
Published sources are the various memoirs and newspapers
mentioned before.

Good descriptions in English of the Hofburg chapel service
are those of *The New York Times* of July 4, 1914, and of the
British envoy in *B.D.*, XI, p. 26. The angry witness who has
recorded the Emperor's apparent indifference is Nikitsch, pp.
219–220. On the absence of foreign royalty, see Kautsky, I, pp.
11–12 and 14; *D.D.F.*, X, p. 652; *Ö.-U.*, VIII, pp. 312 and 336;
Nikitsch, p. 221; Margutti, p, 151, and the *Berliner Tageblatt*
of July 2, 1914.

How the aristocracy broke into the cortège is told in
Nikitsch, p. 220; Windischgraetz, pp. 51–52; *D.D.F.*, X, pp.
712–714; Kiszling, pp. 303–304; and Seton-Watson, p. 104.
More details, as well as some pointed criticism, will be found
in Fritz Fellner, ed., *Das politische Tagebuch Josef Redlichs
1908–1919*, I (Graz, 1953), p. 236; and in the contemporary
press, particularly the *Arbeiter-Zeitung, N.F.P.,* and *Reichspost,*
whose No. 310 of July 5 contains the editorial comparing Franz
Ferdinand's funeral with that given to the airmen. The French
writer commenting on Vienna's "tact, dignity, and kindness"
is Muret, *Revue de Paris*, LX, p. 115. Franz Joseph's letter to
Montenuovo was published in the official *Wiener Zeitung* of
July 7, 1914; the words "on the Emperor's orders" will be found
on Montenuovo's handwritten instructions of June 30 ("Seiner
k. und k. Apost. Majestät Obersthofmeisteramt") in the
Austrian Archives.

Concerning the trip from Vienna to Artstetten, the tragi-
comedy at Pöchlarn station, and the final funeral services, our
best sources are Nikitsch, pp. 220–225; Eisenmenger, pp. 265–
266; and the dispatches to the *Reichspost*.

CHAPTER XIV: The Investigation

The detailed reports on the progress of the investigation which Potiorek sent to his superiors in Vienna as often as three times a day form the primary source for this chapter. Most of them are printed in *Ö.-U.*, VIII. Since the published Austrian documents end with August 1, 1914, however, there are some important unpublished Potiorek reports in the Austrian Archives, notably on the arrest of Mičić, Milović, and Milošević, on the capture of the Serbain border guard Grbić, and on the strange scene between Princip and Čabrinović on August 15. (Potiorek to Bilinski, August 11, 16, and 23, 1914. The critical reader may also be interested to know that a comparison of the earlier documents in the archives with the versions printed in *Ö.-U.* has shown no essential discrepancies between the two.) Additional facts on Ilić's loss of nerve, and on the circumstances of Grabež's, Čubrilović's, and Popović's, arrest, can be found in the transcript of the Sarajevo trial. Judge Pfeffer's memoirs (unless otherwise noted the quotations cited here follow the translations in Albertini and in *KSF.*, IV, p. 719) should be used with caution; his version of events frequently clashes with that of the reports written at the time. His press statement referred to was given to the *Budapesti Hirlap* of July 2, and is summed up in the *Arbeiter-Zeitung* of July 3, 1914.

The story of how the defendants communicated secretly from cell to cell was first revealed by Jevtić (pp. 54–56) and confirmed by Vaso Čubrilović to Albertini (II, p. 59). For allegations of mistreatment in prison, and for a convincing refutation of these charges, see Rebecca West's overwrought *Black Lamb and Grey Falcon*, I (New York, 1941), p. 373; Mousset, pp. 175–176 and 346, and the same author's article in *Revue d'Histoire Diplomatique*, XXXIX, 59; Pfeffer, *Istraga*, pp. 27, 50, 54–55; Jevtić, pp. 47–48; Seton-Watson, p. 150; Herczeg, p. 19; and Albertini, II, p. 45 n. How Mehmedbašić escaped into Montenegro, and how the authorities there successfully frustrated his pursuers, is told in the Austrian diplomatic correspondence (*Ö.-U.*, VIII, pp. 314, 392–393, 414, 432, 451, 475, 502, 580–

581, 709–710) and in the amusing dispatch of the French Minister in Cetinje, M. Delaroche-Vernet, to Paris in *D.D.F.*, X, pp. 766–767.

CHAPTER XV: War

The story of the investigation made by the Vienna Foreign Ministry's emissary has been told by Friedrich von Wiesner himself in several articles: most fully in "Meine Depesche vom 13. Juli 1914," in Eduard von Steinitz, ed., *Rings um Sasonov* (Berlin, 1928), but also in "Der Sarajevoer Mord," *Das Neue Reich,* VI, pp. 972–973, and "Die unwiderlegt gebliebene Begründung für das Ultimatum Österreichs an Serbien vom Juli 1914," *KSF.*, V (1927), pp. 499–501. The crucial telegram in which Wiesner summed up his conclusions is printed in *Ö.–U.*, VIII, pp. 436–437; Potiorek's emphatic disagreement with Wiesner's findings in Conrad, IV, 82–85.

[Alexander] Freiherr von Musulin, *Das Haus am Ballplatz* (Munich, 1924), pp. 222–223, and Cormons, pp. 165–166, have some details on how the Austrian ultimatum was drafted, and why its completion took so long. The ultimatum itself, and Vienna's instructions to Giesl, will be found in *Ö.–U.*, VIII, pp. 284–289, 515, 518–519, and 594–595. For the unusual circumstances of its presentation, see *ibid.*, p. 596; Steinitz, ed., *Zwei Jahrzehnte im Nahen Orient, Aufzeichnungen des Generals der Kavallerie Baron Wladimir Giesl* (Berlin, 1927), pp. 266–267; and Albertini, II, p. 285.

For some of the reasons behind the startling absence of any reference to the Black Hand in the Austrian ultimatum, see Wiesner, "Depesche," in Steinitz, *Rings,* pp. 185–186, and "Das Gutachten von Gooss," *B.M.*, X (1932), pp. 558–560; Ludwig Bittner, "Österreich-Ungarn und Serbien," *Historische Zeitschrift,* CXLIV (1931), pp. 91–92, and "Die Schwarze Hand," *B.M.*, X (1932), pp. 64–65; and Albertini, II, pp. 28 and 64–68. The information contained in the Austrian dossier sent to the powers after relations with Serbia were broken is no better; see *Ö.-U.*, VIII, pp. 665–704, and Wiesner, *KSF.*, V, pp. 503–542. The reference to "occasional hints" about the Black Hand in the Austrian diplomatic documents is based on *Ö.-U.*,

VIII, pp. 84, 118–120, 282–284, 325, 330–331, 365, and 854. Why the Austrian Legation in Belgrade should have been so ill-informed about Apis' organization is difficult to explain (see, *e.g., Ö.-U.,* VIII, pp. 232 and 317–318), even when proper allowances are made by citing the ignorance of other foreign missions, shown in, Johannes Lepsius and others, ed., *Die Grosse Politik der Europäischen Kabinette 1871–1914* (hereafter cited as *G.P.*), XXXVIII (Berlin, 1926), pp. 358–361; and *D.D.F.,* 3rd series, X, pp. 333–335, 362–363, 495–497, 535–538, 565–567, 630–631, and 649–650. The contents of the folder "Secret Society, The Black Hand in Serbia," are described in Bittner, *B.M.,* X, pp. 55–61.

There exists some evidence that the Belgrade government undertook an investigation into the crime's origins after June 28, although it never published the results, and never even admitted that such an inquiry had taken place. On this subject, see *I.B.,* IV, p. 96; Herczeg, pp. 21–27, and Jovan Jovanović's letter to *B.M.,* XIII (1935), p. 881. What connection—if any—there existed between such an investigation and Ciganović's disappearance is not clear, however.

For the Serbian reply to the Austrian ultimatum, and for some of the circumstances of its preparation and presentation, see *Ö.-U.,* VIII, 660–663; Wegerer, *P.M.,* IX, pp. 860–864; Giesl, *ibid.,* XI, pp. 466–467; Steinitz *Zwei,* p. 268; and Jovanović, *Murder,* p. 7. Franz Joseph's "If the monarchy must perish . . ." is cited by the usually reliable Conrad (IV, p. 162).

CHAPTER XVI: The Trial

That the problem of the trial's political implications must have caused some serious thoughts in Vienna is indicated by an unpublished letter from Potiorek to Bilinski of September 12, 1914, in the Austrian Archives. "The draft of the indictment for the trial of the plotters is nearly finished," wrote the Governor, "and before long, the question will have to be considered and decided whether the main trial is to take place in a few weeks, or only after the end of the war. I am not in favor of postponing the trial." An even plainer letter from the Foreign Minister, Count Berchtold, to Bilinski of October

1, 1914—in Bruno Adler, *Der Schuss in den Weltfrieden* (Stuttgart, 1931), pp. 169–170—ordering a trial before the end of the war, and demanding a sentence "which should correspond to the vast international consequences of the crime" is of doubtful authenticity.

Charges made by some writers that the trial was "strictly secret" (Wendel, p. 327) are strictly incorrect. A few spectators found admittance, and the trial proceedings were reported in the Austrian as well as in the neutral press. (See, for example, the Swiss *Neue Zürcher Zeitung* in addition to *The New York Times* dispatches mentioned in the text.) A comparison of the various press reports makes it appear as if one single agency, if not one single correspondent, supplied the entire coverage, however. The most detailed reports will be found in the official *Wiener Zeitung*. The rest of the press merely seems to have carried shorter versions of the same dispatches.

The best explanations of the points of Bosnian law involved —the paragraphs under which the defendants were tried are cited in their entirety—is in *Sérajevo, la conspiration Serbe,* pp. 151–154. The local press and Pharos have some colorful details about the setting of the trial, but all quotations are from Mousset, the French version of the trial transcript. The sole exception is Princip's "Do you think I am an animal" outcry during the recess, which is from Pharos, p. 159. It is borne out by Feldbauer's later reference to it, which is a part of the official record (Mousset, p. 574). On the argument over Princip's birthdate, Bogićević, *Sar. At.,* pp. 423–424, has information contained in neither Pharos nor Mousset.

The one real link that may actually have existed between the Masons and the Black Hand was mentioned by Apis and a codefendant of his at the 1917 Salonica trial; Ljuba Jovanović-Čupa, one of the Black Hand's charter members, apparently was a Mason, and may have patterned such rites as the Black Hand's initiation ceremony after Masonic ritual. (*Saloniki-Prozess,* pp. 51, 68, and 201.)

Examples of General Erich Ludendorff's bigoted nonsense can be found in his *Vernichtung der Freimaurerei durch Enthüllung ihrer Geheimnisse, II. Teil* (Munich, 1928) and *Wie der Weltkrieg 1914 "gemacht" wurde* (Munich, 1934). Milder English versions are Durham and C. H. Norman, "Grand Orient," *B.M.*, IX (1931), pp. 177–182. The *Mercure de France* article is L[éon] de Poncins, "L'Attentat de Sérajevo et la Franc-maçonnerie," *M.d.F.*, CCXI (1929), pp. 121–131. It is convincingly answered in the same magazine by Mousset, in an article that is also entitled "L'Attentat de Sarajevo et la Franc-maçonnerie," and in another article, signed "L.D.," "L'Attentat de Sarajevo et les Responsabilités de la Guerre," *ibid.*, CCXI, pp. 733–736, and CCXIII, pp. 731–737. For the charges leveled against the Hungarians, see Žibert, *passim;* Renouvin, pp. 15–16; Stojanović, pp. 106–107; for innuendoes against the Austrians, Recouly, pp. 175–194; Steed, I, pp. 396–403; and Rebecca West, I, pp. 348–350. The reader has his choice.

Other superstitions are expounded in Eisenmenger, pp. 136–137; Muret, p. 119 (for the myth that Princip was Archduchess Stephanie's illegitimate son); and A[lbert] T'Serstevens, *Taïa, roman contemporain* (Paris, 1929), which is mentioned in the text. This novel's fraudulent basis is explained in Poncins, "Une nouvelle version de Mayerling et de Serajevo," *Mercure de France,* CCXVII (1930), pp. 347–354, and in Basil Thomson's aptly named *Queer People* (London, n.d.), pp. 238–240. As a final curiosity, there is the story of Bishop Lànyi's dream during the night of June 27, 1914, in which the Archduke's former Hungarian language teacher claimed to have received a letter from his one-time pupil, informing him of "my and my wife's death today as victims of a political assassination." (Adelt, p. 2; and *B.M.*, IX, pp. 1115–1117.)

CHAPTER XVII: The Penalty

This chapter, too, is based almost entirely on the Mousset version of the trial record. Only two details are taken from other sources. How Čabrinović wept, and how Princip remained calm as each made his final statement is described in the *Sarajevoer Tagblatt* of October 24, 1914; and a reproduction of the telegram reporting the execution of the three condemned men is shown in Bogićević, *Sar. At.,* following p. 444.

There is a more graphic account of the execution scene in Cornelius Zimka, *Das Drama von Sarajevo* (second edition, Leipzig, 1915), pp. 138–139, but it lacks all substantiation.

EPILOGUE: "On This Historic Spot . . ."

Magrini and Albertini, II, contain some reliable information on the post-1914 fate of Tankosić as well as others among the plotters. Worth consulting on Ciganović are Weisner, "Milan Ciganović," *KSF.*, V (1927), pp. 1041–1048, and the briefer notices in the same periodical, V, pp. 1036 and 1140.

The indispensable source for the Salonica trial is the transcript mentioned before (*Tajna prevratna organizatsija*). Comments on the motives behind it, and additional documents, will be found in Albertini, II, pp. 30–31; Bogićević, "Mord," and *Procès de Salonique;* Gabrilović, *J.M.H.*, XXVII; [Popović,] *B.M.*, X, p. 1108; Svetozar Pribitéhévitch [Pribićević], *La Dictature du Roi Alexandre* (Paris, 1933); Schmitt, *J.M.H.*, XVI, 170, and XXVII, 413; [Seton-Watson,] "Serbia's Choice," *The New Europe* (London), VIII, pp. 121–128; Hans Uebersberger, "Das entscheidende Aktenstück zur Kriegsschuldfrage 1914," *Auswärtige Politik,* X (1943), pp. 429–438; and Vucinich, p. 104.

Apis' confession here is given in the Gavrilović version just mentioned, which differs slightly from that of Uebersberger. The version of his last will and testament follows Bogićević, *Procès,* pp. 68–69, rather than text published in the Belgrade newspaper *Politika* of September 3, 1925, which is translated in *B.M.*, III, pp. 686–687. Also from Bogićević (pp. 94–99) is Lieutenant Colonel Dabic's report on Dimitrijević's execution. The retrial of Apis and the subsequent discussion in Yugoslavia are summarized in Vucinich, p. 105. A major reason for retrying the case may have been the desire to bring discredit on the royal house. An English version of the record of the new trial, though promised, so far has not been released. See Taylor, *The Observer,* November 16, 1958, p. 5.

On the later fate of Curinaldi and Zistler, see Albertini, II, pp. 47 and 59; on that of Pfeffer, *KSF.*, IV, pp. 640–641, 661, and 718–719; on that of Grbić, Potiorek's dispatch to Vienna of August 16, 1914, in the Austrian Archives. The sources for Bilinski's argument with Potiorek are *Ö.-U.*, VIII, Conrad, IV, and Theodor Sosnosky, "Der Letzte Akt vor dem Weltkrieg," *Wiener Zeitung*, January 6, 14, and 21, 1934 (which is based on the files of the *Kriegsarchiv*). Facts and rumors on the Governor's wartime role can be found in Glaise-Horstenau, "Feldzeugmeister Potiorek," *B.M.*, XII, pp. 144–148; C.R.M.F. Cruttwell, *A History of the Great War 1914–1918* (Second Edition, Oxford, 1936), pp. 53 and 90–92; and Margutti, pp. 423–426 and 430. In addition to Potiorek's dispatches to Vienna urging strong action against Serbia after the Sarajevo crime in *Ö.-U.*, VIII, there is an unpublished telegram of a similar nature in the Austrian Archives, which while unsigned, clearly seems to have been written by the General. (Telegram to the War Ministry, Res. Nr. 4754, Received July 6, 1914.) The obituary quoted is that of Glaise; the reference to his former antagonist, Bilinski, comes from Sieghart, p. 29. For a translation of two Belgrade press reports about Pašić and his unpublished memoirs see *KSF.*, V, pp. 174–175.

On the death of Mitar Kerović, Marko Perina, and Trifko Grabež see Mousset, p. 676, and Seton-Watson, p. 121 n. The meeting between Čabrinović and Franz Werfel is described in a story which first appeared in 1923, "Cabrinowitsch, Ein Tagebuch aus dem Jahre 1915," *Erzählungen aus zwei Welten,* I (Stockholm, 1948), pp. 21–28. As a historical document, it is of questionable value, since Werfel's mystic mind and mystic style blur all lines between fact and fiction. The meeting may also have inspired an early novel; see Annemarie von Putt-kamer, *Franz Werfel* (Würzburg, 1952), pp. 16–18.

On the conditions of Princip's imprisonment, no reliable evidence exists, and we must do with the doubtful material in *Princips Bekenntnisse;* Pharos, p. 165; and Nikitsch, pp. 226–227. His death certificate is reproduced in Bogićević, *Sar. At.,* facing p. 445. Facts on Popović, Čubrilović, and Mehmedbašić can be found in Albertini, II, p. 47; *B.M.*, X, p. 1098; West, *New Statesman, XLVII,* p. 824; Rebecca West, II, p. 770; Seton-Watson, p. 149; Tomasevich, pp. 92–97, and 708; and T'Ser-stevens, "Étapes."

For information concerning the postwar fate of some of the Sarajevo survivors, the author is greatly indebted to personal communications received from Professor Wayne Vucinich of Stanford University and from Professor Vojislav Bogićević of Sarajevo. An English visitor's recent report on Čubrilović and Popović is that of Richard West, "Martyr Princip," *The New Statesman and Nation,* XLVII (1954), p. 824. Some caution is indicated here; West never quite makes it clear whether or not he talked with the two men, and in one important reference he apparently confuses Vaso Čubrilović with the politician Branko Čubrilović. The meeting with Franz Ferdinand's two sons in Duchau concentration camp is recounted in Funder, pp. 489–490.

"The Serbs carry on a hero cult" was Professor Čubrilović's comment on the many ways in which various groups were paying homage to the assassins' memory in Yugoslavia (Albertini, II, p. 47 n.). How the assassins were reburied in Sarajevo is told in *B.M.,* VIII, pp. 573–574, and Rebecca West, II, p. 380; how the memorial to the victims (for a photograph see Pharos, facing p. 165) was destroyed and the assassins were praised is told in Albertini, II, p. 47; *KSF.,* VI, pp. 711–713, VIII, pp. 91, 434, 574, 886, and XIII, p. 347; Mousset, *Revue d'Histoire Dipl.,* XXXIX, p. 61; Pelletier, *L'Illustration,* CLXXXVIII, p. 434; Seton-Watson, p. 159; and West, p. 824. Photographs of the memorial tablet for Princip erected in 1930, a translation of its inscription, and reports of the unveiling ceremony are to be found in *B.M.,* pp. 281, 284–285, 289; "La Commémoration d'un grand drame," *L'Illustration,* CLXXV, (1930), p. 217; "In Memory of an Assassin," *The Literary Digest,* CIV (1930), p. 13; and *Politika* of February 3, 1930, which is translated in *B.M.,* VIII, pp. 281–284. Perhaps the cruelest comment on it all was made by an old friend of the Austrian monarchy, Sir Winston Churchill, who wrote (in *The Unknown War* [New York, 1932], p. 54): "He [Princip] died in prison, and a monument erected in recent years by his fellow countrymen records his infamy, and their own."

Index

Albert I, King of Belgium, 171
Alexander, Prince Regent of Serbia, 49, 248, 249, 250
Alexander, Obrenović, King of Serbia, 44, 50, 51
Anarchism. *See* Assassination
Apis. *See* Dimitrijević, Col. Dragutin
Appel, Gen. Michael von, 114, 123–24, 146, 147–48
Arbeiter Zeitung, 163
Arnstein, Maj., 124, 142
Artstetten, burial at, 168, 173, 177, 178, 180, 181
Artamonov, Col. Victor, 57, 208
Assassination, 19, 35–36, 37, 44, 51, 53, 77, 78; unsuccessful attempts at, 4, 36, 47, 50–51, 53, 55, 92, 121–23
Assassination of Franz Ferdinand, 119, 136–37, 214, 230, 231, 242, 243, 249; attempts to prevent, 71, 72, 74–76, 77, 224; first attempt at, 3–4, 121–23, 182, 183; investigations of, 125, 137, 145, 182, 183–86, 187, 192, 196, 197–98, 199 200–01, 204; planning of, 54, 55–56, 57, 93, 100, 110–11, 112, 127; reactions to, 146–47, 148, 149, 150, 151, 152–53, 154–56, 157, 158–59, 163–65, 199;

reasons for, 28, 56–57, 64–65, 66, 94; theories about, 226–29; Wiesner's report on, 200–01; *see also* Assassins; Franz Ferdinand, Archduke
Assassins, 3–4, 44–45, 51, 63–64, 66–67, 69, 72, 73, 74, 76, 78, 80, 81, 82, 83, 84, 85, 86, 88–90, 93, 94, 96, 98, 99, 110, 111, 112, 114, 118, 260–61; arrest of, 124–25, 138–40, 187–88, 189, 193; border crossing of, 68–69, 70, 78–83; confessions of, 183–85, 186, 187, 188, 189, 192, 193, 194–96, 198, 216–17, 223–24, 225–26; defense pleas for, 232–41; memorials to, 261; selection of, 59, 92–94, 95–96; sentences of, 243–45, 246, 257; trial of, 60, 61, 64, 65–66, 81, 82, 83–84, 86, 94–95, 120, 126, 211, 212, 213–16, 217–26, 241–43; *see also* Čabrinović, Nedjelko; Čubrilović, Vaso; Grabež, Trifko; Mehmedbašić, Muhamed; Princip, Gavrilo
Austro-Hungarian Empire, 25–26, 27, 33, 35, 159; alliance with Germany of, 208–09; knowledge of Black Hand in, 48, 117, 195, 204–05, 206;

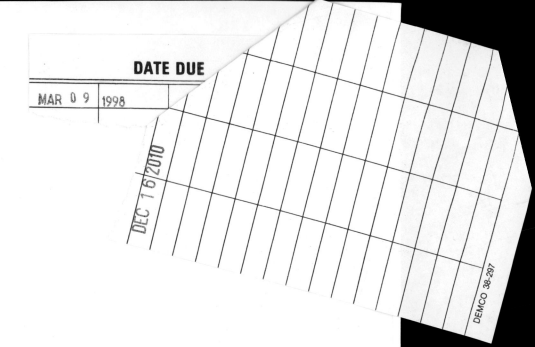